D1020108

Major Modern Black American Writers

Writers of English: Lives and Works

MAJOR MODERN
BLACK AMERICAN
WRITERS

Edited and with an Introduction by

Harold Bloom

CHELSEA HOUSE PUBLISHERS
New York   Philadelphia

Jacket illustration: Jacob Lawrence (b. 1917), *Photographer's Shop* (1951) (courtesy of Jacob Lawrence, the Francine Seders Gallery, Seattle, WA, and the Milwaukee Art Museum, Gift of Milprint, Inc., a Division of Philip Morris Industrial).

CHELSEA HOUSE PUBLISHERS

Editorial Director Richard Rennert
Executive Managing Editor Karyn Gullen Browne
Copy Chief Robin James
Picture Editor Adrian G. Allen
Creative Director Robert Mitchell
Art Director Joan Ferrigno
Production Manager Sallye Scott

Writers of English: Lives and Works

Senior Editor S. T. Joshi
Series Design Rae Grant

Staff for MAJOR MODERN BLACK AMERICAN WRITERS

Assistant Editor Mary Sisson
Editorial Assistant Scott Briggs
Picture Researcher Ellen Dudley

© 1995 by Chelsea House Publishers, a division of Main Line Book Co.

Introduction © 1995 by Harold Bloom

Printed and bound in the United States of America.

First Printing

1 3 5 7 9 8 6 4 2

Library of Congress Cataloging-in-Publication Data

Major modern black American writers / edited and with an introduction by Harold Bloom.
     p.   cm.—(Writers of English)
     Includes bibliographical references.
     ISBN 0-7910-2219-6.—ISBN 0-7910-2244-7 (pbk.)
   1. American literature—Afro-American authors—History and criticism. 2. American literature—Afro-American authors—Bio-bibliography. 3. American literature—20th century—History and criticism. 4. American literature—20th century—Bio-bibliography. 5. Afro-Americans in literature. I. Bloom, Harold. II. Series.
PS153.N5M245 1994
810.9′896073—dc20   94-4336
                                                                                        CIP

▨ Contents

◙ User's Guide

THIS VOLUME PROVIDES biographical, critical, and bibliographical information on the twelve most significant modern black American writers. Each chapter consists of three parts: a biography of the author; a selection of brief critical extracts about the author; and a bibliography of the author's published books.

The biography supplies a detailed outline of the important events in the author's life, including his or her major writings. The critical extracts are taken from a wide array of books and periodicals, from the author's lifetime to the present, and range in content from biographical to critical to historical. The extracts are arranged in chronological order by date of writing or publication, and a full bibliographical citation is provided at the end of each extract. Editorial additions or deletions are indicated within carets.

The author bibliographies list every separate publication—including books, pamphlets, broadsides, collaborations, and works edited or translated by the author—for works published in the author's lifetime; selected important posthumous publications are also listed. Titles are those of the first edition; variant titles are supplied within carets. In selected instances dates of revised editions are given where these are significant. Pseudonymous works are listed but not the pseudonyms under which these works were published. Periodicals edited by the author are listed only when the author has written most or all of the contents. Titles enclosed in square brackets are of doubtful authenticity. All works by the author, whether in English or in other languages, have been listed; English translations of foreign-language works are not listed unless the author has done the translation.

The Life of the Author
Harold Bloom

NIETZSCHE, WITH EXULTANT ANGUISH, famously proclaimed that God was dead. Whatever the consequences of this for the ethical life, its ultimate literary effect certainly would have surprised the author Nietzsche. His French disciples, Foucault most prominent among them, developed the Nietzschean proclamation into the dogma that all authors, God included, were dead. The death of the author, which is no more than a Parisian trope, another metaphor for fashion's setting of skirt-lengths, is now accepted as literal truth by most of our current apostles of what should be called French Nietzsche, to distinguish it from the merely original Nietzsche. We also have French Freud or Lacan, which has little to do with the actual thought of Sigmund Freud, and even French Joyce, which interprets *Finnegans Wake* as the major work of Jacques Derrida. But all this is as nothing compared to the final triumph of the doctrine of the death of the author: French Shakespeare. That delicious absurdity is given us by the New Historicism, which blends Foucault and California fruit juice to give us the Word that Renaissance "social energies," and not William Shakespeare, composed *Hamlet* and *King Lear*. It seems a proper moment to murmur "enough" and to return to a study of the life of the author.

Sometimes it troubles me that there are so few masterpieces in the vast ocean of literary biography that stretches between James Boswell's great *Life* of Dr. Samuel Johnson and the late Richard Ellmann's wonderful *Oscar Wilde*. Literary biography is a crucial genre, and clearly a difficult one in which to excel. The actual nature of the lives of the poets seems to have little effect upon the quality of their biographies. Everything happened to Lord Byron and nothing at all to Wallace Stevens, and yet their biographers seem equally daunted by them. But even inadequate biographies of strong writers, or of weak ones, are of immense use. I have never read a literary biography from which I have not profited, a statement I cannot make about any other genre whatsoever. And when it comes to figures who are central to us—Dante, Shakespeare, Cervantes, Montaigne, Goethe, Whitman, Tolstoi, Freud, Joyce, Kafka among them—we reach out eagerly for every scrap that the biographers have gleaned. Concerning Dante and Shakespeare we know much too little, yet when we come to Goethe and Freud, where we seem to know more than everything, we still want to know more. The death of the author, despite our current resentniks, clearly was only a momentary fad. Something vital in every authentic lover of literature responds to Emerson's battle-cry sentence: "There is no history, only biography." Beyond that there is a deeper truth, difficult to come at and requiring a lifetime to understand, which is that there is no literature, only autobiography, however mediated, however veiled, however transformed. The events of Shakespeare's life included the composition of *Hamlet,* and that act of writing was itself a crucial act of living, though we do not yet know altogether how to read so doubled an act. When an author takes up a more overtly autobiographical stance, as so many do in their youth, again we still do not know precisely how to accommodate the vexed relation between life and work. T. S. Eliot, meditating upon James Joyce, made a classic statement as to such accommodation:

> We want to know who are the originals of his characters, and what were the origins of his episodes, so that we may unravel the web of memory and invention and discover how far and in what ways the crude material has been transformed.

When a writer is not even covertly autobiographical, the web of memory and invention is still there, but so subtly woven that we may never unravel it. And yet we want deeply never to stop trying, and not merely because we are curious, but because each of us is caught in her own network of memory and invention. We do not always recall our inventions, and long before we age we cease to be certain of the extent to which we have invented our memories. Perhaps one motive for reading is our need to unravel our own webs. If our masters could make, from their lives, what we read, then we can be moved by them to ask: What have we made or lived in relation to what we have read? The answers may be sad, or confused, but the question is likely, implicitly, to go on being asked as long as we read. In Freudian terms, we are asking: What is it that we have repressed? What have we forgotten, unconsciously but purposely: What is it that we flee? Art, literature necessarily included, is regression in the service of the ego, according to a famous Freudian formula. I doubt the Freudian wisdom here, but indubitably it is profoundly suggestive. When we read, something in us keeps asking the equivalent of the Freudian questions: From what or whom is the author in flight, and to what earlier stages in her life is she returning, and why?

Reading, whether as an art or a pastime, has been damaged by the visual media, television in particular, and might be in some danger of extinction in the age of the computer, except that the psychic need for it continues to endure, presumably because it alone can assuage a central loneliness in elitist society. Despite all sophisticated or resentful denials, the reading of imaginative literature remains a quest to overcome the isolation of the individual consciousness. We can read for information, or entertainment, or for love of the language, but in the end we seek, in the author, the person whom we have not found, whether in ourselves or in others. In that quest, there always are elements at once aggressive and defensive, so that reading, even in childhood, is rarely free of hidden anxieties. And yet it remains one of the few activities not contaminated by an entropy of spirit. We read in hope, because we lack companionship, and the author can become the object of the most idealistic elements in our search for the wit and inventiveness we so desperately require. We read biography, not as a supplement to reading the author, but as a second, fresh attempt to understand what always seems to evade us in the work, our drive towards a kind of identity with the author.

This will-to-identity, though recently much deprecated, is a prime basis for the experience of sublimity in reading. *Hamlet* retains its unique position in the Western canon not because most readers and playgoers identify themselves with the prince, who clearly is beyond them, but rather because they find themselves again in the power of the language that represents him with such immediacy and force. Yet we know that neither language nor social energy created Hamlet. Our curiosity about Shakespeare is endless, and never will be appeased. That curiosity itself is a value, and cannot be separated from the value of *Hamlet* the tragedy, or Hamlet the literary character. It provokes us that Shakespeare the man seems so unknowable, at once everyone and no one as Borges shrewdly observes. Critics keep telling us otherwise, yet something valid in us keeps believing that we would know Hamlet better if Shakespeare's life were as fully known as the lives of Goethe and Freud, Byron and Oscar Wilde, or best of all, Dr. Samuel Johnson. Shakespeare never will have his Boswell, and Dante never will have his Richard Ellmann. How much one would give for a detailed and candid *Life of Dante* by Petrarch, or an outspoken memoir of Shakespeare by Ben Jonson! Or, in the age just past, how superb would be rival studies of one another by Hemingway and Scott Fitzgerald! But the list is endless: think of *Oscar Wilde* by Lord Alfred Douglas, or a joint biography of Shelley by Mary Godwin, Emilia Viviani, and Jane Williams. More than our insatiable desire for scandal would be satisfied. The literary rivals and the lovers of the great writers possessed perspectives we will never enjoy, and without those perspectives we dwell in some poverty in regard to the writers with whom we ourselves never can be done.

There is a sense in which imaginative literature *is* perspectivism, so that the reader is likely to be overwhelmed by the work's difficulty unless its multiple perspectives are mastered. Literary biography matters most because it is a storehouse of perspectives, frequently far surpassing any that are grasped by the particular biographer. There are relations between authors' lives and their works of kinds we have yet to discover, because our analytical instruments are not yet advanced enough to perform the necessary labor. Perhaps a novel, poem, or play is not so much a regression in the service of the ego, as it is an amalgam of *all* the Freudian mechanisms of defense, all working together for the apotheosis of the ego. Freud valued art highly, but thought that the aesthetic enterprise was no rival for psychoanalysis, unlike religion and philosophy. Clearly Freud was mistaken; his own anxieties about his indebtedness to Shakespeare helped produce the weirdness of his joining in the lunacy that argued for the Earl of Oxford as the author of Shakespeare's plays. It was Shakespeare, and not "the poets," who was there before Freud arrived at his depth psychology, and it is Shakespeare who is there still, well out ahead of psychoanalysis. We see what Freud would not see, that psychoanalysis is Shakespeare prosified and systematized. Freud is part of literature, not of "science," and the biography of Freud has the same relations to psychoanalysis as the biography of Shakespeare has to *Hamlet* and *King Lear*, if only we knew more of the life of Shakespeare.

Western literature, particularly since Shakespeare, is marked by the representation of internalized change in its characters. A literature of the ever-growing inner self is in itself a large form of biography, even though this is the biography of imaginary beings, from Hamlet to the sometimes nameless protagonists of Kafka and Beckett. Skeptics might want to argue that all literary biography concerns imaginary beings, since authors make themselves up, and every biographer gives us a creation curiously different from the same author as seen by the writer of a rival *Life*. Boswell's Johnson is not quite anyone else's Johnson, though it is now very difficult for us to disentangle the great Doctor from his gifted Scottish friend and follower. The life of the author is not merely a metaphor or a fiction, as is "the Death of the Author," but it always does contain metaphorical or fictive elements. Those elements are a part of the value of literary biography, but not the largest or the crucial part, which is the separation of the mask from the man or woman who hid behind it. James Joyce and Samuel Beckett, master and sometime disciple, were both of them enigmatic personalities, and their biographers have not, as yet, fully expounded the mystery of these contrasting natures. Beckett seems very nearly to have been a secular saint: personally disinterested, heroic in the French Resistance, as humane a person ever to have composed major fictions and dramas. Joyce, self-obsessed even as Beckett was preternaturally selfless, was the Milton of the twentieth century. Beckett was perhaps the least egoistic post-Joycean, post-Proustian, post-Kafkan of writers. Does that illuminate the problematical nature of his work, or does it simply constitute another problem? Whatever the cause, the question matters. The only death of the author that is other than literal, and that matters, is the fate only of weak writers. The strong, who become canonical, never die, which is what the canon truly is about. To be read forever is the Life of the Author.

◈ Introduction

JAY WRIGHT'S POETRY develops a powerful image of creation-by-twinning, in which a poem becomes a limbo dance, a gateway out of the Middle Passage of the slave trade, a gateway that is also a logbook, and so a poem for passage. The limbo is a West Indian dance in which the dancer must perform under a bar that is gradually lowered until a kind of spiderman dance is necessary, with spread-eagled arms and legs. By tradition, the limbo refers to the notorious Middle Passage, the route of slave ships from Africa to America, during which the slaves were pushed into so little space that they had to go through the contortions of becoming human spiders. In the poetic art of Jay Wright, the limbo becomes a metaphor for Wright's own aesthetic project, which quests for a gateway out of the Middle Passage by making "a log for passage," a logbook of initiation by twinning, a mode of creation in West African Dogon mythology, where Amma or Yahweh twins himself as Nommo or Adam, a prefiguration that clears into the figure of a Black Son of God, a human gateway out of a universal Middle Passage. Standing in the Albuquerque Graveyard, the young Jay Wright had a vision of the prefiguration:

> I am going back
> to the Black limbo,
> an unwritten history
> of our own tensions.

In his major phase now, as a fully matured strong poet, Jay Wright begins to fulfill this prefigurative prophecy. Dogon mythology had taught him that each being—even every object—has its own language, its own twin or double, its Nommo or Adam. In his *Dimensions of History*, Wright had promised that "The bones will set themselves to a dance," to a resurrected limbo, and that he would make "a logbook of judgments." He has become, in his *Elaine's Book* and in his new volume, *Boleros*, a true Pindaric poet, the chanter of great odes worthy of Hölderlin or of Hart Crane, of Rilke or of Paul Celan. The limbo has fused with creation-by-twinning into an intricate mythology parallel to the visions of William Blake or of W. B. Yeats. In the latest Jay Wright I hear a magnificent litany in which the Middle Passage merges into the middle term of life itself, as the poet stands in the gateway of a New Hampshire field and beholds the Sublime:

> ... in a body
> that could father us without a hint of solace,
> and induce us to dance out of the first dream,
> into betrayal, and the word that takes its first step into death.

—H. B.

◈ ◈ ◈

Maya Angelou
b. 1928

MAYA ANGELOU was born Marguerite Johnson in St. Louis, Missouri, on
April 4, 1928. Her life has been both remarkably varied and occasionally
grim (she was raped at the age of eight by her mother's boyfriend), and she
has won greater critical acclaim for her several autobiographical volumes
than for her poetry and drama. She attended public schools in Arkansas
and California, studied music privately, and studied dance with Martha
Graham. In 1954–55 she was a member of the cast of *Porgy and Bess*, which
went on a twenty-two-nation world tour sponsored by the U.S. Department
of State. Some of her songs were recorded on the album *Miss Calypso* (1957).
Later she acted in several off-Broadway plays, including one, the musical
Cabaret for Freedom (1960), that she wrote with Godfrey Cambridge.

In addition to these artistic pursuits, Angelou held a variety of odd jobs
in her late teens and early twenties, including streetcar conductor, Creole
cook, nightclub waitress, prostitute, and madam. She has been married
twice: first, around 1950, to a white man, Tosh Angelos (whose surname
she adapted when she became a dancer), and then, from 1973 to 1981, to
Paul Du Feu. She bore a son, Guy, at the age of sixteen.

When she was thirty Angelou moved to Brooklyn. There she met John
Oliver Killens, James Baldwin, and other writers who encouraged her to
write. While practicing her craft, however, she became involved in the civil
rights movement. She met Martin Luther King, Jr., was appointed the
northern coordinator of the Southern Christian Leadership Conference,
and organized demonstrations at the United Nations. She fell in love with
the South African freedom fighter Vusumzi Make, and they left for Egypt,
where in 1961–62 Angelou worked as associate editor of the *Arab Observer*,
an English-language newspaper in Cairo. She broke up with Make when
he criticized her independence and lack of subservience to him.

In 1963 Angelou went to Ghana to be assistant administrator of the
School of Music and Drama at the University of Ghana's Institute of African
Studies. In the three years she was there she acted in several additional

plays, served as feature editor of the *African Review*, and was a contributor to the Ghanaian Broadcasting Corporation. Returning to the United States, she was a lecturer at the University of California at Los Angeles and has subsequently been a visiting professor or writer in residence at several other universities.

Angelou's first published book was *I Know Why the Caged Bird Sings* (1969), an autobiography of the first sixteen years of her life; a tremendous critical and popular success, it was nominated for a National Book Award and was later adapted for television. Two more autobiographical volumes appeared in the 1970s, *Gather Together in My Name* (1974) and *Singin' and Swingin' and Gettin' Merry Like Christmas* (1976), along with three volumes of poetry: *Just Give Me a Cool Drink of Water 'Fore I Diiie* (1971), *Oh Pray My Wings Are Gonna Fit Me Well* (1975), and *And Still I Rise* (1978). She wrote several more dramas, including the unpublished *And Still I Rise!*, a medley of black poetry and music that was successfully staged in 1976; two screenplays (directing one of them and writing the musical scores for both); and several television plays, including a series of ten one-hour programs entitled *Blacks, Blues, Black*. She also continued to pursue her acting career and was nominated for a Tony Award in 1973 for her Broadway debut, *Look Away*. She was appointed a member of the American Revolution Bicentennial Council by President Gerald R. Ford in 1975.

In the last fifteen years Angelou has solidified her reputation with two more autobiographies, *The Heart of a Woman* (1981) and *All God's Children Need Traveling Shoes* (1986), along with two more volumes of poetry, *Shaker, Why Don't You Sing?* (1983) and *I Shall Not Be Moved* (1990). The peak of her fame was perhaps achieved when in 1993 she composed a poem, "On the Pulse of Morning," for the inauguration of President Bill Clinton. Angelou's latest prose work, *Wouldn't Take Nothing for My Journey Now*, a collection of essays and sketches, also appeared that year and, like most of its predecessors, was a best-seller.

Maya Angelou, who has received honorary degrees from Smith College, Mills College, and Lawrence University, currently resides in Sonoma, California.

◈ *Critical Extracts*

MAYA ANGELOU   There was shuffling and rustling around me, then Henry Reed was giving his valedictory address, "To Be or Not to Be." Hadn't he heard the whitefolks? We couldn't *be*, so the question was a waste of time. Henry's voice came out clear and strong. I feared to look at him. Hadn't he got the message? There was no "nobler in the mind" for the Negroes because the world didn't think we had minds, and they let us know it. "Outrageous fortune"? Now, that was a joke. ⟨. . .⟩

I had been listening and silently rebutting each sentence with my eyes closed; then there was a hush, which in an audience warns that something unplanned is happening. I looked up and saw Henry Reed, the conservative, the proper, the A student, turn his back to the audience and turn to us (the proud graduating class of 1940) and sing, nearly speaking,

> "Lift ev'ry voice and sing
> Till earth and heaven ring
> Ring with the harmonies of Liberty . . ."

It was the poem written by James Weldon Johnson. It was the music composed by J. Rosamond Johnson. It was the Negro national anthem. Out of habit we were singing it.

Our mothers and fathers stood in the dark hall and joined the hymn of encouragement. A kindergarten teacher led the small children onto the stage and the buttercups and daisies and bunny rabbits marked time and tried to follow:

> "Stony the road we trod
> Bitter the chastening rod
> Felt I the days when hope, unborn, had died.
> Yet with a steady beat
> Have not our weary feet
> Come to the place for which our fathers sighed?"

Every child I knew learned that song with his ABC's and along with "Jesus Loves Me This I Know." But I personally had never heard it before. Never heard the words, despite the thousands of times I had sung them. Never thought they had anything to do with me.

On the other hand, the words of Patrick Henry had made such an impression on me that I had been able to stretch myself tall and trembling and say, "I know not what course others may take, but as for me, give me liberty or give me death."

And now I heard, really for the first time:

> "We have come over a way that with tears
> has been watered,
> We have come, treading our path through
> the blood of the slaughtered."

While the echoes of the song shivered in the air, Henry Reed bowed his head, said, "Thank you," and returned to his place in the line. The tears that slipped down many faces were not wiped away in shame.

We are on top again. As always, again. We survived. The depths had been icy and dark, but now a bright sun spoke to our souls. I was no longer simply a member of the proud graduating class of 1940; I was a proud member of the wonderful, beautiful Negro race.

Maya Angelou, *I Know Why the Caged Bird Sings* (New York: Random House, 1969), pp. 177–79

SIDONIE ANN SMITH   Maya Angelou's autobiography, like ⟨Richard⟩ Wright's, opens with a primal childhood scene that brings into focus the nature of the imprisoning environment from which the self will seek escape. The black girl child is trapped within the cage of her own diminished self-image around which interlock the bars of natural and social forces. The oppression of natural forces, of physical appearance and processes, foists a self-consciousness on all young girls who must grow from children into women. Hair is too thin or stringy or mousy or nappy. Legs are too fat, too thin, too bony, the knees too bowed. Hips are too wide or not wide enough. Breasts grow too fast or not at all. The self-critical process is incessant, a driving demon. But in the black girl child's experience these natural bars are reinforced with the rusted iron social bars of racial subordination and impotence. Being born black is itself a liability in a world ruled by white standards of beauty which imprison the child *a priori* in a cage of ugliness: "What you looking at me for?" This really isn't me. I'm white with long blond hair and blue eyes, with pretty pink skin and straight hair, with a delicate mouth. I'll try again. The black and blue bruises of the soul multiply and compound as the caged bird flings herself against these bars:

> The Black female is assaulted in her tender years by all those
> common forces of nature at the same time that she is caught in
> the tripartite crossfire of masculine prejudice, white illogical hate
> and Black lack of power.

Within this imprisoning environment there is no place for this black girl
child. She becomes a displaced person whose pain is intensified by her
consciousness of that displacement:

> If growing up is painful for the Southern Black girl, being
> aware of her displacement is the rust on the razor that threatens
> the throat.
> It is an unnecessary insult.

If the black man is denied his potency and his masculinity, if his autobiography narrates the quest of the black male after a "place" of full manhood,
the black woman is denied her beauty and her quest is one after self-accepted
black womanhood. Thus the discovered pattern of significant moments
Maya Angelou superimposes on the experience of her life is a pattern of
moments that trace the quest of the black female after a "place," a place
where a child no longer need ask self-consciously, "What you looking at
me for?" but where a woman can declare confidently, "I am a beautiful,
Black woman."

Sidonie Ann Smith, "The Song of a Caged Bird: Maya Angelou's Quest After Self-
Acceptance," *Southern Humanities Review* 7, No. 4 (Fall 1973): 368

ANNIE GOTTLIEB   *Gather Together in My Name* is a little shorter
and thinner than its predecessor; telling of an episodic, searching and wan-
dering period in Maya Angelou's life, it lacks the density of childhood. In
full compensation, her style has both ripened and simplified. It is more
telegraphic and more condensed, transmitting a world of sensation or emotion or understanding in one image—in short, it is more like poetry. (Maya
Angelou published a book of poems, *Just Give Me a Cool Drink of Water
'Fore I Diiie*, in between the two autobiographical volumes.)

"Disappointment rode his face bareback." "Dumbfounded, founded in
dumbness." "The heavy opulence of Dostoevsky's world was where I had
lived forever. The gloomy, lightless interiors, the complex ratiocinations of
the characters and their burdensome humors, were as familiar to me as

loneliness." "The South I returned to . . . was flesh-real and swollen belly poor." "I clenched my reason and forced their faces into focus." Even in these short bits snipped out of context, you can sense the palpability, the precision and the rhythm of this writing. 〈. . .〉

In *Gather Together in My Name*, the ridiculous and touching posturing of a young girl in the throes of growing up are superimposed on the serious business of survival and responsibility for a child. Maya Angelou's insistence on taking full responsibility for her own life, her frank and humorous examination of her self, will challenge many a reader to be as honest under easier circumstances. Reading her book, you may learn, too, the embrace and ritual, the dignity and solace and humor of the black community. You will meet strong, distinctive people, drawn with deftness and compassion; their blackness is not used to hide their familiar but vulnerable humanity any more than their accessible humanity can for a moment be used to obscure their blackness—or their oppression. Maya Angelou's second book about her life as a young black woman in America is engrossing and vital, rich and funny and wise.

> Annie Gottlieb, "Growing Up and the Serious Business of Survival," *New York Times Book Review*, 16 June 1974, pp. 16, 20

SANDRA M. GILBERT   I can't help feeling that Maya Angelou's career has suffered from the interest her publishers have in mythologizing her. *Oh Pray My Wings Are Gonna Fit Me Well* is such a painfully untalented collection of poems that I can't think of any reason, other than the Maya Myth, for it to be in print: it's impossible, indeed, to separate the book's flap copy, with its glossy celebration of "Maya Angelou . . . one of the world's most exciting women . . . Maya, the eternal female" from the book itself. All this is especially depressing because Angelou, "eternal female" or not, is a stunningly talented prose writer, whose marvelous *I Know Why the Caged Bird Sings* has quite properly become a contemporary classic. Why should it be necessary, then, for her to represent herself publicly as the author of such an embarrassing tangle as

> I'd touched your features inchly
> heard love and dared the cost.
> The scented spiel reeled me unreal
> and found my senses lost.

And why, instead of encouraging Angelou, didn't some friendly editor Block (as *The New Yorker* would say) the following Metaphor:

> A day
> drunk with the nectar of
> nowness
> weaves its way between
> the years
> to find itself at the flophouse
> of night. . . .

To be fair, not all the verse in *Oh Pray . . .* is quite as bad as these two examples. A few of the colloquial pieces—"Pickin Em Up and Layin Em Down" or "Come. And Be My Baby"—have the slangy, unpretentious vitality of good ballads. "The Pusher" ("He bad / O he bad"), with its echoes of Brooks's "We real cool", achieves genuine scariness. And "John J." might be a portrait in verse of Bailey, the handsome brother Angelou renders so beautifully in *I Know Why. . . .* But these are only four or five poems out of the thirty-six in this collection. And most of the others, when they're not awkward or stilted, are simply corny. The writer whose unsentimental wit and passionate accuracy gave us such a fresh account of growing up black and female really doesn't need to publish "No one knows / my lonely heart / when we're apart" or "No lady cookinger than my Mommy / smell that pie / see I don't lie / No lady cookinger than my Mommy" (from "Little Girl Speakings"). Angelou can hardly be accused of self-parody: for one thing, most of the poetry here is too unself-conscious, too thoughtless, to be in any sense parodic. But, for whatever reason, the wings of song certainly don't seem to fit her very well right now.

Sandra M. Gilbert, "A Platoon of Poets," *Poetry* 128, No. 5 (August 1976): 296–97

EUGENE REDMOND   A multi-tiered ballet-symphony conceived and directed by writer-director Maya Angelou, *And Still I Rise!* was exuberantly received by full houses during four August weekends at the Oakland Ensemble Theatre. ⟨. . .⟩

Black-based, with dramatic tentacles and sub-themes that are global (indeed, galaxial!), *And Still I Rise!* is an admirable adaptation of subtle, poignant and humorous verse-songs from a rich cross-spread of Afro-American poets. Household names such as Paul Laurence Dunbar, Gwendolyn

Brooks, Langston Hughes and Nikki Giovanni, are mixed with an ample sprinkling of lesser known bards—Frank Horne, Richard A. Long, Joyce Carol Thomas and Ray Garfiend Dandridge. Spices from the "traditional" song-book (those "black and unknown bards") and Miss Angelou's own volumes make up the remainder of this tasty drama. These items form a histrionic bridge between Africa and the New World via six sub-themes (Childhood, Youth, Love, Work, Religion, and The Old Souls) that evoke nostalgia, fear, humor and pride. ⟨. . .⟩

As a dramatic exploration of black survival and endurance, *And Still I Rise!* is coincidentally an enormous praise-song, a totemic tribute to those gone souls and a challenge to those living and unborn. Maya Angelou has brought years of formidable experience, research and travel to bear on her serious interest in the black cultural legacy. *And Still I Rise!* congeals a substantial body of her own portfolio as writer-actress-dancer-singer-director into relentless drama. And we are all the better for it.

> Eugene Redmond, [Review of *And Still I Rise!*], *Black Scholar* 8, No. 1 (September 1976): 50–51

SONDRA O'NEALE   Unlike her poetry, which is a continuation of traditional oral expression in Afro-American literature, Angelou's prose follows classic technique in nonpoetic Western forms. The material in each book while chronologically marking her life is nonetheless arranged in loosely structured plot sequences which are skillfully controlled. In *Caged Bird* the tenuous psyche of a gangly, sensitive, withdrawn child is traumatically jarred by rape, a treacherous act from which neither the reader nor the protagonist has recovered by the book's end. All else is cathartic: her uncles' justified revenge upon the rapist, her years of readjustment in a closed world of speechlessness despite the warm nurturing of her grandmother, her grand-uncle, her beloved brother Bailey, and the Stamps community; a second reunion with her vivacious mother; even her absurdly unlucky pregnancy at the end does not assuage the reader's anticipatory wonder: isn't the act of rape by a trusted adult so assaultive upon an eight-year-old's life that it leaves a wound which can never be healed? Such reader interest in a character's future is the craft from which quality fiction is made. Few autobiographers however have the verve to seize the drama of such a moment, using one specific incident to control the book but with an underlining implication that the incident will not control a life.

The denouement in *Gather Together in My Name* is again sexual: the older, crafty, experienced man lasciviously preying upon the young, vulnerable, and, for all her exposure by that time, naïve woman. While foreshadowing apprehension guided the reader to the central action in the first work, Maya presses the evolvement in *Gather Together* through a limited first-person narrator who seems to know less of the villain's intention than is obvious to the reader. Thrice removed from the action, the reader sees that L. D. Tolbrook is nothing but a slick pimp, that his seductive sexual refusals can only lead to a calamitous end; that his please-turn-these-few-tricks-for-me-baby-so-I-can-get-out-of-an-urgent-jam line is an ancient inducement for susceptible females, but Maya the actor in the tragedy cannot. She is too much in love. Maya, the author, through whose eyes we see a younger, foolish "self," so painstakingly details the girl's descent into the brothel that Black women, all women, have enough vicarious example to avoid the trap. Again, through using the "self" as role model, not only is Maya able to instruct and inspire the reader but the sacrifice of personal disclosure authenticates the autobiography's integral depth.

> Sondra O'Neale, "Reconstruction of the Complete Self: New Images of Black Women in Maya Angelou's Continuing Autobiography," *Black Women Writers (1950–1980): A Critical Evaluation,* ed. Mari Evans (New York: Anchor Books/Doubleday, 1984), pp. 32–33

CHRISTINE FROULA   Mr. Freeman's abuse of Maya ⟨in *I Know Why the Caged Bird Sings*⟩ occurs in two episodes. In the first, her mother rescues her from a nightmare by taking her into her own bed, and Maya then awakes to find her mother gone to work and Mr. Freeman grasping her tightly. The child feels, first, bewilderment and terror: "His right hand was moving so fast and his heart was beating so hard that I was afraid that he would die." When Mr. Freeman subsides, however, so does Maya's fright: "Finally he was quiet, and then came the nice part. He held me so softly that I wished he wouldn't ever let me go. . . . This was probably my real father and we had found each other at last." After the abuse comes the silencing: Mr. Freeman enlists the child's complicity by an act of metaphysical violence, informing her that he will kill her beloved brother Bailey if she tells anyone what "they" have done. For the child, this prohibition prevents not so much telling as asking, for, confused as she is by her conflicting feelings, she has no idea what has happened. One day, however, Mr. Freeman stops her as she is setting out for the library, and it is then that he commits the actual rape on the terrified child, "a breaking and entering when even the senses are torn apart." Again threatened with violence if she tells, Maya retreats to her bed in a silent delirium, but the story emerges when her mother discovers her stained drawers, and Mr. Freeman is duly arrested and brought to trial. ⟨. . .⟩

Maya breaks her silence when a woman befriends her by taking her home and reading aloud to her, then sending her off with a book of poems, one of which she is to recite on her next visit. We are not told which poem it was, but later we find that the pinnacle of her literary achievement at age twelve was to have learned by heart the whole of Shakespeare's *Rape of Lucrece*—nearly two thousand lines. Maya, it appears, emerges from her literal silence into a literary one. Fitting her voice to Shakespeare's words, she writes safe limits around the exclamations of her wounded tongue and in this way is able to reenter the cultural text that her words had formerly disrupted. But if Shakespeare's poem redeems Maya from her hysterical silence, it is also a lover that she embraces at her peril. In Angelou's text, Shakespeare's Lucrece represents that violation of the spirit which Shakespeare's and all stories of sleeping beauties commit upon the female reader. Maya's feat of memory signals a double seduction: by the white culture that her grandmother wished her black child not to love and by the male culture which imposes upon the rape victim, epitomized in Lucrece, the double silence of a beauty that serves male fantasy and a death that serves male honor. The black child's identification with an exquisite rape fantasy of white male culture violates her reality. Wouldn't everyone be surprised, she muses, "when one day I woke out of my black ugly dream, and my real hair, which was long and blond, would take the place of the kinky mass that Momma wouldn't let me straighten? My light-blue eyes were going to hypnotize them. . . . Because I was really white and because a cruel fairy stepmother, who was understandably jealous of my beauty, had turned me into a too-big Negro girl, with nappy black hair, broad feet, and a space between her teeth that would hold a number two pencil." Maya's fantasy bespeaks her cultural seduction, but Angelou's powerful memoir, recovering the history that frames it, rescues the child's voice from this seduction by telling the prohibited story.

Christine Froula, "The Daughter's Seduction: Sexual Violence and Literary History," *Signs* 11, No. 4 (Summer 1986): 634–37

DOLLY A. McPHERSON Through the genre of autobiography, Angelou has celebrated the richness and vitality of Southern Black life and the sense of community that persists in the face of poverty and racial prejudice, initially revealing this celebration through a portrait of life as experienced by a Black child in the Arkansas of the 1930s (*I Know Why the Caged Bird Sings*, 1970). The second delineates a young woman struggling to create an existence that provides security and love in post–World War II America (*Gather Together in My Name*, 1974). The third presents a young, married adult in the 1950s seeking a career in show business and experiencing her first amiable contacts with Whites (*Singin' and Swingin' and Gettin' Merry Like Christmas*, 1976). The fourth volume (*The Heart of a Woman*, 1981) shows a wiser, more mature woman in the 1960s, examining the roles of being a woman and a mother. In her most recent volume, Angelou demonstrates that *All God's Children Need Traveling Shoes* (1986) to take them beyond familiar borders and to enable them to see and understand the world from another's vantage point.

While the burden of this serial autobiography is essentially a recapturing of her own subjective experiences, Angelou's effort throughout her work is to describe the influences—personal as well as cultural, historical and social—that have shaped her life. Dominant in Angelou's autobiography is the exploration of the self—the self in relationship with intimate others: the family, the community, the world. Angelou does not recount these experiences simply because they occurred, but because they represent stages of her spiritual growth and awareness—what one writer calls "stages of self." ⟨. . .⟩

A study of Maya Angelou's autobiography is significant not only because the autobiography offers insights into personal and group experience in America, but because it creates a unique place within Black autobiographical tradition, not because it is better than its formidable autobiographical predecessors, but because Angelou, throughout her autobiographical writing, adopts a special stance in relation to the self, the community and the world. Angelou's concerns with family and community, as well as with work and her conceptions of herself as a human being, are echoed throughout her autobiography. The ways in which she faces these concerns offer instruction into the range of survival strategies available to women in America and reveal, as well, important insights into Black traditions and culture.

Dolly A. McPherson, *Order out of Chaos: The Autobiographical Works of Maya Angelou* (New York: Peter Lang, 1990), pp. 5–6

CAROL E. NEUBAUER   Within four years of the publication of *Just Give Me a Cool Drink 'Fore I Diiie*, Maya Angelou completed a second volume of poetry, *Oh Pray My Wings Are Gonna Fit Me Well* (1975). By the time of its release, her reputation as a poet who transforms much of the pain and disappointment of life into lively verse had been established. During the 1970s, her reading public grew accustomed to seeing her poems printed in *Cosmopolitan*. Angelou had become recognized not only as a spokesperson for blacks and women, but also for all people who are committed to raising the moral standards of living in the United States. The poems collected in *My Wings*, indeed, appear at the end of the Vietnam era and in some important ways exceed the scope of her first volume. Many question traditional American values and urge people to make an honest appraisal of the demoralizing rift between the ideal and the real. Along with poems about love and the oppression of black people, the poet adds several that directly challenge Americans to reexamine their lives and to strive to reach the potential richness that has been compromised by self-interest since the beginnings of the country.

One of the most moving poems in *My Wings* is entitled "Alone," in which carefully measured verses describe the general alienation of people in the twentieth century. "Alone" is not directed at any one particular sector of society but rather is focused on the human condition in general. No one, the poet cautions, can live in this world alone. This message punctuates the end of the three major stanzas and also serves as a separate refrain between each and at the close of the poem:

> Alone, all alone
> Nobody, but nobody
> Can make it out here alone.

Angelou begins by looking within herself and discovering that her soul is without a home. Moving from an inward glimpse to an outward sweep, she recognizes that even millionaires suffer from this modern malaise and live lonely lives with "hearts of stone." Finally, she warns her readers to listen carefully and change the direction of their lives:

> Storm clouds are gathering
> The wind is gonna blow
> The race of man is suffering.

For its own survival, the human race must break down barriers and rescue one from loneliness. The only cure, the poet predicts, is to acknowledge common interests and work toward common goals. ⟨. . .⟩

In one poem, "Southern Arkansia," the poet shifts her attention from the general condition of humanity to the plight of black people in America. The setting of this tightly structured poem is the locale where Angelou spent most of her childhood. At the end of the three stanzas, she poses a question concerning the responsibility and guilt involved in the exploitation of the slaves. Presumably, the white men most immediately involved have never answered for their inhumane treatment of "bartered flesh and broken bones." The poet doubts that they have ever even paused to "ponder" or "wonder" about their proclivity to value profit more than human life.

Carol E. Neubauer, "Maya Angelou: Self and Song of Freedom in the Southern Tradition," *Southern Women Writers: The New Generation*, ed. Tonette Bond Inge (Tuscaloosa: University of Alabama Press, 1990), pp. 134–35

GLORIA T. HULL   *I Shall Not Be Moved* is Maya Angelou's fifth book of poetry. Because of who she is as actress, activist, woman of letters, and acclaimed autobiographer (*I Know Why the Caged Bird Sings* and succeeding volumes), she is able to command our ear. As I listen, what I hear in her open, colloquial poems is racial wit and earthy wisdom, honest black female pain and strength, humor, passion, and rhetorical force. What I miss— probably because of my academic training and my own predilections as reader and practicing poet—is verbal ingenuity, honed craft, intellectual surprise, and flawless rhythms. Each of her books has at least one striking poem that stands as a centerpiece. Here, it is the title-inspiring work, "Our Grandmothers," which begins:

> She lay, skin down on the moist dirt,
> the canebrake rustling
> with the whispers of leaves, and
> loud longing of hounds and
> the ransack of hunters crackling the near branches.
>
> She muttered, lifting her head a nod toward freedom,
> I shall not, I
> shall not be
> moved.

With slavery figuring so prominently in recent African American women's writings, it is not surprising that this keystone poem of Angelou's mines that tenacious reality.

Gloria T. Hull, "Covering Ground," *Belles Lettres* 6, No. 3 (Spring 1991): 1–2

ROBERT FULGHUM   After five volumes of autobiography and five volumes of poetry, Maya Angelou offers us this very small volume of 24 poetically entitled essays so carefully crafted they cover only 54 actual pages of writing. Her publisher, Random House, has assigned the book to the publishing category "Inspiration/Self-Help." But *Wouldn't Take Nothing for My Journey Now* really belongs in an even more prestigious location in a bookstore, labeled "Wisdom Literature." ⟨. . .⟩

Angelou has dedicated this book to Oprah Winfrey. Not a casual gesture, it is a salute to the speaker at the head table of the banquet of sisterhood.

Maya Angelou has, of course, become one of these wise women herself, as her new book so clearly demonstrates. At the end of the first essay, she writes: "Women should be tough, tender, laugh as much as possible, and live long lives. The struggle for equality continues unabated, and the woman warrior who is armed with wit and courage will be among the first to celebrate victory." As of this past January, millions of Americans realize how certainly this celebration is underway. ⟨. . .⟩

To read these essays carefully, slowly, even one a day over a month, is to feel you are there with Maya Angelou on her day away, leaning back in the shade of an old tree on a hot afternoon; after an arduous journey you have come home. The companion who has waited for you is older than you are. She knows where you've been. Like the prodigal son, she too has wandered in foreign lands and returned again and again to the place where she began. She has known pain and sorrow, sinfulness and saintliness. Yet she can sing and dance, recite poems, speak with words of silence and make you laugh or cry. There is no finer company than hers. She has something to tell you now. Listen. She is wise.

Robert Fulghum, "Home Truths and Homilies," Washington Post Book World, 19 September 1993, p. 4

❖ *Bibliography*

I Know Why the Caged Bird Sings. 1969.
Just Give Me a Cool Drink of Water 'Fore I Diiie: The Poetry of Maya Angelou.
    1971, 1988 (with *Oh Pray My Wings Are Gonna Fit Me Well*).
Gather Together in My Name. 1974, 1985.
Oh Pray My Wings Are Gonna Fit Me Well. 1975.

Singin' and Swingin' and Gettin' Merry Like Christmas. 1976.

And Still I Rise. 1978.

Weekend Glory. 198-.

The Heart of a Woman. 1981.

Poems. 1981, 1986.

Shaker, Why Don't You Sing? 1983.

All God's Children Need Traveling Shoes. 1986.

Now Sheba Sings the Songs. 1986.

Conversations with Maya Angelou. Ed. Jeffrey M. Elliot. 1989.

I Shall Not Be Moved. 1990.

Maya Angelou Omnibus. 1991.

On the Pulse of Morning. 1993.

Soul Looks Back in Wonder. 1993.

Lessons in Living. 1993.

Life Doesn't Frighten Me. 1993.

Wouldn't Take Nothing for My Journey Now. 1993.

I Love the Look of Words. 1993.

And My Best Friend Is Chicken. 1994.

James Baldwin
1924–1987

JAMES ARTHUR BALDWIN was born on August 2, 1924, in Harlem, New York City, to Emma Berdis Jones and an unknown father. When James was three years old his mother married David Baldwin, the son of a slave, who was a factory worker and lay preacher; the couple would subsequently have eight children. Baldwin joined the Church of Mount Calvary of the Pentecostal Faith in 1938 and became a preacher, although in later years he expressed scorn and regret over his youthful religious activities. He attended De Witt Clinton High School, a largely white school in the Bronx, from 1938 to 1942. After working at a series of menial jobs in New Jersey, he moved to Greenwich Village in 1944 in order to support his family after the death of his stepfather the previous year. He met Richard Wright, whose writing exerted considerable influence on him. Failing in the attempt to write a novel, he began writing reviews in the *Nation* and the *New Leader* and gained notoriety by a controversial essay, "The Harlem Ghetto: Winter 1948," in *Commentary* for February 1948.

Later that year Baldwin won a Rosenwald Foundation Fellowship; in November he used much of the grant money to emigrate to Paris, where he remained for the next nine years, although returning frequently to New York. He associated with many of the American expatriates in Paris—Saul Bellow, Truman Capote, Herbert Gold—along with Jean-Paul Sartre, Jean Genet, and other French writers. One friend, the painter Lucien Happersberger, invited Baldwin to spend time at his home in Switzerland in 1951, where Baldwin completed his most highly regarded novel, *Go Tell It on the Mountain* (1953). This novel, drawing upon his childhood experiences, deals with the religious and social maturation of a boy in a repressive and racist society.

A Guggenheim Fellowship awarded in 1954 allowed Baldwin the leisure to work on his next book, *Giovanni's Room* (1956). This is one of the first modern novels to deal frankly with homosexuality. *Another Country* (1962), a novel on which Baldwin worked for six years, is a wide-ranging treatment

16

of homosexual, bisexual, and interracial love; it was a tremendous popular success. He also published two noted collections of essays, *Notes of a Native Son* (1955) and *Nobody Knows My Name* (1961). Returning to the United States in 1957, Baldwin became actively involved in the civil rights movement, meeting with Martin Luther King, Jr., and becoming spokesman for the Congress on Racial Equality (CORE) and the Student Nonviolent Coordinating Committee (SNCC).

In 1963 Baldwin published the controversial *The Fire Next Time*, a collection of two essays that predict social apocalypse in America if the question of racial harmony is not addressed. The play *Blues for Mr. Charlie* (1964), a violent depiction of racism in the South, also provoked outrage from white critics. *No Name in the Street* (1972) is a still more unrestrained exposé of American racism. Nevertheless, Baldwin was labeled an "Uncle Tom" by Eldridge Cleaver in *Soul on Ice* (1968) for his lack of support of African nationalism.

Later works by Baldwin display a more subdued approach to racial issues. Such nonfictional works as *The Devil Finds Work* (1976) and *The Evidence of Things Not Seen* (1985) sensitively and complexly explore the history of race relations in the United States. Baldwin's later novels—*Tell Me How Long the Train's Been Gone* (1968), *If Beale Street Could Talk* (1974), *Little Man, Little Man* (1976), and *Just Above My Head* (1979)—combine autobiography with intricacy of character portrayal; but some critics feel that they merely repeat themes and motifs expressed better in his earlier works.

James Baldwin died of stomach cancer in St. Paul de Vence, France, on December 1, 1987.

Critical Extracts

LANGSTON HUGHES   I think that one definition of the great artist might be the creator who projects the biggest dream in terms of the least person. There is something in Cervantes or Shakespeare, Beethoven or Rembrandt or Louis Armstrong that millions can understand. The American native son who signs his name James Baldwin is quite a ways off from fitting such a definition of a great artist in writing, but he is not as far off as many another writer who deals in picture captions or journalese in the hope of capturing and retaining a wide public. James Baldwin writes down to nobody, and he is thought-provoking, tantalizing, irritating, abusing and amusing. And he uses words as the sea uses waves, to flow and beat, advance and retreat, rise and take a bow in disappearing. ⟨. . .⟩

Few American writers handle words more effectively in the essay form than James Baldwin. To my way of thinking, he is much better at provoking thought in the essay than he is in arousing emotion in fiction. I much prefer *Notes of a Native Son* to his novel, *Go Tell It on the Mountain*, where the surface excellence and poetry of his writing did not seem to me to suit the earthiness of his subject matter. In his essays, words and material suit each other. The thought becomes poetry, and the poetry illuminates the thought.

> Langston Hughes, "From Harlem to Paris," *New York Times Book Review*, 26 February 1956, p. 26

ROBERT BONE   The best of Baldwin's novels is *Go Tell It on the Mountain* (1953), and his best is very good indeed. It ranks with Jean Toomer's *Cane*, Richard Wright's *Native Son*, and Ralph Ellison's *Invisible Man* as a major contribution to American fiction. For this novel cuts through the walls of the store-front church to the essence of Negro experience in America. This is Baldwin's earliest world, his bright and morning star, and it glows with metaphorical intensity. Its emotions are his emotions; its language, his native tongue. The result is a prose of unusual power and authority. One senses in Baldwin's first novel a confidence, control, and mastery of style that he has not attained again in the novel form.

The central event of *Go Tell It on the Mountain* is the religious conversion of an adolescent boy. In a long autobiographical essay, which forms a part of *The Fire Next Time*, Baldwin leaves no doubt that he was writing of his own experience. During the summer of his fourteenth year, he tells us, he succumbed to the spiritual seduction of a woman evangelist. On the night of his conversion, he suddenly found himself lying on the floor before the altar. He describes his trancelike state, the singing and clapping of the saints, and the all-night prayer vigil which helped to bring him "through." He then recalls the circumstances of his life that prompted so pagan and desperate a journey to the throne of Grace.

The overwhelming fact of Baldwin's childhood was his victimization by the white power only indirectly, as refracted through the brutality and degradation of the Harlem ghetto. The world beyond the ghetto seemed remote, and scarcely could be linked in a child's imagination to the harrowing conditions of his daily life. And yet a vague terror, transmitted through his parents to the ghetto child, attested to the power of the white world. Meanwhile, in the forefront of his consciousness was a set of fears by no means vague.

To a young boy growing up in the Harlem ghetto, damnation was a clear and present danger: "For the wages of sin were visible everywhere, in every wine-stained and urine-splashed hallway, in every clanging ambulance bell, in every scar on the faces of the pimps and their whores, in every helpless, newborn baby being brought into this danger, in every knife and pistol fight on the Avenue." To such a boy, the store-front church offered a refuge and a sanctuary from the terrors of the street. God and safety became synonymous, and the church, a part of his survival strategy.

> Robert Bone, *The Negro Novel in America* (New Haven: Yale University Press, 1958 [rev. ed. 1965]), pp. 218–19

MARCUS KLEIN   The invisibility of the Negro in America has in fact been James Baldwin's underlying metaphor ⟨. . .⟩, and when he has been most responsive to his materials he has made of invisibility, the failure of identity, a lyric of frustration and loss. What is most revealing for the case Baldwin comes to represent, however, is that the fury in his frustration and the pathos in his loss have led him, in a progress of three novels and far too many personal essays, even further from the clarity with which he began. What promised to be a dramatic recognition of the actual conditions of invisibility in his first novel, *Go Tell It on the Mountain* (1953), became a rhetoric of privileged alienation. As a Negro, Baldwin was society's victim. As a victim, he was alienated. As an alienatee, he presented himself with vast moral authority. In the space of a few years the rhetoric and the authority have done him less and less service, and he has been left to fall back on an iteration of the word "love." Love in its demonstration has become, finally, a fantasy of innocence.

The plight in invisibility has remained a plight for Baldwin, despite his uses of it as an instrument of moral authority and despite the fury in his words. His heroes are victims, caught between despair and spite, their spitefulness directed sometimes against the very sympathy which as victims they earn. They are heroes who cannot make themselves felt in the world, heroes for whom society almost provides but then doesn't quite provide a clear, felt identity. The story Baldwin tells repeatedly, in his novels, his stories, his writing for the theater, and in his essays, is of the attempt of a heroic innocent to achieve what Baldwin usually calls "identity"—"identity" is by all measure his favorite word, but on occasion the word is "manhood" or "maturity"—and the thwarting, then, of this hero by his society. The hero is prevented from entering the world. He does not achieve the definition provided by a place in the world. If sometimes in a final movement he does locate himself in a peripheral place and in a special expression of the self, in the expatriate community of Paris, perhaps, or the world of jazz, more often he finds himself shunted into one or another expression of neurosis— religious mania in Go Tell It on the Mountain and in Baldwin's play The Amen Corner, homosexuality elsewhere, a nightmare violence such as that in the first movement of Another Country (1962). And the hero's fulfillment stands, then, ironically and bitterly, for the quantity of his pain.

Marcus Klein, "James Baldwin: A Question of Identity," After Alienation: American Novels at Mid-Century (Cleveland: World Publishing Co., 1962), pp. 147–48

STEPHEN SPENDER   Baldwin's power is in his ability to express situations—the situation of being a Negro, and of being white, and of being human. Beyond this, he is perhaps too impatient to be a good novelist, and although he is a powerful essayist, his experiences are so colored with feelings that he seems unable to relate the thoughts which arise from his feelings to parallel situations that have given rise to other men's thoughts. Thus it seems important to him in his feelings about American Negroes that he should write as though there were no other Negroes, no other oppressed peoples anywhere in the world. He states: "Negroes do not, strictly, or legally speaking, exist in any other" country but the United States where "they are taught really to despise themselves from the moment their eyes open on the world." One suspects that for Mr. Baldwin it is sacrilege to suggest that there are Negroes outside America; and from this there follows the implication that the Negro problem is *his* problem that can only be discussed on *his* terms. Hence too his contempt for most people who, in the main, agree with him, especially for poor despised American liberals.

He has, as a Negro, a right, of course, to despise liberals, but he exploits his moral advantage too much. ⟨. . .⟩

Although Mr. Baldwin considers love is the only answer to the American race problem, it is not at all evident from his book ⟨*The Fire Next Time*⟩ that he loves white Americans, and at times it is even doubtful whether he loves his own people. Not that I blame him for this. What I do criticize him for is postulating a quite impossible demand as the only way of dealing with a problem that has to be solved.

Stephen Spender, "James Baldwin: Voice of a Revolution," *Partisan Review* 30, No. 2 (Summer 1963): 256–58

SUSAN SONTAG   The truth is that *Blues for Mister Charlie* isn't really about what it claims to be about. It is supposed to be about racial strife. But it is really about the anguish of tabooed sexual longings, about the crisis of identity which comes from confronting these longings, and about the rage and destructiveness (often, self-destructiveness) by which one tries to surmount this crisis. The surface may be ⟨Clifford⟩ Odets, but the interior is pure Tennessee Williams. What Baldwin has done is to take the leading theme of the serious theater of the fifties—sexual anguish— and work it up as a political play. Buried in *Blues for Mister Charlie* is the plot of several successes of the last decade: the gruesome murder of a hand- some virile young man by those who envy him his virility.

Susan Sontag, "Going to Theater, etc." (1964), *Against Interpretation and Other Essays* (New York: Farrar, Straus & Giroux, 1966), p. 155

FERN MARJA ECKMAN   James Arthur Baldwin was born in Har- lem which is geographically part of the United States but sociologically an island surrounded by the rest of the country. He was born a Negro. And to some extent this accidental conjunction of time and place has dictated his course. But it does not define who he is.

This slight, dark man is salt rubbed in the wounds of the nation's con- science. He is the shriek of the lynched. He is an accusing finger thrust in the face of white America. He is a fierce, brilliant light illuminating the unspeakable and the shameful. Gadfly and bogey man, triumphant and despairing, he has been an impassioned spokesman for the ranks of unheard Negroes, a spokesman initially appointed—and anointed—by the whites.

But first and foremost he is a writer, an American phenomenon, one of the nation's great creative artists. Like every creative artist, Baldwin mirrors the mountains, valleys and plains of his environment. In his frail person, he embodies the paradoxes and the potentials of the integration battle in the United States.

In his oratory, and sometimes, in his prose, there are apt to be passages clouded by confusion; and his political innocence has made a number of his allies apprehensive. But his emotional impact is uncompromising: harsh, violent and beautiful.

Three times now his books have secured a niche on the bestseller list, confirming his commercial attractions and enhancing his literary prestige. His old-young features with their medieval cast have been exposed frequently enough in photographs, interviews and lectures to have seemed ubiquitous. Luminaries on several continents clamor to meet him.

But all of this is part of the glittering panoply of the public Baldwin. And: "The James Baldwin the public knows is not the Jimmy I know," says his sister and secretary, Mrs. Gloria Davis Karefa-Smart.

Jimmy Baldwin, jagged as a sliver, belongs to a generation of angry, middle-aged men. He is a nonconformist, a partially reconstructed expatriate, a flagrant individualist disavowed by the bulk of middle-class Negroes, who recoil from his unorthodox conduct and even less orthodox standards.

Fern Marja Eckman, *The Furious Passage of James Baldwin* (New York: M. Evans & Co., 1966), pp. 11–12

DAVID LITTLEJOHN   *Another Country* has, in its frantic new writer's world called New York, much of the same necessity, the same quality of desperate exorcism as Baldwin's earlier works. But things here are less under control. Almost all of the thinking, the non-imaginative thinking of Baldwin's essays is sandwiched into the fiction, bearing a suggestion that the man is now writing more from his ideas than his imagination. The piercing one-note tone of repetitiousness of so much of this long book supports this dissatisfying notion. Another dangerous sign is the confusion of narrative authority, very like the confusions of self-identity which mar so many of Baldwin's latest and weakest essays. His own opinions mingle with those of his characters, subjectivity jars with objectivity in such a way as to indicate that the author is unaware of the difference: i.e., that James Baldwin, through the 1950's the sole master of *control* in American prose, in the 1960's has begun to lose control.

What is there to salvage and prize? A number of things. More often than not, between the explosions, *Another Country* reminds the reader that James Baldwin is still one of the genuine stylists of the English language. ⟨. . .⟩

There are moments, too—especially towards the end of the novel—when Baldwin shows himself a worthy heir of Proust, suavely analyzing the mixed motives of lovers in pairs and threes and fours, their whirlpools of self-torment over the feelings of others. Eric, in particular, is so poignantly honest it wounds. And the conclusions of the book, Ida's conclusion, Eric's conclusion, are not only genuine but, for once, sympathetic and humane.

Still, all these make up—what? five percent? ten percent? of the book. Most of what we have to fall back on, finally, is the same bed of nails we began with, that four-hundred-page torture in a new-New York accent. And what good, even to a white man, is a bed of nails?

As of all "painful" works, no one reader can speculate how useful the pain may be for another. One may ask whether it is "realistic"—where there *are* such people? Baldwin, in this novel, has convinced me there are, and that they are not always the freakishly odd exceptions. The book strikes me, moreover, as precisely and exactly of its time and of its place, as much so as other honest, unfictionlike American novels such as *Herzog* or Clancy Sigal's *Going Away*. What its real value for Americans will prove, I think, for Americans who can separate the good from the bad—like so many Negro works, it is a remarkably "American" book—is that of the first open and direct statement, however unpleasant, of some underlying psychological truths of the race war, and of much else that is wrong with America as well. It reads like a record of the climactic sessions in a long, national psychoanalysis—*here* is what is really wrong, it seems to cry, for all of its own confusion, a many-men's sickness that only *one* man has been able to define, out loud.

David Littlejohn, *Black on White: A Critical Survey of Writing by American Negroes* (New York: Grossman Publishers, 1966), pp. 130, 132–33

IRVING HOWE   Now, after having read Baldwin's new novel *Tell Me How Long the Train's Been Gone*, I have come to feel that the whole problem of Negro writing in America is far more complex that I had ever recognized, probably more complex that even Ellison had supposed, and perhaps so complex as to be, at this moment, almost beyond discussion. *Tell Me How Long the Train's Been Gone* is a remarkably bad novel, signaling the collapse of a writer of some distinction. But apart from its intrinsic qualities, it helps make clear that neither militancy nor its refusal, neither a program of aesthetic autonomy nor its denial, seems enough for the Negro novelist who wishes to transmute the life of his people into a serious piece of fiction. No program, no rhetoric, no political position makes that much difference. What does make the difference I would now be hard pressed to say, but as I have been thinking about the Negro writers I know or have read, I have come to believe that their problems are a good deal more personal than we have usually supposed. For the Negro writer, if he is indeed to be a *writer*, public posture matters less than personal identity. His problem is to reach into his true feelings, be they militant or passive, as distinct from the feelings he thinks he should have, or finds it fashionable to have, about the life of his fellow blacks. The Negro writer shares in the sufferings of an exploited race, and it would be outrageous to suppose that simply by decision he can avoid declaring his outrage; but he is also a solitary man, solitary insofar as he is a writer, solitary even more because he is a black writer, and solitary most of all if he is a black man who writes. Frequently he is detached from and in opposition to other blacks; unavoidably he must find himself troubled by his relationship to the whole looming tradition of Western literature, which is both his and never entirely his; and sooner or later he must profoundly wish to get away from racial polemic and dialectic, simply in order to reach, in his own lifetime, some completeness of being. As it seems to me, James Baldwin has come to a point where all of these problems crush down upon him and he does not quite know who he is, as writer, celebrity, or black man; so that he now suffers from the most disastrous of psychic conditions—a separation between his feelings and his voice.

Irving Howe, "James Baldwin: At Ease in Apocalypse," *Harper's Magazine* 237, No. 3 (September 1968): 95

ALFRED KAZIN   As a writer Baldwin is as obsessed by sex and family as Strindberg was, but instead of using situations for their dramatic value, Baldwin likes to pile up all possible emotional conflicts as assertions.

But for the same reason that in *Giovanni's Room* Baldwin made everybody white just to show that he could, and in *Tell Me How Long the Train's Been Gone* transferred the son-father quarrel to a quarrel with a brother, so one feels about *Another Country* that Baldwin writes fiction in order to use up his private difficulties; even his fiction piles up the atmosphere of raw emotion that is his literary standby. ⟨. . .⟩

But in *Notes of a Native Son, Nobody Knows My Name, The Fire Next Time*, Baldwin dropped the complicated code for love difficulties he uses in his novels and simplified himself into an "angry Black" very powerfully indeed—and this just before Black nationalists were to turn on writers like him. The character who calls himself "James Baldwin" in *his* nonfiction novel is more professionally enraged, more doubtfully an evangelist for his people, than the actual James Baldwin, a very literary mind indeed. But there is in *Notes of a Native Son* a genius for bringing many symbols together, an instinctive association with the 1943 Harlem riot, the streets of smashed plate glass, that stems from the all too understandable fascination of the Negro with the public sources of his fate. The emphasis is on heat, fire, anger, the sense of being hemmed in and suffocated; the words are tensed into images that lacerate and burn. Reading Baldwin's essays, we are suddenly past the discordancy that has plagued his fiction—a literal problem of conflict, for Baldwin's fiction shows him trying to transpose facts into fiction without sacrificing the emotional capital that has been his life.

Alfred Kazin, *Bright Book of Life: American Novelists and Storytellers from Hemingway to Mailer* (Boston: Little, Brown, 1973), pp. 222–24

JOYCE CAROL OATES   A spare, slender narrative, told first-person by a 19-year-old black girl named Tish, *If Beale Street Could Talk* manages to be many things at the same time. It is economically, almost poetically constructed, and may certainly be read as a kind of allegory, which refuses conventional outbursts of violence, preferring to stress the provisional, tentative nature of our lives. ⟨. . .⟩

Baldwin certainly risked a great deal by putting his complex narrative, which involves a number of important characters, into the mouth of a young girl. Yet Tish's voice comes to seem absolutely natural and we learn to know her from the inside out. Even her flights of poetic fancy—involving rather subtle speculations upon the nature of male-female relationships, or black-white relationships, as well as her articulation of what it feels like to be pregnant—are convincing. Also convincing is Baldwin's insistence upon the primacy of emotions like love, hate, or terror: it is not sentimentality, but basic psychology, to acknowledge the fact that one person will die, and another survive simply because one has not the guarantee of a fundamental human bond, like love, while the other has. ⟨. . .⟩

If Beale Street Could Talk is a moving, painful story. It is so vividly human and so obviously based upon reality, that it strikes us as timeless—an art that has not the slightest need of esthetic tricks, and even less need of fashionable apocalytic excesses.

> Joyce Carol Oates, [Review of *If Beale Street Could Talk*], *New York Times Book Review*, 19 May 1974, pp. 1–2

SHIRLEY S. ALLEN   From the very beginning of the novel ⟨*Go Tell It on the Mountain*⟩ Baldwin clearly indicates the central importance of religious symbolism. The title, taken from a Negro spiritual, suggests not only the basic Christian setting of the action, but also the kind of symbolism we are to expect. In different versions of the folk hymn the command, "Go tell it," refers to the good news (gospel) that "Jesus Christ is born" or to the message of Moses to the Pharaoh, "Let my people go." The ambiguity of the allusion in the title is intentional and also suggests the unity of Old Testament and New Testament faith that is characteristic of the Christian belief described in the novel—the teachings of a sect formed from Baptist practices and Calvinist doctrines, grounded in frequent reading of the King James translation of the Bible, and influenced by the needs, hopes, and artistic expression of Negro slaves. ⟨. . .⟩ Baldwin's use of Biblical allusion in the title and the first epigraph to give symbolic meaning to John's conversion and to interpret the event is typical of his use of symbolism throughout the novel. Each of the three parts has a title and two epigraphs referring to the Bible or Christian hymns, and each of the prayers in Part Two begins with a quotation from a hymn. Two of Gabriel's sermons, based on Biblical texts, are paraphrased at some length. The thoughts and spoken words of almost all the characters are larded with passages from the King James version, and the major characters are identified with their favorite texts of scripture. The doctrines, ritual, songs, and visual symbols of the Baptist church are equally pervasive in the words and events of the novel.

But all this religious apparatus, like the central scene of the tarry service itself, is used not simply as psychological and social milieu for the action, but also to give symbolic expression and archetypal meaning to the characters and events. Biblical allusion in Go Tell It on the Mountain serves some of the same purposes as the Homeric myth in Ulysses and the Olympic paraphernalia in The Centaur, but Baldwin's use of the religious apparatus is more like that of Dostoyevsky in the Brothers Karamazov than that of Joyce and Updike in one important respect: the symbolism arises naturally out of the setting. This very integration of symbolic apparatus and milieu is perhaps the reason critics have missed the symbolism—a case of not seeing the forest in the trees. ⟨. . .⟩

The effect of this religious symbolism is to keep the reader aware of the universal elements in John's struggle so that its significance will not be lost amid the specific details and particular persons complicating his conflict. The symbolism prevents us, for example, from mistaking John's peculiar problem as a black taking his place in a society dominated by whites for the more basic problem, common to all humanity, of a child taking his place in adult society. The symbolism also keeps us from being sidetracked by the specific personality of Gabriel or the fact that he is not John's real father, since he is named for the angel of the Annunciation and therefore symbolically is the agency of fatherhood. We are to see John in the larger view as a human child struggling against dependency and finding a sense of his own selfhood through the initiation rite practiced in his community, even though Baldwin has fully realized that struggle in the specific circumstances of Harlem, the fully rounded human characteristics of the Grimes family, and the particular heritage of American Negro religion.

Shirley S. Allen, "Religious Symbolism and Psychic Reality in Baldwin's Go Tell It on the Mountain," CLA Journal 19, No. 2 (December 1975): 175, 177–79

TRUDIER HARRIS   Sex that was transformed into godhead in If Beale Street Could Talk is eliminated altogether in Just Above My Head. Realizing that he perhaps could not keep his characters at the level of the gods and still enable them to live in this world, Baldwin initially returned to the worldliness of sex in Just Above My Head as well as to some of the familiar conflicts between males and females that were visible in his earlier fiction. In the conclusion of the novel, however, Baldwin leaves Julia, though in this world, yet beyond the petty realities of role playing and sex. The brotherhood he had underscored with Tish, Fonny, their families, and the Puerto Ricans in *If Beale Street Could Talk* is picked up again with the extended families in *Just Above My Head*, particularly as it is manifested at the end of the novel with Hall's family and with Julia and Jimmy.

Having moved beyond sex, wives, mothers, sisters, and lovers, the major black male and female characters in *Just Above My Head* are truly at peace when they have transcended physical contact (though Hall has not yet transcended desire) and can also exist at an implied larger-than-life level. Julia has gone through many storms to arrive at the calm she manifests on the day of the barbecue. And Hall has gone through a lot to realize that Julia can no longer be possessed physically. They have given up each other's bodies for mutual respect and peaceful coexistence. Lest we conclude that such a platonic view might suggest the end of the family, keep in mind that Hall still has Ruth and his children, Odessa and Tony. He has them, and he has Julia. Somewhere in the midst of that seeming overdose is the suggestion that perhaps the extended family, the communal family, minimizes the acute tension that individuals feel who are isolated in nuclear families. Remember, again, that Florence and Elizabeth are in many ways isolated; especially is this true of Florence and her desire to escape from "niggers." Ruth voluntarily gave up her repressive nuclear family, and Ida voluntarily left Harlem to escape what she imagined would be confinement from her environment if she remained within her nuclear family. The concept of the extended family—across oceans, across nations and nationalities, across sexes—as a viable alternative to the restrictions of the nuclear family surfaced in *If Beale Street Could Talk* with Fonny and Frank becoming a part of the Rivers family, and with the Puerto Ricans in New York adopting Tish and Fonny. Conflicts that may arise ultimately seem small because the support group is larger; such is the case with the extended families in *Just Above My Head*. Before the establishment of peace, however, it must be clear who can touch whom, who must play which roles for whom, and what all expectations are. It is only after all those things have been clarified that Hall and Julia can be so peaceful with each other. They have sacrificed parochial experience for international experience, and they have thereby broken free of some of the restraints that so characterized the interactions between black men and black women in Baldwin's earlier fiction. Their situation does not allow us to conclude that the black man has completely given up his desire for mastery over black women; it does suggest, however,

that at least one kind of black woman has escaped from the limitations of
that desire. Hall and Julia may or may not point the way to the future in
Baldwin's works, but they do show that at least one healthy pattern of
resolution to the conflicts between black men and black women in Baldwin's
fiction has been meticulously worked out.

> Trudier Harris, *Black Women in the Fiction of James Baldwin* (Knoxville: University
> of Tennessee Press, 1985), pp. 210–11

JANE CAMPBELL   Baldwin transmutes the messianic myth into
that of an artist-priest whose visionary powers allow transcendence of oppression so that she or he can ultimately change history. To Baldwin, the
personal and racial past are inseparable; therefore, to grasp racial history,
one must first confront personal history. Beyond knowledge lies change,
and within each sensitive intellectual lodge the tools for transforming history.
Go Tell It on the Mountain, like *Invisible Man*, exemplifies distrust of collective
effort in favor of individual action. Moreover, although Baldwin's work
anticipates the urge to explore and reconstruct history, an urge permeating
Afro-American literature of the sixties, seventies, and eighties, *Go Tell It
on the Mountain* does not reckon with African history or culture.

The introspection Baldwin demands of his leaders prohibits him from
employing the romance, with its de-emphasis on subjectivity. Instead, he
turns to the confessional mode to convey his protagonist's guilt, confession,
and transcendence. By using flashbacks disguised as prayers to present personal histories, Baldwin underscores the spiritual dimensions of those histories, at the same time focusing on the points of congruence between the
personal and racial past. Finally, one must applaud Baldwin's recognition
of the centrality of religion in black life and his ingenuity in employing a
fictional mode that clearly suggests spiritual and religious concerns.

In a sense, Baldwin's entire canon might be called confessional, but critics
have done surprisingly little to illuminate Baldwin's use of the form. Most
refer to *Go Tell It on the Mountain* as an autobiographical novel, based on
the author's now legendary conversion to the ministry. But to term a novel
"autobiographical" tells only part of the story; to some extent, most fiction
may derive from the writer's life. The term autobiographical, though it does
link episodes and characters to their creator, fails to elucidate much about
the way the artist transforms these elements into art. Moreover, authors

often augment or alter the actual when they transmute it into fiction. Baldwin, for example, as quoted by Fern M. Eckman, says that Richard, John Grimes' biological father, is "completely imaginary," but at least one critic has theorized that Richard's characterization is unsuccessful because Baldwin was too close to his material to achieve aesthetic distance. Looking at Go Tell It on the Mountain as confessional probably discloses more about Baldwin's transformation of life into art than viewing the work as autobiography.

Jane Campbell, "Retreat into the Self: Ralph Ellison's Invisible Man and James Baldwin's Go Tell It on the Mountain," Mythic Black Fiction: The Transformation of History (Knoxville: University of Tennessee Press, 1986), pp. 101–2

HORACE A. PORTER   There is, of course, genuine merit, even if shrouded in the thick smoke of his fiery black rhetoric, in certain of his insights about America's vision of itself. There are, for example, as he observes on several occasions, people in the world who exist far beyond the confines of the American imagination. But what I call the tragedy concerns Baldwin's abdication of his responsibility as a serious writer—a serious writer like Henry James—in the course of his decision, enthusiasm, and willingness to assume the role of racial spokesman and representative. An accomplished writer and cosmopolite, Baldwin knows with acute awareness how hopelessly interdependent the world has become. If America is the premier example of "retarded adolescence," as Baldwin calls it, what country, if not his own, would he suggest even figuratively has achieved adulthood or maturity—his beloved France, England, Brazil, Nigeria? Furthermore, in "Everybody's Protest Novel" Baldwin argues passionately that a human being is considerably more than "merely a member of a Society or a Group or a deplorable conundrum to be explained by science." But he willingly becomes a representative of people of color around the globe: "What they don't know about me is what they don't know about Nicaragua." ⟨. . .⟩

It almost seems as though the gods conspire against Baldwin. On the one hand, they grant him the rare and priceless gift of supreme literary intelligence. On the other, they provide a set of personal circumstances, including the historical moment, that leads him to assume the arduous task of illuminating and seeking to solve the so-called American dilemma. They made him black. To paraphrase Louis Armstrong singing "What Did I Do

to Be So Black and Blue," "His only sin was in his skin." Given Baldwin's
Harlem boyhood of poverty and anonymity, it makes perfect sense and it
is certainly to his eternal credit that he strongly identifies with black Americans, and that he, so to speak, cut his teeth on *Uncle Tom's Cabin* and
Native Son. It is understandable that he was inclined to exhort and persuade
the hard-hearted and to articulate the rage of the disesteemed. The temper
of the times, the civil rights movement, gave him the historical stage on
which to voice with moral clarity and authority what the consequences of
America's moral evasion and racial bigotry would be.

But, finally, the threatening possibility that he clairvoyantly sees in
"Everybody's Protest Novel" ensnarls him too. With the publication of *The
Fire Next Time*, Baldwin is typecast as an angry spokesman—"a black Tom
Paine," as *Time* magazine put it. The limitation that he had diagnosed in
"Everybody's Protest Novel"—a limitation imposing itself on the writer
from without and simultaneously corroborating or inscribing itself from deep
within—imposed itself on him.

Horace A. Porter, *Stealing the Fire: The Art and Protest of James Baldwin* (Middletown,
CT: Wesleyan University Press, 1989), pp. 164–65

MEL WATKINS   As a writer, then, Baldwin is part of the tradition
of black-American polemical essayists that include David Walker, Henry
Highland Garnet, Frederick Douglass, Booker T. Washington, and W. E.
B. Du Bois. But he is just as much a part of the tradition of American
Romantic moralists—a group that includes Ralph Waldo Emerson, Henry
David Thoreau, and John Jay Chapman. This dual approach, the ability to
assume the voice of black as well as white Americans, accounts, in great
part, for his popularity and acceptance among Americans on both sides of
the racial issue.

His appeal to America's mainstream society notwithstanding, he became,
as Albert Murray pointed out in *The Omni-Americans* (1970), a hero of
"the Negro revolution, a citizen spokesman, as eloquent . . . as was citizen
polemicist Tom Paine in the Revolution of '76." But, most often, he did
not, as Murray asserts, "write about the economic and social conditions of
Harlem." Quite the contrary, Eldridge Cleaver was more accurate when
⟨. . .⟩ he wrote that Baldwin's work "is void of a political, economic, or even
a social reference." For Baldwin's technique was to write through events,

to penetrate the external veneer of sociological generality and probe the darker underside—"the real world" that Jesse Jackson alluded to at the 1988 Democratic convention—focusing finally on the enigmas that resided beneath the social and economic, enigmas that ultimately plagued his own psyche as well as our own. His influence and popularity, then, depended largely on the extent to which his psyche corresponded to the mass American psyche.

Mel Watkins, "An Appreciation," *James Baldwin: The Legacy*, ed. Quincy Troupe (New York: Simon & Schuster, 1989), p. 117

Bibliography

Go Tell It on the Mountain. 1953.

Notes of a Native Son. 1955.

Giovanni's Room. 1956.

Nobody Knows My Name: More Notes of a Native Son. 1961.

Another Country. 1962.

The Fire Next Time. 1963.

Nothing Personal (with Richard Avedon). 1964.

Blues for Mr. Charlie. 1964.

Going to Meet the Man. 1965.

The Amen Corner. 1968.

Tell Me How Long the Train's Been Gone. 1968.

An Open Letter to My Sister, Miss Angela Davis. 1970.

A Rap on Race (with Margaret Mead). 1971.

No Name in the Street. 1972.

One Day, When I Was Lost: A Scenario Based on Alex Haley's The Autobiography of Malcolm X. 1972.

A Dialogue (with Nikki Giovanni). 1973.

If Beale Street Could Talk. 1974.

Little Man, Little Man: A Story of Childhood. 1976.

The Devil Finds Work: An Essay. 1976.

Just Above My Head. 1979.

Jimmy's Blues: Selected Poems. 1983.

The Price of the Ticket: Collected Nonfiction 1948–1985. 1985.

The Evidence of Things Not Seen. 1985.

Gypsy and Other Poems. 1989.
Conversations with James Baldwin. Ed. Fred L. Standley and Louis H. Pratt.
1989.

Imamu Amiri Baraka
b. 1934

IMAMU AMIRI BARAKA was born Everett LeRoy Jones on October 7, 1934, in Newark, New Jersey. Although his original intention was to join the ministry, upon graduating from high school in 1951 he attended Rutgers University on a science scholarship, at which time he changed his name to LeRoi Jones. He transferred to Howard University in 1952, but found the conservative political atmosphere at this black school stifling and left after two years.

Between 1954 and 1957, Jones served in the air force's Strategic Air Command, spending much of this time stationed in Puerto Rico. It was in the air force that he began his first attempts at writing poetry. His experiences in the military, however, increased his suspicion of the white power structure, and his failure to conform to military discipline led to a dishonorable discharge in 1957. The next year he moved to Greenwich Village and began working as a jazz critic for such magazines as *Jazz Review*, *Downbeat*, and *Metronome*. It was in the Village that Jones became associated with Beat poets such as Allen Ginsberg and Charles Olson. Also in 1958 he married a Jewish woman, Hettie Cohen, with whom he had two children. With her, he founded the avant-garde poetry magazine *Yugen*, which lasted from 1958 to 1973. She has recently written a book about her marriage with Baraka, *How I Became Hettie Jones* (1990).

Baraka's first major book was a collection of poetry, *Preface to a Twenty Volume Suicide Note* (1961). He continued to be very active in the New York literary scene, editing an anthology of new writing, *The Moderns* (1963), and a study of black music, *Blues People* (1963). He also taught courses in contemporary poetry and creative writing at the New School for Social Research and Columbia University, where he completed his M.A. in literature in 1964.

That same year his plays *Dutchman* and *The Slave* were produced, the former winning an Obie Award as best play of the season. In 1965 he had published a novel, *The System of Dante's Hell,* and received a Guggenheim

Fellowship. However, Jones became increasingly discontented and later withdrew from the Village, divorced his wife, and moved to Harlem.

It was also at this time that he changed his name to Imamu Amiri Baraka. The names generally signify the following: Imamu, a Muslim philosopher/ poet/priest; Amiri, an African warrior/prince; and Baraka, spiritual conversion from Christianity to Islam as well as elimination of the slave name Jones. The new name was indicative of a more politically and socially committed point of view: in the late 1960s Baraka worked as a writer and activist for black unity both in Harlem and in his hometown of Newark, with the United Brothers of Newark and the Black Community Development and Defense Organization.

Baraka's poetry and plays began to incorporate both an increasingly radical political orientation (inspired in part by his visit to Cuba in 1960) and an increasing use of specifically black forms of speech. Such plays as *The Motion of History* and *S-1* are openly Marxist, and Baraka created a sensation with such collections as *Four Black Revolutionary Plays* (1969) and *The Motion of History and Other Plays* (1978). Such poetry collections as *The Dead Lecturer* (1964) and *Black Magic* (1969) also reflected his political concerns. Baraka became personally involved in the struggle for civil rights when he was arrested in 1967 during the Newark riots; at his trial he was convicted of a misdemeanor, but the verdict was later overturned on appeal.

Baraka has continued to be a prolific poet (*Hard Facts*, 1975; *Selected Poetry*, 1979), essayist (*Raise Race Rays Raze*, 1971; *Daggers and Javelins*, 1984), and anthologist (*Confirmation: An Anthology of AfricanAmerican Women*, 1983). Since 1979 he has been a member of the African Studies department of the State University of New York at Stony Brook. He married Amina Baraka (originally Sylvia Robinson) in 1966; they have five children. In 1984 he published his autobiography.

❖ *Critical Extracts*

DENISE LEVERTOV   His special gift is an emotive music that might have made him predominantly a "lyric poet," but his deeply felt preoccupation with more than personal issues enlarges the scope of his poems beyond what the term is often taken to mean.

> . . . Lighter, white man
> talk. They shy away. My won
> dead souls, my, so called
> people. Africa
> is a foreign place. You are
> as any other sad man here
> american.

I feel that sometimes his work is muddled, and after the event he convinces himself that it had to be that way; in other words, his conception of when a poem is ready to be printed differs from mine. But while he is not the craftsman ⟨Gilbert⟩ Sorrentino is, he is developing swiftly and has a rich potential. Certain poems—especially "The Clearing," "The Turncoat," "Notes for a Speech"—show what he can do. They are beautiful poems, and others that are less complete have passages of equal beauty.

Since beauty is one of the least precise words in the language I had better define what I mean by it in this instance: the beauty in Jones's poems is sensuous and incantatory, in contrast to the beauty in Sorrentino's which is a sensation of exactitude, a hitting of nails on the head with a ringing sound. In his contribution to the notes on poetics at the back of the Grove Press anthology, *The New American Poetry*, Jones speaks of García Lorca as one of the poets he has read intensely; and what is incantatory (magical) in his work, while it is natural to him, may well have been first brought to the surface by the discovery of an affinity in the magic of Lorca.

Denise Levertov, "Poets of the Given Ground," *Nation*, 14 October 1961, p. 252

M. L. ROSENTHAL   LeRoi Jones ⟨. . .⟩ has the natural gift for quick, vivid imagery and spontaneous humor, and his poems are filled with sardonic or sensuous or slangily knowledgeable passages. His first book, *Preface to a Twenty Volume Suicide Note* (1960), was interesting—as much of our newer poetry is—for the structural similarity of some of its pieces to jazz improvisation. Thus, the ending of what is perhaps the best poem in the volume, 'Way Out West':

> . . . Insidious weight
> of cankered dreams. Tiresias'
> weathered cock.

Walking into the sea, shells
caught in the hair. Coarse
waves tearing the tongue.

Closing the eyes. As
simply an act. You float

The spiraling, dreaming movement of associations, spurts of energetic
pursuit of melody and motifs, and driftings away of Jones's poems seem very
much an expression of a new way of looking at things, and of a highly
contemporary aesthetic, of a very promising sort. The perspectives include
traditional directions and symbols, yet are not dominated by them. Jones,
a Negro intellectual and playwright, at first seemed to be finding a tangential
way of making use of Negro experience and its artistic and psychological
aspects in such a way as to enable himself, at the same time, to develop
within the normal context of American poetry of this period. As he came
into some prominence, however, and, for the time being at least, began to
ally himself with the new tendencies toward intransigent hostility to the
'white' civilization, his poetry became more militant in its projection of
that hostility.

     M. L. Rosenthal, *The New Poets: American and British Poetry Since World War II*
(New York: Oxford University Press, 1967), pp. 189–90

LARRY NEAL   Jones' particular power as a playwright does not rest
solely on his revolutionary vision, but is instead derived from his deep
lyricism and spiritual outlook. In many ways, he is fundamentally more a
poet than a playwright. And it is his lyricism that gives body to his plays.
Two important plays in this regard are *Black Mass* and *Slave Ship*. *Black
Mass* is based on the Muslim myth of Yacub. According to this myth Yacub,
a Black scientist, developed the means of grafting different colors of the
Original Black Nation until a White Devil was created. In *Black Mass*,
Yacub's experiments produce a raving White Beast who is condemned to
the coldest regions of the North. The other magicians implore Yacub to
cease his experiments. But he insists on claiming the primacy of scientific
knowledge over spiritual knowledge. The sensibility of the White Devil
is alien, informed by lust and sensuality. The Beast is the consummate
embodiment of evil, the beginning of the historical subjugation of the
spiritual world.

Black Mass takes place in some prehistorical time. In fact, the concept of time, we learn, is the creation of an alien sensibility, that of the Beast. This is deeply weighted play, a colloquy on the nature of man, and the relationship between legitimate spiritual knowledge and scientific knowledge. It is LeRoi Jones' most important play mainly because it is informed by a mythology that is wholly the creation of the Afro-American sensibility. 〈...〉

Slave Ship presents a more immediate confrontation with history. In a series of expressionistic tableaux it depicts the horrors and the madness of the Middle Passage. It then moves through the period of slavery, early betrayal, and the final act of liberation. There is no definite plot (LeRoi calls it a pageant), just a continuous rush of sound, groans, screams, and souls wailing for freedom and relief from suffering. This work has special affinities with the New Music of Sun Ra, John Coltrane, Albert Ayler, and Ornette Coleman. Events are blurred, rising and falling in a stream of sound. Almost cinematically, the images flicker and fade against a heavy backdrop of rhythm. The language is spare, stripped to the essential. It is a play which almost totally eliminates the need for a text. It functions on the basis of movement and energy—the dramatic equivalent of the New Music.

Larry Neal, "The Black Arts Movement," *Drama Review* 12, No. 4 (Summer 1968): 36–37

THEODORE R. HUDSON   In a general way, Jones is a romantic in the sense that many literary historians and scholars consider the post-Romantic Period of symbolists, imagists, realists, naturalists, dadaists, impressionists, and other modern writers as latter day romantics or as part of a romantic continuum. He is a romantic in more specific ways as well. Like Emerson and certain other romantic writers, in a transcedentalistic way Jones places great faith in intuition, in feelings. As he applies this faith in an ethnocentric way, he would have blacks place faith in what he assumes to be their singular mystical impulses. He is antirational in the way that romantics of Western European literature were opposed to the "cold" rationality of neoclassicism. Moreover, in connection with this reliance upon innate urgings and promptings, Jones inescapably asserts, as Blake and other romantic mystics contended, that man is divine, although, as Baraka, Jones would argue that the white man has perverted his, the white man's, divinity.

Also, Jones is, like those romantics who would not conform to neoclassical religious dogma and traditions, romantic in that he is disdainful of the organized and orthodox religion of the majority and in that he has been himself a religous speculator and seeker. Next, Jones is romantic in his concern for the well-being, freedom, and dignity of the economically and politically weak, the dispossessed, the oppressed, and the downtrodden, as were the past century's romantic political and social libertarians and romantic champions of "humble" people. Further, Rousseau-like in his concern for the full development of man's potential, Jones sees his contemporary social, cultural, and political institutions as destructive of (black) man, so he would have man destroy, change, or control these institutions so that they, in his opinion, serve man rather than have man serve them. Further, Jones, like the Shelleys of the Romantic Period, is a visionary who sees creative artists as providers of philosophical and ideological bases of change. Next, in regard to technique, Jones, like many romantics of the past, will have little to do with conventional and prescribed forms and techniques, insists upon using the "language of the people," and constantly strives for new ways of writing, searching for what he calls a "post-American form." And it is obvious that Jones, as have countless romantics, uses his creative imagination to inform and shape his literary work.

Theodore R. Hudson, *From LeRoi Jones to Amiri Baraka* (Durham, NC: Duke University Press, 1973), pp. 179–80

CLYDE TAYLOR   The mark of LeRoi Jones' poetry is the mark of his personality on the printed page. He is the most personal so far of the Afro-American poets. For him poetry is the flow of being, the process of human electricity interacting with the weight of time, tapped and possibly trapped on paper. Feelings, impressions, moods, passions move unedited through a structure of shifting images. Quick poems, light on their feet, like a fancy middle-weight. Mostly, his poems carry no argument, no extractable, paraphraseable statement. They operate prior to the pros and cons of rational, persuasive, politic discourse. Even after several readings, one is likely to remember mainly a flavor, a distinct attutude of spirit, an insistent, very personal voice.

His poetry is written out of a heavy anti-rationalist, anti-didactic bias. Its obligation is to the intentions of its own feelings. Its posture is in defiance of criticism. The critic is for him the sycophant and would-be legislator of official (white) reality, an implacable enemy, the best symbol of the spiritually dead pseudo-intellectuality of the West. (Lula in *Dutchman* is a white critic, if you watch closely.) Against the strictures and constipations of this official reality, his poetry is an imposition upon the reader of the actuality, the majesty even (hence, LeRoi) of his subjectivity. The personalism of his earlier poetry, particularly, is a challenge to the ready-to-wear definitions of the sociologically defined "Negro writer" lying in wait for him.

The arrogance of *Preface to a Twenty Volume Suicide Note* and *The Dead Lecturer* is in this personalism and intimacy, not in any pretensions of impeccability of character. The poetry alternately invites the reader to jam his face into his own shit or to love or condemn the poet. It is the work of a spiritual gambler who wants to think of himself as waging heavy stakes. A reflection of this spirituality is its absoluteness. All his poems give the notion of being end-of-the-line thoughts, where attempts to reach an understanding dance on the edge of ambiguity. They are the works of an apprentice guru, "stuntin' for disciples," he later decided.

A major source of this creative orientation came from the streets. The hipsterism that nourished his poetry has to be regarded respectfully since whatever its limitations hipsterism was the germ of several cultural and social revolutions still turning in the world today. Hipsterism was a counter-assertion to brand-name, white values and the conformism of middle America, a serio-comic celebration of energies and forms unaccounted for, a mysticism (with some odd resemblances to Zen and other spiritual disciplines) of rhythms and tempos inside of and beyond metronomic, bureaucratic time, reflective of the polyrhythmic time of black music (particularly bebop) and of the fluid, open time-space sensation of a pot high. Hipsterism was a new, Afro-American ontology, a style of knowing the world and acknowledging in the parody of one's own posture the craziness of a materialistic, hyper-rationalist, racist, self-contradictory square world on the one hand and the absurdity of a universe that mocked human values in its variousness and arbitrariness on the other.

Clyde Taylor, "Baraka as Poet," *Modern Black Poets: A Collection of Critical Essays*, ed. Donald B. Gibson (Englewood Cliffs, NJ: Prentice-Hall, 1973), pp. 127–28

KIMBERLY W. BENSTON   Baraka's literary career, more than that of any other Afro-American writer, has illustrated the ethic/aesthetic of "change." The impulse to harness the energy of black life's chaos is consonant with the desire for political and cultural transformation. Thus "the revolution = change," and Malcolm X, the exemplar of cultural revolution, "was killed, for saying, / and feeling, and being / change" (from "Poem for Black Hearts"). At the core of Baraka's art is the insistence upon the formlessness of life-giving energy and the energetic or fluid nature of all form. It is no wonder that events in his work are violent, his images often alarmingly brutal. The only fruition or finality honored is that of death, which produces a sudden enlargement of vision—the realization that personality, or the "deadweight" of any fixed idea or being, is inevitably annihilated by history's progress: "The only constant is change."

In the purgatorial domain of his "ever-blacker" life, the artist learns to submit to his people's pure energy. He must surrender the shape of his own life, freeing his soul to flow into the black nation. The most extreme form of such identity-loss is the ceremonial dismemberment of the poet, so that he is no longer a man but instead becomes his singing, fateful words and purest deeds, a man reduced to the barest of essences:

> When I die, the consciousness I carry I will to
> black people. May they pick me apart and take the
> useful parts, the sweet meat of my feelings. And leave
> the bitter bullshit white parts
> alone.
>   [from "leroy"]

This poem had begun in a pastoral dimension, a realm of accomplished forms and stilled gestures, a realm suffused with sadness:

> I wanted to know my mother when she sat
> looking sad across the campus in the late 20's
> into the future of the soul.

The violent ending is a stunning reversal of the poem's opening: the history of black consciousness is a generation-by-generation stripping of "sweet meat" from "bitter bullshit white parts." Here, Baraka sustains the hope that a static resolution of black experience can be avoided by willing the collective purification of his specific personality: "leroy" dies and Imamu is born.

Kimberly W. Benston, *Baraka: The Renegade and the Mask* (New Haven: Yale University Press, 1976), pp. 261–62.

WERNER SOLLORS   Despite Baraka's insistence that he was concerned with Black culture as Black people live it, his cultural nationalism never allowed much room for Black culture and Black consciousness as it actually existed; instead, he tended to view Black culture as something Black people could *learn*, or even as something that might have to be forced on people by intellectuals who had renounced their own backgrounds. Thus, being "Black" in the sense of Baraka's nationalism may mean being immersed in a disciplined acceptance of certain codes, may mean being "modernized." It seems doubtful that people generally, or Black people in particular, have to be de-brainwashed against "l'art pour l'art" or "New Criticism." Baraka's strategies often reveal that he is really thinking of his own past when he attempts to exorcise absurd drama, or that he silently equates people's consciousness with popular culture, which convinces him that de-brainwashing is necessary. While rhetorically people-oriented, tradition-conscious, and folk-directed, Baraka may be a modernizer who attempts to impose new synthetic religious-cultural constructions which he calls Black. Thus it is at least paradoxical that Karenga propagated a Napoleonic military organization as very Black, while denouncing the blues as "invalid," since they teach resignation. And it is equally puzzling that many writers of the Black Arts Movement were formally Western avant-gardists, although they expressed strong ethnic exhortation. The demand for a "collective" art was often a camouflage for individualistic, modernizing artists who feigned collectivity. Despite all the invocation of "the people," despite the claims that alienation has been transcended in Black cultural nationalism, there remains a struggle between the elitist writer and the people who are to learn the right Black consciousness from him. Writing "for the people" may mask a deep-seated opposition to the people. In this context, the elements of opposition to other groups of people—women, Jews, homosexuals—are indicative of a larger opposition between artist and people.

Werner Sollors, *Amiri Baraka/LeRoi Jones: The Quest for a "Populist Modernism"* (New York: Columbia University Press, 1978), pp. 193–94

LLOYD W. BROWN   *Slave Ship* predates Baraka's major socialist dramas by several years. But the play's historical themes, and historically defined structure, make it a direct forerunner of *The Motion of History* (1976) and *S-1* (1976). And this remains true despite the fact that *Slave Ship* is not committed to socialist ideology. The perception of history in all three plays is intrinsic to Baraka's emphasis on the theater as a teaching device. In black nationalist drama like *Slave Ship* the reenactment of history fulfills a major assumption of black nationalism: the full understanding of black history is crucial to a vital sense of black identity because the crippling of black pride in the past has been partly the result of white distortions of black history. Moreover, the very process of reenactment becomes a form of celebration, the celebration of that black ethnicity which emerges from the exploration of the past.

On the whole this approach to the play as teaching device and as celebration is similar to the fundamental premise of Baraka's socialist drama, although in the latter there is a far more explicit self-consciousness about the teaching role. The norms of "scientific socialism" reflect a certain commitment to education: the inevitability of the socialist revolution is partly the consequence of politically enlightening the masses. Art, especially dramatic art, facilitates the revolutionizing process by depicting the past and its impact on the present. While the black nationalist's historical sense enhances the discovery and celebration of a distinctive black culture, the historical perspectives of scientific socialism encourage the social awareness that will hasten revolution across racial lines. As Baraka himself describes *The Motion of History* and *S-1*, "both plays are vehicles for a simple message, viz., the only solution to our problems . . . is revolution! And that revolution is inevitable. *The Motion of History* brings it back through the years, focusing principally on the conscious separation created between black and white workers who are both exploited by the same enemy."

Both plays also reflect a continuing weakness in Baraka's committed art. In this socialist phase, as in the black nationalist period, he suffers from a tendency to indulge in ideological wish-fulfillment at the expense of social realities. Hence the earlier habit of exaggerating the depth and breadth of black nationalism in America has been replaced by unconvincing images of one great socialist rebellion in all the countries of the world (*The Motion of History*) and by the highly unlikely spectacle of the American labor union movement as an anticapitalist, prorevolutionary force. Of course these "weaknesses" are less troublesome if we are inclined to accept the underlying purpose of such plays: they are concerned less with strict social realism as such, and more with the advocacy of social change. ⟨. . .⟩

This kind of drama does have its built-in limitations, of course. The characters are rudimentary types conceived in very broad terms, so broad indeed that the revolutionary figures of *S-1* are indistinguishable not only from each other but from their counterparts in *The Motion of History*. Scenes in which ideological conflicts are presented are severely underdeveloped, largely because the extreme sketchiness of the characterization limits the possibilities of the very confrontations that are supposed to dramatize the clash of ideas. And as a result of all this the audience is left with a theater of rhetoric in which potentially interesting situations and personalities are inundated with a flood of repetitive statements from all sides of the political landscape. Ironically enough Baraka's lack of emotional control in his ideological statements and his increasing indifference to characterization have resulted in a thin, one-dimensional drama that contravenes his own ideal of dramatic art as one that fuses word, act, and idea. Instead what he has produced is largely a loosely connected series of scenes filled with shopworn clichés of reactionaries and revolutionaries alike. At its worst this method exemplifies the predominance of ideological word over dramatic art, the very kind of imbalance that Baraka himself abhors in theory.

Lloyd W. Brown, *Amiri Baraka* (Boston: Twayne, 1980), pp. 162–65

HENRY C. LACEY   Like the train of its setting, *Dutchman* moves with tremendous bursts of energy and periodic lulls. As the train pulls out of the station, the tension accelerates immediately with Lula's increasingly abusive treatment of Clay, who, by virtue of his apparent naivete, wins the sympathy of the audience. Midway through the play, however, this incessant goading threatens to completely exasperate the audience, to drain them all too hastily. The maturing dramatist effectively counters this by ending the first scene. By dividing the action into two scenes, he not only gives the audience a chance to regroup emotionally, he also manages to give the play a greater sense of depth. After those few seconds of darkness, the audience views the opening action of scene II with the distinct feeling that a great deal has happened, as well as the hope that Clay has started to better acquit himself with Lena. This hope is short-lived, however, for the dramatist starts anew the pattern of scene I as the train pulls out at the beginning of scene II. ⟨. . .⟩

Along with his masterful manipulation of suspense and tension, Baraka shows his growth in the ease with which he combines the mythic and the literal in *Dutchman*. We are prepared for his duality of meaning from the opening lines of the text. *Dutchman* takes place *"In the flying underbelly of the city. Steaming hot, and summer on top, outside. Underground. The subway heaped in modern myth."* The setting suggests that the play will delve into the troubling, but too often denied truths of race relations, American style. This setting, like the encounter between the exaggeratedly "real" characters, is, indeed, meant to represent a more elusive inner or psychic reality. As if he wanted to make sure no one mistook this work for the overt naturalism of, say, *The Toilet*, Baraka gives important alternative directions: *"Dimlights and darkness whistling by against the glass. (Or paste the lights, as admitted props right on the subway windows.)"* He seeks to synthesize the naturalistic and expressionistic modes, to take the best each has to offer. This is evidenced not only in his approach to setting, but also in the characterization of *Dutchman*. Lula and Clay are simultaneously "real" persons and highly symbolic types. The powerful effect of the drama, derived from this synthesis of artistic modes, has been compared frequently to that of Albee's *The Zoo Story*, another lean, parable-like work concerned with the tragic consequences of failure to communicate.

The play's title and setting have prompted many commentators to explore its mythic implications. Hugh Nelson asserts, rather convincingly, that Baraka converts the legend of "the Flying Dutchman" into modern myth. Seeing Lula as the doomed Dutchman and Clay as the pure lover who could release her from her deathly existence, Nelson notes striking similarities in the legendary ship and Baraka's train. The cold, impersonal train, like the doomed ship, seems to operate "according to some diabolical plan. It goes nowhere, never emerges from its darkness; reaching one terminus, it reverses itself and speeds back towards the other with brief pauses at identical stations. . . ." Like the crew of the "Dutchman," Baraka's passengers exhibit the same spiritual torpor in acceding to the wishes of their "captain," Lula. Other commentators have noted the implication of the myth of Adam and Eve—and on occasion, Lilith—in the story of Clay and Lula. It is obvious that Baraka drew upon all these elements in the creation of *Dutchman*.

Henry C. Lacey, *To Raise, Destroy, and Create: The Poetry, Drama, and Fiction of Imamu Amiri Baraka (LeRoi Jones)* (Troy, NY: Whitston Publishing Co., 1981), pp. 73–75

AMIRI BARAKA   I had come into poetry from a wide-open perspective—anti-academic because of my experience, my social history and predilections. Obviously, as an African American I had a cultural history that should give me certain aesthetic proclivities. In the US and the Western world generally, white supremacy can warp and muffle the full recognition of a black person of this history, especially an "intellectual" trained by a system of white supremacy. The dead bourgeois artifact I'd cringed before in *The New Yorker* was a material and spiritual product of a whole way of life and perception of reality that was hostile to me. I dug that even as a young boy weeping in San Juan. Coming out of Howard and getting trapped in the Air Force had pulled me away from the "good job" path which is also called The Yellow Brick Road. The Yalla heaven of the undead!

I'd come to the Village *looking*, trying to "check," being open to all flags. Allen Ginsberg's *Howl* was the first thing to open my nose, as opposed to, say, instructions I was given, directions, guidance. I dug *Howl* myself, in fact many of the people I'd known at the time warned me off it and thought the whole Beat phenomenon a passing fad of little relevance. I'd investigated further because I was looking for something. I was precisely open to its force as the statement of a new generation. As a line of demarcation from "the silent generation" and the man with the (yellow) grey flannel skin, half brother of the one with the grey flannel suit. I took up with the Beats because that's what I saw taking off and flying and somewhat resembling myself. The open and implied rebellion—of form and content. Aesthetic as well as social and political. But I saw most of it as Art, and the social statement as merely our lives as dropouts from the mainstream. I could see the young white boys and girls in their pronouncement of disillusion with and "removal" from society as being related to the black experience. That made us colleagues of the spirit. Yet I was no stomp-down bohemian. I had enough of the mainstream in me, of lower-middle-class craving after order and "respectability," not to get pulled all the way over to Wahooism. Yet as wild as some of my colleagues and as cool as I usually was, the connection could be made because I was black and that made me, as Wright's novel asserted, an *outsider*.

Amiri Baraka, *The Autobiography of LeRoi Jones* (New York: Freundlich Books, 1984), pp. 156–57

WILLIAM J. HARRIS   Baraka not only set the tone of the black poem in the 1960s—violent, defiant, and independent—in the 1980s he has become the senior revolutionary voice of the black community. Graying hair notwithstanding, he is as fiery and militant as ever. Even though it is not as easy today to trace Baraka's influence, we can immediately see it in the work of Jayne Cortez, Ntozake Shange, and Lorenzo Thomas as well as its continuance in the work of Sonia Sanchez and Askia Touré. The current generation of writers responds to Baraka as a symbol of the engaged and socially committed third-world artist, referring to him "as a major and as a world poet," to quote Quincy Troupe's introduction of Baraka at a black art poetry reading in April, 1984. Because for a long period at the beginning of his Marxist stage Baraka could not get his books published by major publishers, his continuing importance was glimpsed only at black meetings, where he was treated with great respect. Perhaps it is useful to see Baraka as the new W. E. B. Du Bois for the black community, the distinguished, learned, and committed dissenter. Perhaps a measure of his influence is the dedication of a forthcoming issue of the black journal *Steppingstones* to a celebration of his work.

At fifty-one, with over thirty books behind him, Baraka is still an enigma to the American literary establishment, which cannot come to terms with this difficult and brilliant maverick. Possibly the establishment's reluctance to recognize him as it finally recognized the other two great contemporary mavericks, Mailer and Ginsberg, rests on the real—as opposed to the meta-physical—threat he poses. At most, the ramifications of Ginsberg's and Mailer's arts threaten consciousness, while Baraka's art threatens property and the actual structure of society. Or, perhaps, Baraka simply has too big a mouth, too much readiness to say the wrong thing. Whatever the reason for Baraka's exclusion, the American literary scene would be enriched by his more obvious presence: we need him to expand the definition of the American poem and to show us how to demonstrate moral commitment. At the very least, we need him to show us that a major poet does not have to heed the rules the establishment has proclaimed to be "universal."

William J. Harris, *The Poetry and Poetics of Amiri Baraka: The Jazz Aesthetic* (Columbia: University of Missouri Press, 1985), pp. 138–39

ROBERT ELLIOT FOX The revolutionary tradition of black Americans which Baraka and others speak of has always found its most vital and persistent expression in the arts, especially music. It advocates freedom, change, roots, and it is not materialistic in orientation. This may help us to explain why works like *A Black Mass* and *Slave Ship* are so much more powerful and effective as art than works like *The Motion of History*, when all three are so clearly polemical. The former dramas derive from the (pre-Baraka) early cultural-nationalist phase, the latter from the Marxist-Leninist-Maoist (M-L-M) phase, and this appears to provide the key, rather than any serious diminution of power or skill on Baraka's part. The Marxist work is intellectually determined, whereas the cultural-nationalist pieces are emotionally felt. For Baraka—indeed, for the majority of artists and intellectuals in America—the international capitalist/communist struggle must remain an abstraction in a way that it can never be for our counterparts in the Third World. Racism, on the other hand, is experienced far more concretely. *The Motion of History* and many of Baraka's recent poems display too overtly a materialist skeleton hung with the papier-mâché of ideology, while *Slave Ship*, contrastingly, is a ritual reenactment, an historical communion.

The strength of successful works of a socialist orientation derives not from the persuasiveness of their informing ideology but rather from their energy of opposition, the power of their portrayal of injustice—precisely those virtues which characterize many non-socialist protest writings. However, the studied polemic, the doctrinal script are always inferior to those works in which the political import is broadly fused with imaginative power—in which we are compelled by life, not lectures. A polemical and polarizing ideology can never lead us out of the "labyrinth of history" or navigate us safely around the "confusing land-masses of myth" (Wilson Harris).

In his cultural-nationalist period, Baraka sought to blacken the zero of white values and to make that hermeneutical circle, unrevealing of black experience, a rooted sphere through the added dimension of a "spirit reach." Excessively ritualized and mythologized, the black value system then espoused still had the virtue of organizing black energies in reconstructive channels. However, in Baraka's latest phase, designated by the alphabetical incantation M-L-M, the ceremonialized, celebrative sphere is flattened once more into an area of materialist conflict.

If one desires an antidote to Baraka's Marxist rhetoric derived from a black perspective, one could profitably turn to Richard Wright's *American Hunger* (1944). By making a significant individual contribution to the scope and presence of Afro-American literature, Wright did more to advance the cause of blackness than the Communist Party ever did, and the same is true of Baraka. There is nothing original in his present political commitment; all the positions he has held in the course of his career have been held before in Afro-American history. What is original and vital is his artistry. Chairman Baraka simply can't cut it, compared with LeRoi Jones/Amiri Baraka as tale-teller, as black word magician, as, in essence, one of the blues people.

> Robert Elliot Fox, *Conscious Sorcerers: The Black Postmodernist Fiction of LeRoi Jones/ Amiri Baraka, Ishmael Reed, and Samuel R. Delany* (Westport, CT: Greenwood Press, 1987), pp. 31–32

JAMES DE JONGH   The existential intensity of the Harlems of Oliver Pitcher and William Browne is summarized in the opening statement of "Return of the Native," the only Harlem poem by Amiri Baraka/LeRoi Jones:

> Harlem is vicious
> modernism, BangClash.
> Vicious the way it's made.
> Can you stand such beauty.
> So violent and transforming.

Baraka makes much the same point in "City of Harlem," from his volume of essays entitled *Home:*

> The legitimate cultural tradition of the Negro in Harlem (and America) is one of wild happiness, usually at some black man's own invention—of speech, of dress, of gait, the sudden twist of a musical phrase, the warmness or hurt of someone's voice. But that culture is also one of hatred and despair. Harlem must contain all of this and be capable of producing all these emotions.

Harlem was a pivotal issue for Baraka as he made the transition from the antibourgeois individualism of his Greenwich Village bohemianism of the 1950s to the consciousness of a group identity in the black nationalism of the 1960s. In the earlier phase, Baraka's attitude toward the cultural signifi-cance of Harlem had been negative: "Harlem is today the veritable capital city of the Black Bourgeoisie. The Negro Bohemian's flight to Harlem is not a flight from the world of color but the flight of any would-be Bohemian from ... 'the provinciality, philistinism and moral hypocrisy of American life.' By the late 1950s and early 1960s, though, Baraka's view of Harlem was changing:

> In a very real sense, Harlem is the capital of Black America. . . . But even the name Harlem, now, means simply Negroes (even though some other peoples live there too). The identification is international as well: even in Belize, the capital of predominantly Negro British Honduras, there are vendors who decorate their carts with flowers and the names and pictures of Negro culture heroes associated with Harlem like Sugar Ray Robinson. Some of the vendors even wear T-shirts that say "Harlem, U.S.A.," and they speak about it as a Black Paris.

This is the Harlem of "vicious modernism": "The place, and place / meant of black people. Their heavy Egypt. (Weird word!)." Harlem's value is a consciousness of self that is loving, hoping, celebratory, significant, and, therefore, joyful, for all its pain. With this Harlem the poet can identify without reservation:

> Their minds, mine.
> the black hope, mine. In Time,
> We slide along in pain or too
> happy. So much love
> for us. All over, so much of
>
> what we need.

James De Jongh, *Vicious Modernism: Black Harlem and the Literary Imagination* (Cambridge: Cambridge University Press, 1990), pp. 111–12

▨ *Bibliography*

Jan. 1st 1959: Fidel Castro (editor). 1959.
April 13. 1959.
Spring & Soforth. 1960.
Cuba Libre. 1961.
The Disguise. 1961.
Preface to a Twenty Volume Suicide Note. 1961.
Blues People: Negro Music in White America. 1963.

The Moderns: An Anthology of New Writing in America (editor). 1963.

Dutchman and The Slave. 1964.

The Dead Lecturer. 1964.

The System of Dante's Hell. 1965.

In-formation (editor). 1965.

Home: Social Essays. 1966.

The Baptism. 1966.

Afro-American Festival of the Arts Magazine (editor). 1966, 1969 (as *Anthology of Our Black Selves*).

Black Art. 1966.

Slave Ship. 1967.

A Poem for Black Hearts. 1967.

A Traffic of Love. 1967.

Striptease. 1967.

The Baptism and The Toilet. 1967.

Arm Yourself, or Harm Yourself! A Message of Self-Defense to Black Men! 1967.

Tales. 1967.

Black Music. 1967.

Answers in Progress. c. 1967.

The Cricket: Black Music in Evolution (with Larry Neal and A. B. Spellman). 1968, 1969 (as *Trippin': A Need for Change*).

Black Fire: An Anthology of Afro-American Writing (editor; with Larry Neal). 1968.

Short Speech to My Friends. 1969.

Black Magic: Sabotage; Target Study; Black Art: Collected Poetry 1961–1967. 1969.

Four Black Revolutionary Plays: All Praise to the Black Man. 1969.

In World War 3 Even Your Muse Will Get Killed! 197-.

New Era in Our Politics: The Revolutionary Answer to Neo-colonialism in Newark Politics. 197-.

A Black Value System. 1970.

J-E-L-L-O. 1970.

It's Nation Time. 1970.

In Our Terribleness: Some Elements and Meaning in Black Style (with Fundi [Billy Abernathy]). 1970.

Raise Race Rays Raze: Essays Since 1965. 1971.

Strategy and Tactics of a Pan-African Nationalist Party. 1971.

Kawaida Studies: The New Nationalism. 1972.

Spirit Reach. 1972.

African Congress: A Documentary of the First Modern Pan-African Congress (editor). 1972.

Beginning of a National Movement. 1972.

Afrikan Revolution. 1973.

Crisis in Boston!!!! 1974.

Black People and Imperialism. 1974.

Toward Ideological Clarity. 1974.

The Meaning and Development of Revolutionary Kawaida. 1974.

Creating a Unified Consciousness. c. 1974.

Revolutionary Party: Revolutionary Ideology. c. 1974.

Hard Facts: Excerpts. 1975.

Three Books (The System of Dante's Hell, Tales, The Dead Lecturer). 1975.

The Motion of History and Other Plays. 1978.

Caution: A Disco Near You Wails Death Funk. 1978.

What Was the Relationship of the Lone Ranger to the Means of Production? 1978.

The Sidney Poet Heroical. 1979.

Spring Song. 1979.

AM/TRAK. 1979.

Selected Plays and Prose. 1979.

Selected Poetry. 1979.

Afro-American Literature and Class Struggle. 198-.

Important Sonnet. 1980.

In the Tradition: For Black Arthur Blythe. c. 1980.

Reggae or Not. 1981.

Confirmation: An Anthology of AfricanAmerican Women (editor; with Amina Baraka). 1983.

Daggers and Javelins: Essays 1974–1979. 1984.

The Autobiography of LeRoi Jones. 1984.

Three Articles. c. 1985.

The Music: Reflections on Jazz and Blues (with Amina Baraka). 1987.

An Amiri Baraka/LeRoi Jones Poetry Sampler. 1991.

The LeRoi Jones/Amiri Baraka Reader. Ed. William J. Harris and Amiri Baraka. 1991.

Thornton Dial: Image of the Tiger (with others). 1993.

Conversations with Amiri Baraka. Ed. Charlie Reilly. 1994.

⬧ ⬧ ⬧

Gwendolyn Brooks
b. 1917

GWENDOLYN ELIZABETH BROOKS was born on June 7, 1917, in Topeka, Kansas, but grew up in Chicago. At the age of seven she began to write poetry, and her first poem was published when she was thirteen. Some of these poems were sent to James Weldon Johnson and Langston Hughes, who encouraged her work. As Willard Motley had done before her, Brooks began a weekly column for the *Chicago Defender* when she was sixteen. After graduation in 1936 from Wilson Junior College, she worked as publicity director for the NAACP Youth Council in Chicago. Brooks married Henry Lowington Blakely II in 1939; they have two children.

Brooks's career was launched in 1945 with the publication of her first book of poems, *A Street in Bronzeville*. Its acclaim was immediate; Brooks received a grant from the National Institute of Arts and Letters the next year, as well as a Guggenheim Fellowship. Her next book, *Annie Allen* (1949), won her the Pulitzer Prize for poetry: she was the first black American ever to receive the Pulitzer Prize. More poems followed, as well a book of poems for children (*Bronzeville Boys and Girls*, 1956), frequent book reviews, and the novel *Maud Martha* (1953).

In 1967 Brooks attended the Second Fisk University Writers' Conference and as a result became increasingly concerned with black issues. She left Harper & Row, her longtime publisher, for the black-owned Broadside Press, submitted her poetry to black-edited journals only, edited the magazine *Black Position*, and wrote introductions to several anthologies of work by young black writers. In May 1967 she formed a poetry workshop in Chicago for teenage gang members, eventually encountering Don L. Lee (Haki R. Madhubuti) and Carolyn M. Rodgers, who would go on to become distinguished poets in their own right. Brooks's anthology, *Jump Bad* (1971), collects poems written at this workshop. In 1968 she was named Poet Laureate of the State of Illinois.

By the time she was fifty Gwendolyn Brooks had already become an institution. The Gwendolyn Brooks Cultural Center opened at Western

Illinois University (Macomb, Illinois) in 1970. The next year a large anthology, *The World of Gwendolyn Brooks*, appeared, collecting several of her previous books. Between 1969 and 1973 she was separated from her husband, but they reconciled and in 1974 traveled to Ghana, England, and France. In 1976 Brooks became the first black woman elected to the National Institute of Arts and Letters.

Honors continued to accrue during the 1980s. On January 3, 1980, she recited a poem at the White House. In 1981 the Gwendolyn Brooks Junior High School opened in Chicago. She became the first black woman to serve as Consultant in Poetry at the Library of Congress in 1985–86. Although health problems in the 1970s reduced her output, she continues to write poems, poetry manuals for children (*Young Poet's Primer*, 1980; *Very Young Poets*, 1983), and articles for major magazines. A second omnibus of her work, *Blacks*, appeared in 1987.

Brooks has taught at City College, the University of Wisconsin at Madison, Northeastern Illinois University, Elmhurst College, and Columbia College in Illinois. She has received honorary degrees from nearly fifty universities. The first volume of her autobiography, *Report from Part One*, appeared in 1972; a second volume is in progress. Gwendolyn Brooks presently lives in Chicago.

Critical Extracts

STANLEY KUNITZ   If only a single poem could be saved out of this book ⟨*Annie Allen*⟩, I should speak up for the one entitled (from a witty line by Edward Young) "Pygmies Are Pygmies Still, Though Percht on Alps":

> But can see better there, and laughing there
> Pity the giants wallowing on the plain.
> Giants who bleat and chafe in their small grass,
> Seldom to spread the palm; to spit; come clean.
>
> Pygmies expand in cold impossible air,
> Cry fie on giantshine, poor glory which
> Pounds breast-bone punily, screeches, and has
> Reached no Alps: or knows no Alps to reach.

I should vote for this brief poem because of the exquisite rightness of its scale; because, knowing its own limits, it is cleanly and truly separated from the jungle of conception and sensibility that constitutes the not-poem; because the imagery is sharp, the rhythm supple, the word-choice and word-play agreeably inventive; because the small and sequent pleasures of the verse are continually linked and at the last resolved, made one, and magnified. The concluding line is obviously triumphant in its massive concentration; among the other details that please me are the effective manipulation of the off-rhyme, the wallowing and bleating of the giants, the teasing ambiguity of "come clean"; the magical connotations of "giantshine"; the explosive irony in context of the adverb "punily."

How right Gwendolyn Brooks can be, as in projecting the crystalline neatness of—"Pleasant custards sit behind / The white Venetian blind"; or in arriving at the studied casualness of—"Chicken, she chided early, should not wait / Under the cranberries in after-dinner state. / Who had been beaking about the yard of late"; or in producing on occasion the flat, slapping image—"stupid, like a street / That beats into a dead end"; or in distilling her irony into—"We never did learn how / To find white in the Bible"; or in raising her voice without shrillness to the pitch of—"What shall I give my children? who are poor, / Who are adjudged the leastwise of the land, / Who are my sweetest lepers . . ."; or in achieving the beautiful and passionate rhetoric of the lines that close her book—"Rise. / Let us combine. There are no magics or elves / Or timely godmothers to guide us. We are lost, must / Wizard a track through our own screaming weed."

These are as many kinds of rightness, scattered though they be, as are tentatively possessed by any poet of her generation. To make the possession absolute and unique is the task that remains.

Stanley Kunitz, "Bronze by Gold," *Poetry* 76, No. 1 (April 1950): 55–56

HUBERT CREEKMORE   "She was learning to love moments. To love moments for themselves." And this tale of Maud Martha Brown's youth, marriage and motherhood is made up of the moments she loved. With a few exceptions when straightforward narrative takes over, it is presented in flashes, almost gasps, of sensitive lightness—distillations of the significance of each incident—and reminds of Imagist poems or clusters of ideograms from which one recreates connected experience. Miss Brooks' prose style here embodies the finer qualities of insight and rhythm that were notable in her two earlier books of poetry (her *Annie Allen* received the Pulitzer Prize), and gives a freshness, a warm cheerfulness as well as depth of implication to her first novel. In technique and impression it stands virtually alone of its kind.

> Hubert Creekmore, "Daydreams in Flight," *New York Times Book Review*, 4 October 1953, p. 4

ARTHUR P. DAVIS   The range of color in the Negro community is fascinating; but, unfortunately, it tends to create a problem *within* the group similar to that between colored and white America. The *inside* color line has never been as definitely prescribed or as harshly drawn as the outside; nevertheless, the problem *has* existed, and it *has* caused friction, misunderstanding and on occasion heartache and tragedy. For obvious reasons, this color difference within the group has made things particularly difficult for the dark girl. ⟨. . .⟩

Miss Brooks uses again and again some variant of a black-and-tan symbol, often that of a dark girl in love with a tan boy who rejects her. But she is always aware of the larger implications of the theme. Her characters, we feel, are not just poor, lost black girls in an inhospitable world; they are poor, lost humans in a modern world of other rejections equally as foolish as those based on color.

Gwendolyn Brooks has published three works: *A Street in Bronzeville* (1945), a volume which ranks with ⟨Countee Cullen's⟩ *Color* and ⟨Langston Hughes's⟩ *The Weary Blues* as a significant first work; *Annie Allen* (1949), which won for her the Pulitzer Prize in Poetry; and the *Bean Eaters* (1960), her latest work. It is not my intention to deal with all of the poems in these works. I am concerned only with those which either directly or by implication involve the black-and-tan symbol. It is my belief that an understanding of Miss Brooks's use of this symbol will give added meaning and significance to all of her works.

The scene on which Miss Brooks places her characters is always "a street in Bronzeville," and Bronzeville is not just Southside Chicago. It is also Harlem, South Philadelphia, and every other black ghetto in the North. Life in these various Bronzeville streets is seldom gay or happy or satisfying. The Bronzeville world is a world of run-down tenements, or funeral homes, or beauty parlors, of old roomers growing older without graciousness, or "cool" young hoodlums headed for trouble, of young girls having abortions. Unlike the South, it is not a place of racial violence, but in other respects it is worse than the South. It is a drab, impersonalized "corner" of the metropolitan area into which the Negro—rootless and alone—has been pushed. A sombre cloud of futility lies over Bronzeville, and nowhere is its presence more tragically felt than in its black-and-tan situations. ⟨. . .⟩

From the time of Phillis Wheatley on down to the present, practically every Negro poet has protested the color proscription in America. Perhaps it is what every sensitive and honest Negro poet *has* to do if he is to retain his self-respect. Gwendolyn Brooks has followed the tradition, but she has written poetry and not polemic.

Arthur P. Davis, "The Black-And-Tan Motif in the Poetry of Gwendolyn Brooks," *CLA Journal* 6, No. 2 (December 1962): 90–92, 97

DAVID LITTLEJOHN   What she seems to have done is to have chosen, as her handle on the "real" (often the horribly real), the other reality of craftsmanship, of technique. With this she has created a highly stylized screen of imagery and diction and sound—fastidiously exact images, crisp Mandarin diction, ice-perfect sound—to stand between the reader and the subject; to stand often so glittering and sure that all he can ever focus on is the screen. The "subjects"—racial discrimination, mother love, suffering—are dehumanized into *manerismo* figurines, dancing her meters. It is *her* intelligence, *her* imagination, *her* brilliant wit and wordplay that entrap the attention. Always, the subjects are held at arm's length away. Whoever the persona—and she is often forced to make the speakers fastidious, alienated creatures like herself—it is always her mind and her style we are dwelling in.

This can (to a reader still concerned with "subjects") run to excess, when all "idea" is honed away in overcontrol, when all that is left, it seems, is wordplay and allusion and technique: crisp, brisk phrases and images like the taps of steel spike heels, going nowhere. In many of her early poems (especially the *Annie Allen* poems) Mrs. Brooks appears only to pretend to talk of things and of people; her real love is words. The inlay work of words, the *précieux* sonics, the lapidary insets of jeweled images (like those of Gerard

Manley Hopkins) can, in excess, squeeze out life and impact altogether, and all but give the lie to the passions professed in the verbs. The style itself cannot be described briefly. There is enough new-bought diction and shivery tonic phrasing and rhythmic play to fascinate a university seminar in modern poetics for months. She has learned her art superbly. The words, lines, and arrangements have been worked and worked again into poised exactness: the unexpected apt metaphor, the mock-colloquial asides amid jeweled phrases, the half-ironic repetitions—she knows it all. The stylistic critic could only, at his most keen, fault the rare missed stitch of accent, the off-semitone of allusion.

David Littlejohn, *Black on White: A Critical Survey of Writing by American Negroes* (New York: Grossman Publishers, 1966), pp. 90–91

MARGARET T. G. BURROUGHS   Will she be remembered because of a limited vocabulary filled with sensational and titillating four letter words used and excused on the basis of relevancy? I think not.

Will she be remembered because her poetry is filled with rage, hate and violence, that hate which is the antithesis of creativity, that hate which corrupts, destroys, and thwarts creativity? I think not.

Will she be remembered because she has mastered the dexterity to embroider cute designs on the page with a typewriter? I think not.

Miss Brooks and her poetry will be remembered and will speak to generations yet to come because in the first instance she is a creative human being who is concerned with all humanity. She will be remembered because she speaks from the deep wellsprings of her own black experience which shares common universals with all downtrodden and oppressed peoples, black, brown, red, white and yellow.

However above all, there is this fact which should be of great import to all younger poets who would seek to emulate Miss Brooks; Miss Brooks is a student and scholar of poetry and writing. She has done and continues to do her homework, that meticulous dedication which is necessary to produce a meaningful and lasting work of art. Miss Brooks has thoroughly mastered her craft. She knows it inside and out and in all of its aspects. She does not resort to fads, tricks or gimmicks of the moment.

Margaret T. G. Burroughs, " 'She'll Speak to Generations Yet to Come,' " *To Gwen with Love: An Anthology Dedicated to Gwendolyn Brooks*, ed. Patricia L. Brown, Don L. Lee, and Francis Ward (Chicago: Johnson Publishing Co., 1971), pp. 129–30

TONI CADE BAMBARA   Like the younger black poets, Gwen
Brooks since the late Sixties has been struggling for a cadence, style, idiom
and content that will politicize and mobilize. Like the young black poets,
her recent work is moving more toward gesture, sound, intonation, attitude
and other characteristics that depend on oral presentation rather than private
eyeballing. It is important to have the poet herself assess these moves in
her own way so as to establish the ground for future critical biographies.
But "change" and "shift" may be too heavy-handed, somewhat misleading;
for in rereading the bulk of her work, which Report (from Part One) does
prompt one to do, we see a continuum.

Gwen Brooks's works have also been very much of their times. Prior to
the late Sixties, black writers invariably brought up the rear, so to speak,
having to prove competence in techniques already laid down by mainstream
critics. Jim Crow esthetics decreed that writing "negro" was not enough,
not valid—not universal. In these times, however, black writers and critics
are the vanguard. Black works of the Thirties and Forties reflect the "social
consciousness" of the times. There was a drastic reduction in race themes
as compared with the Twenties and an adoption of a "global" perspective;
concern about European War II or whatever. The works of the Forties and
Fifties gave credence to the shaky premise on which "protest" literature
rests—that the oppressor simply needed information about grievances to
awaken the dormant conscience. The works of these times, on the other
hand, reflect quite another sensibility.

As Gwen Brooks says, "I knew there were injustices, and I wrote about
them, but I didn't know what was behind them. I didn't know what kind
of society we live in. I didn't know it was all organized." Or, assessing her
appeal-to-the-Christian-heart period: "But then, I wasn't reading the books
I should have read when I was young. If I'd been reading W. E. B. Du Bois,
I would have known." Or, "I thought I was happy, and I saw myself going
on like that for the rest of my days, I thought it was the way to live. I wrote
. . . But it was white writing, the different trends among whites. Today I
am conscious of the fact that my people are black people: it is to them that
I appeal for understanding."

Toni Cade Bambara, [Review of Report from Part One], New York Times Book Review,
7 January 1973, p. 1

GLORIA T. HULL   Verbal economy ⟨. . .⟩ is accomplished more
easily in an imperative or declarative mood. Consequently, these moods
predominate in Miss Brooks's poetry and, combined with her short lines
and generalizing statements, produce gnomic saws and aphorisms. The whole
of her famous sonnet, "First fight. Then fiddle," is a classic instance of her
speaking in this mode. She adopts the same tone in her later "Second
Sermon on the Warpland," part two of which begins: "Salve salvage in the
spin. / Endorse the splendor splashes" (*Mecca*). Her penchant for simple
declaratives is illustrated by these Eliotic lines:

> The onlÿ sanity is a cup of tea.
> The music is in minors.
>   (*Mecca*)

Her prediliction for raw statement often results in a string of one-word
modifiers appended to a declaration she has just made:

> Peanut is
> Richard—a Ranger and a gentleman.
> A signature. A Herald. And a Span.

Such a juxtaposition of phrases without supplying the grammatical, logical,
or emotional links leaves this rich but potentially-difficult creative task to
the reader and holds her overt statement of her idea down to its minimum
length.

This second set of qualities comprising the economical use of language
almost totally characterizes Miss Brooks's *Annie Allen*, the book for which
she won the Pulitzer Prize and which, ironically, is generally least liked—
particularly by young blacks who reject it for reasons which directly relate
to its rugged, intellectual style. Don L. Lee's reaction is typical:

> *Annie Allen* (1949), important? Yes. Read by blacks? No. *Annie
> Allen* more so than *A Street in Bronzeville* seems to have been
> written for whites. . . . This poem ("The Anniad") is probably
> earth-shaking to some, but leaves me completely dry.

Miss Brooks says that when she wrote "The Anniad," she "was fascinated
by what words might do there in the poem," and calls it "labored, a poem
that's very interested in the mysteries and magic of technique" (*Report from
Part One*).

Finally, Miss Brooks has a characteristic way of handling three minor
devices. First, her alliteration is often heavy and unsubtle—as a glance back
through the quotations will show. Second, she uses rhyme and quick rhyme

to integrate her free verse ("In the Mecca," for instance). And last, she sometimes personifies abstractions and non-human entities—a practice which may reflect her animistic beliefs, and certainly contributes to her quaint, colloquial tone. Examples occur plentifully in her poetry: "clawing the suffering dust," "the sick and influential stair," and "The ground springs up; / hits you with gnarls and rust."

In isolation, these peculiarities of style identified in Miss Brooks's poetry seem to be stilted and artificial. Yet it is obvious that she is able to make them work for her, with relatively few lapses or outright failures. She has taken definitive techniques of diction, verbal economy, and sound which are the shared tools of every poet and used them in an individual way to give herself a recognizably distinctive poetic voice.

Gloria T. Hull, "A Note on the Poetic Technique of Gwendolyn Brooks," *CLA Journal* 19, No. 2 (December 1975): 283–85

HORTENSE J. SPILLERS   For over three decades now, Gwendolyn Brooks has been writing poetry which reflects a particular historical order, often close to the heart of the public event, but the dialectic that is engendered between the event and her reception of it is, perhaps, one of the more subtle confrontations of criticism. We cannot always say with grace or ease that there is a direct correspondence between the issues of her poetry and her race and sex, nor does she make the assertion necessary at every step of our reading. Black and female are basic and inherent in her poetry. The critical question is *how* they are said. Here is what the poet has to say about her own work:

> My aim, in my next future, is to write poems that will somehow successfully "call" all black people: black people in taverns, black people in alleys, black people in gutters, schools, offices, factories, prisons, the consulate; I wish to reach black people in mines, on farms, on thrones; *not* always to "teach"—I shall wish often to entertain, to illumine [emphasis Brooks]. My newish voice will not be an imitation of the contemporary young black voice, which I so admire, but an extending adaptation of today's G. B. voice.

Today's G. B. voice is one of the most complex on the American scene precisely because Brooks refuses to make easy judgments. In fact, her disposition to reserve judgment is directly mirrored in a poetry of cunning, laconic surprise. Any descriptive catalog can be stretched and strained in her case: I have tried "uncluttered," "clean," "robust," "ingenious," "unorthodox," and in each case a handful of poems will fit. This method of grading and cataloguing, however, is essentially busywork, and we are still left with the main business: What in this poetry is stunning and evasive?

To begin with, one of Brooks's most faithfully anthologized poems, "We Real Cool," illustrates the wealth of implication that the poet can achieve in a very spare poem:

> We real cool. We
> Left school. We
> Lurk late. We
> Strike straight. We
> Sing sin. We
> Thin gin. We
> Jazz June. We
> Die soon.

The simplicity of the poem is stark to the point of elaborateness. Less then lean, it is virtually coded. Made up entirely of monosyllables and end-stops, the poem is no non-sense at all. Gathered in eight units of three-beat lines, it does not necessarily invite inflection, but its persistent bump on "we" suggests waltz time to my ear. If the reader chooses to render the poem that way, she runs out of breath, or trips her tongue, but it seems that such "breathlessness" is exactly required of dudes hastening toward their death. Deliberately subverting the romance of sociological pathos, Brooks presents the pool players—"seven in the golden shovel"—in their own time. They make no excuse for themselves and apparently invite no one else to do so. The poem is their situation as *they* see it. In eight (could be nonstop) lines, here is their total destiny. Perhaps comic geniuses, they could well drink to this poem, making it a drinking/revelry song.

Hortense J. Spillers, "Gwendolyn the Terrible: Propositions on Eleven Poems," *Shakespeare's Sisters: Feminist Essays on Women Poets*, ed. Sandra M. Gilbert and Susan Gubar (Bloomington: University of Indiana Press, 1979), pp. 233–34

HARRY B. SHAW   Perhaps the most important technique that Miss Brooks uses in developing her social themes is her masterful control of artful ambiguity. Demanding a great deal of creative response from the reader, her poems are all the more an embodiment of the black experience because the technique of indirection which is vital to black survival is so prevalent in them. Using the black experience and the condition of oppression at the hands of the white man as the underlying social theme of virtually all her poetry, Miss Brooks records the black man's anguish, protest, pride, and hope in his thralldom with the artful ambiguity characteristic of black United States folk poetry. The general approach of her poetry to the life around her reflects the tradition of the black spirituals, black secular slave songs, and blues ballads with their double and triple meanings that hide the underlying and sometimes subliminal meaning that was a form of unoffensive, inconspicuous, or even invisible protest.

As an extension of the intuitive beauty of ambiguity in art used to vent the pent-up feelings of a people whose survival has demanded acquiescence, Miss Brooks's poetry often couches the predominant social themes in such ostensibly displayed conventional themes as death, religion, war, sexual and Platonic love, and peace, to name a few. She also uses many commonplace concrete subjects, such as movies, pool players, old age, apartment dwellings, and physical deformity, that are so innocent or asocial in appearance that they may beguile the unperceptive reader into a superficial reading and, therefore, perhaps a superficial appreciation, missing the heart of the poetry's black message.

Miss Brooks's ability to use the tangible to explain the intangible to reveal the tangible in its proper perspective along with her continuous complexity and subtlety are assets in the overall efficacy of her poetry in conveying social messages. Her poetry is aligned with the black tradition of artful ambiguity and indirection and therefore communicates with a subconscious sophistication that is not possible with expression made solely on the conscious level.

Harry B. Shaw, *Gwendolyn Brooks* (Boston: Twayne, 1980), pp. 182–83

R. BAXTER MILLER   The simple plot and structure of "In the Mecca" (the poem) present an urban setting. For convenience one can divide the narrative into three sections. Part I sets forth the return home from work of Mrs. Sallie Smith, mother of nine. The focus here is on the neighbors that she encounters and on the characterizations of her children. In the second part, the shortest, the woman notices that Pepita, one of her girls, is missing. This prompts the first search through the tenement and allows for further characterization and biblical parody. Part II also concerns the paradox of American myth. The longest section is Part III, which constitutes almost half of the verse. Here the police retrace the Smiths' search. Because of its themes and styles, Part III is probably the richest. The following contribute to its power: militant declarations, interracial lovemaking, rhetorical questions, and Christian myth. The poem ends with the discovery of Pepita's corpse under the bed of Jamaican Edward.

"In the Mecca" represents opposite strains of the Anglo-American tradition. One finds a naturalistic version of Walt Whitman, by way of the industrial age, and the redemptive, if frustrated, potential that characterizes the world of T. S. Eliot. But these influences work so that the peculiarities of the Black American experience transform them into a new and creative vision. By adapting to the social forces of the sixties, the poet uses a new milieu. Her canvas is a most demanding time in American history. For this and other times, Gwendolyn Brooks holds to light the soundness of body and mind against the decline of courage and assurance, a lapse which emerged with modernity and the shadow of the holocaust. She continues to believe that imaginative and verbal power challenge and balance finally the danger which posits the insignificance of human life and the indifference to human extinction. For her generation, the defining emblem is ultimately the whirlwind, the collapse of self-confidence, the failure to transform social ill once more into epic victory and to reclaim from the time before the holocaust, and the later accusation of "reverse discrimination" in the United States, the heroic and bluesesque will of Black hope. Whereas for Margaret Walker, cleansing has been the metaphor for the perspective which woman takes on historical and cosmic evil, the depth here every bit as great as Melville's "mystery of iniquity," for Brooks the sign is medication. The artistic process itself plays out the action of healing, while the poem serves as both epic quest and sacramental liberation.

R. Baxter Miller, " 'Define . . . the Whirlwind': Gwendolyn Brooks' Epic Sign for a Generation," *Black American Poets Between Worlds, 1940–1960*, ed. R. Baxter Miller (Knoxville: University of Tennessee Press, 1986), pp. 162–63

D. H. MELHEM   "Bronzeville," Brooks remarks, was a name invented by the *Chicago Defender*. She described it to ⟨Elizabeth⟩ Lawrence as a South Side area of about forty blocks, running north and south from 29th to 69th Streets, and east and west about thirteen blocks from Cottage Grove to State Street (Sept. 28, 1944). An anatomy of Bronzeville appears in the important sociological study *Black Metropolis*, by St. Clair Drake and Horace R. Clayton. These authors analyze the nature and consequences of segregated black life and call for integration to combat its evils. In "Bronzeville 1961," a new chapter for the 1962 edition, Drake and Clayton find that their foci of investigation or "axes of life" remain what they had been in 1945 when the study was first made. The categories are " 'staying alive,' 'getting ahead,' 'having fun,' 'praising god,' and 'advancing the Race.' " In some respects these topics gloss *A Street in Bronzeville*, although skepticism tinges "praising god" and irony touches the "Race Hero" who is "advancing the Race."

A corollary aspect of "advancing the Race" by individual achievement or through social action is "the demand for solidarity" (Drake). This long-standing desire roots Brooks's later concern, most marked in *Beckonings* and "In Montgomery." It partly explains the early sources of her interest and the depth of her later chagrin at the erosion of unity.

Brooks initially planned *A Street in Bronzeville* to portray a personality, event, or idea representing each of thirty houses on a street in the vicinity. The sequence of twenty poems in the first section, "A Street in Bronzeville," is close in tone and milieu to the following five, grouped here as "Five Portraits." All the poems give humanistic and compassionate glimpses of black life. The first section focuses on common existence; the middle one, except for "Hattie Scott," offers longer poems that probe distinct and dra- matic characters. The third and last section, "Gay Chaps at the Bar," comprises the sonnet sequence. Thematically, the volume is largely struc- tured around two units: local/black and national/multiracial. Brooks exposes their interrelationships—personal, social, and national. The theme of entrapment, by community norms, socioeconomic forces, and personal psy- chology, underlies the whole.

> D. H. Melhem, *Gwendolyn Brooks* (Lexington: University Press of Kentucky, 1987), pp. 19–20

GLADYS WILLIAMS   Brooks has been an innovative poet. She is also an artist in whom the forces of tradition and continuity have enriched

her craft. She has written carefully disciplined and well-wrought sonnets in
the tradition of Shakespeare. Metrical craft and poetic form have been as
much a consideration for Brooks as they have been in her antecedents Yeats
and Frost. The metaphysical wit of Eliot, Pound, Frost, and the younger
Robert Lowell have exerted a significant influence on the poet. The basic
and central free-verse tradition that comes to Brooks through Walt Whitman, James Weldon Johnson, Sterling Brown, William Carlos Williams,
and her beloved Langston Hughes is especially strong. Certain features of
her art originate in the black folk art forms—the blues, the ballads, the folk
tales, the sermons Brooks grew up with—as well as in the works of Shakespeare, Frost, Dickinson, et al. The poet's penchant for understatement, her
wry and ironic humor, her terseness, her skill in giving her poetry the sound
of the human voice, and the ethnotropic metaphor she creates are brilliantly
present in her ballads as they are in the folk ballad antecedents. The Brooks
ballad reveals one stream of the multiple literary influences that flow through
her poetry.

> Gladys Williams, "The Ballads of Gwendolyn Brooks," A Life Distilled: Gwendolyn
> Brooks, Her Poetry and Fiction, ed. Maria K. Mootry and Gary Smith (Urbana:
> University of Illinois Press, 1987), pp. 222–23

GEORGE E. KENT   Actually, Annie Allen challenges not so much
by its particularism as by its craft and its universality—further developments
of the resources and approaches present in A Street in Bronzeville. The poems
in A Street offer a deceptively full realistic surface and make use of well-
known devices from the conventions and techniques of poetic realism. There
are abrupt beginnings in A Street and some elliptical syntax, which demand
that the reader drop everything and attend closely, but neither is developed
to the extent manifested in Annie Allen.

One major difference between the two works is that the reader of Annie
Allen is more openly confronted with the necessity to read actively. Although
people and their life stories appear in plots sharply outlined, presenting
easily recognized issues from the daily round of existence, and move to
definite climaxes and decisive conclusions, there are frequent signals of the
presence of more than one perspective—additional comments upon the
human condition available beneath the poems' realistic surface, representing
engagement with the contradictoriness and complexity of experience.

The opening poems of the two works illustrate the difference. A *Street* opens with "the old-marrieds": "But in the crowding darkness not a word did they say. / Though the pretty-coated birds had piped so lightly all the day." Except for the abrupt beginning with "but," there is nothing to discomfit the reader. The syntax is regular except for punctuation of a clause as a full sentence in the second line—certainly no radical break with established practice.

Annie Allen, proper, on the other hand, opens with "the birth in a narrow room": "Weeps out of Western country something new. / Blurred and stupendous. Wanted and unplanned." Whereas in "the old-marrieds" the issue and perhaps the mystery of the story are almost immediately suggested, "the birth" requires careful and repeated readings to grasp the theme: the slow absorption of "reality" by infant life and the creative experiences awaiting the infant between the stages of unreflecting confrontation with existence and realization of its limitations. The poem demands greater reader participation and creativity: an acceptance of the elliptical syntax in the first stanza and grasp of images with mythic functions—not merely of day-to-day "reality." The infant's first movement into time is an almost passive survey of artifacts, with the last image foreshadowing something of the magic of the childhood world: "the milk-glass fruit bowl, iron pot, / The bashful china child tripping forever / Yellow apron and spilling pretty cherries." The second stanza mixes images of reality with expressions and gestures connoting the transforming power of early childhood imagination:

> But prances nevertheless with gods and fairies
> Blithely about the pump and then beneath
> The elms and grapevines, then in darling endeavor
> By privy foyer, where the screenings stand
> And where the bugs buzz by in private cars
> Across old peach cans and old jelly jars.

George E. Kent, *A Life of Gwendolyn Brooks* (Lexington: University Press of Kentucky, 1990), pp. 80–81

Bibliography

A Street in Bronzeville. 1945.
Annie Allen. 1949.

Maud Martha. 1953.
Bronzeville Boys and Girls. 1956.
We Real Cool. 1959.
The Bean Eaters. 1960.
Selected Poems. 1963.
In the Time of Detachment, in the Time of Cold. 1965.
The Wall. 1967.
In the Mecca. 1968.
Martin Luther King, Jr. 1968.
For Illinois 1968: A Sesquicentennial Poem. 1968.
Riot. 1969.
Family Pictures. 1970.
Aloneness. 1971.
The World of Gwendolyn Brooks. 1971.
Elegy in a Rainbow: A Love Poem. 1971.
A Broadside Treasury 1965–1970 (editor). 1971.
Black Steel: Joe Frazier and Mohammad Ali. 1971.
Jump Bad: A New Chicago Anthology (editor). 1971.
Aurora. 1972.
Report from Part One. 1972.
The Tiger Who Wore White Gloves; or, What You Are You Are. 1974.
Beckonings. 1975.
A Capsule Course in Black Poetry Writing (with Keorapetse Kgositsile, Haki
    R. Madhubuti, and Dudley Randall). 1975.
Other Music. 1976.
The Mother. 1978.
Primer for Blacks. 1980.
Young Poet's Primer. 1980.
To Disembark. 1981.
Black Love. 1982.
The Progress. 1982.
Mayor Harold Washington and Chicago, the I Will City. 1983.
Very Young Poets. 1983.
The Near-Johannesburg Boy and Other Poems. 1986.
Blacks. 1987.
Winnie. 1988.
The Second Sermon on the Warpland. 1988.
Gottschalk and the Grande Tarantelle. 1988.

Jane Addams: September 6, 1860–May 21, 1935. 1990.
Children Coming Home. 1991.
Christmas Morning Comes Too Soon. 1992.

Rita Dove
b. 1952

RITA FRANCES DOVE was born on August 28, 1952, in Akron, Ohio, to Ray A. Dove and Elvira Elizabeth Hord. Dove was a precocious child who ranked among the top one hundred high school seniors in the country and was therefore invited to the White House as a "Presidential Scholar." After graduating from high school, Dove entered Miami University at Oxford, Ohio. In 1973 she graduated *summa cum laude*, then entered Tübingen University in what was then West Germany on a Fulbright scholarship. While in Germany, Dove actively sought out Afro-Germans in an attempt to understand their circumstances. Dove discovered that many Afro-German women suffered from the same feelings of rejection and isolation that Dove had felt in the United States. Somewhat optimistically, she wrote about the possibility of unified action among black communities worldwide— action that would inspire a revolution in world consciousness. In 1979 Dove married a German writer, Fred Viebahn, with whom she had one child.

Upon returning from Germany, Dove entered the Iowa Writers Work-shop, where she received an M.F.A. in 1977. She worked principally on her poetry, which thereafter increasingly appeared in magazines and journals. In 1977 *Ten Poems*, Dove's first book of verse, appeared. It reveals her interest in the revolutionary politics of the 1960s as well as the influence of other black revolutionary poets on her work, such as Don L. Lee (Haki R. Madhubuti) and LeRoi Jones (Amiri Baraka). Many of the poems in this first small volume were reprinted along with new verses in her first full-length collection, *The Yellow House on the Corner* (1980). For the most part, the collection was poorly received. Not until the publication of *Museum* (1983) and *Thomas and Beulah* (1986) did Dove receive considerable critical praise. The latter volume also won her a Pulitzer Prize, making her only the second black poet to have won a Pulitzer Prize for poetry (the first was Gwendolyn Brooks). *Thomas and Beulah* is a long narrative poem telling the story of her family from two points of view, her grandfather's and her grandmother's. A chronology at the end of the volume provides a guide to the sometimes confusing overlap of the two stories.

More recently, Dove has published *The Other Side of the House* (1988), a set of poems to accompany photographs by Tamarra Kaida, and *Grace Notes* (1989). Her *Selected Poems* appeared in 1993. She has also written a novel, *Through the Ivory Gate* (1992), and a play, *The Darker Face of the Earth* (1994).

Dove began her teaching career as a professor of English at Arizona State University in 1981. In 1989 she became a professor of English at the University of Virginia. She was a writer in residence at the Tuskegee Institute in 1982 and has served as a member of the literature panel of the National Endowment for the Arts. Since 1987 she has been commissioner of the Schomburg Center for the Preservation of Black Culture at the New York Public Library. In 1993 she became the first black American to be appointed the United States Poet Laureate.

⬙ *Critical Extracts*

PETER STITT   "Shakespeare Say" ⟨in *Museum*⟩ is linear and narra-tive. The moment of telling occurs during an evening when "Champion Jack Dupree, black American blues singer" (as he is identified in the note to the poem) is performing in a Munich nightclub. The mode of narration is not limited to this single period of time, however; to portray the singer's state of mind, the speaker recounts several events in sequential order, first returning to "That afternoon" when "two students / from the Akademie / showed him the town." Later in the poem, we are presented with a general-ized description of the evening in question ("And tonight // every song he sings / is written by Shakespeare"), while still later we learn what happens as Champion Jack is "going down / for the third set / past the stragglers / at the bar."

The quality of this poem is evident in Dove's accuracy of description and in how she interlaces Champion Jack's songs with her narrative to flesh out his portrait:

> Champion Jack in love
> and in debt,

> in a tan walking suit
> with a flag on the pocket,
> with a red eye
> for women, with a
> diamond-studded
> ear, with sand
> in a mouthful of mush—
> *poor me*
> *poor me*
> *I keep on drifting*
> *like a ship out*
> *on the sea.*

In line with the imagery in the song he sings, Jack is described variously as looking like a ship ("a flag on the pocket"), as looking like a pirate (the "red eye" and the earring), and as sounding like an inverted Demosthenes (whereas the Greek orator, according to legend, filled his mouth with pebbles and declaimed to the sea in an effort to strengthen his voice, Jack seems to have filled his mouth with "sand," so great is his sense of sorrow).

In contrast to the narrative and linear structure of "Shakespeare Say," "The Copper Beech" is a descriptive poem in circular form (description in poetry is almost always static with regard to time). Though the poem contains twenty-five lines arranged into nine stanzas, it takes its form not from these distinguishing external features but from the progression inherent in its five sentences. The first sentence establishes setting, character, and theme: "Aristocrat among patriarchs, this / noble mutation is the best / specimen of Rococo // in the park of the castle / at Erpenberg." The second sentence delves into the past to tell how a Baroness brought the tree from South America, and the next sentence furthers interpretation: "This trailing beech became Erpenberg's / tree of grief, their // melancholy individualist, / the park philosopher."

The fourth sentence furthers the description, while the concluding provides a final description/interpretation that unites the whole:

> The aesthetic principles
> of the period: branches
>
> pruned late to heal
> into knots, proud flesh ascending
> the trunk:
>
> living architecture.

The movement of the poem is not narrative, not progressive through time, but accretive around an instance of perception; the form is therefore circular rather than linear. Rita Dove is a poet of considerable skill and promise. The poems in Museum are as intellectually interesting as they are attractive in rhythm and image.

Peter Stitt, "The Circle of the Meditative Moment," Georgia Review 38, No. 2 (Summer 1984): 403–4

LINDA GREGERSON   In Museum, as its title and its cover art-work announce, the author has advanced to full prominence ⟨her⟩ preoccupations with displacement and multiple frames for point of view, frames that are rather superimposed than synthesized. The book is structured and conceived with great deliberation and coherence, from its section titles and sequencing epigraphs, its attributions and its dedication: "for nobody," reads a page at the front, "who made us possible." The book's recurrent thematics are those of light and shade, the exotic and the domestic, reticence (with its furthest limit a nearly Delphic impenetrability, like the hush in a museum) and disclosure ⟨. . .⟩ On both geographical and temporal coordinates, the sweep of the book is large: from Argos to Erpenberg to the poet's native Ohio, from the Western Han Dynasty to the nuclear age. Nor are these distances a species of lush window dressing: Dove believes in history and is capable of mining it for the lucid intersections of imagination and pragmatic ways-and-means, for the junctures where solitary virtuosity finds both its intractable limits (as Catherine of Alexandria was "deprived of learning and / the chance to travel") and its most urgent motives. And according to that other perspective on history, as captured in books or museums, Dove is concerned to render the altered status of a subject when it has been set aside for special delectation, like the fish in the archeologist's stone or like Fiammetta in Boccaccio's mind: the creature lifted to visibility by the pressure of a gaze is also partly stranded there, unsponsored even while it is wholly possessed. In technical terms—their use of the luminous image, their economics of plotting and musical phrase, their reliable modulations of syntax and levels of diction—these poems continue the same expert craftsmanship that marked Dove's earlier work. In their collective argument—and it is a profound one—they go much further.

Linda Gregerson, [Review of The Yellow House on the Corner and Museum], Poetry 145, No. 1 (October 1984): 47–48

HELEN VENDLER   *Thomas and Beulah* manages to keep intact the intensity of the drama and inexplicability of life and marriage. The mutual criticism of Dove's Akron couple, their enterprise and defeat, while specified to a degree that is satisfying as fiction, will remind readers of analogous episodes in the years 1900–1969 undergone by their own parents or grandparents. Dove does not suggest that black experience is identical with white experience, but neither does she suggest that it is always different. Beulah's experience of motherhood—her terror of doing it wrong, the exhaustion of having no privacy, her irritation at the grown girls—is universal. But Beulah's anger when her daughters take her to the Goodyear company picnic after Thomas's death will be personally familiar only to black readers:

> Now this *act of mercy:* four daughters
> dragging her to their husbands' company picnic,
> white families on one side and them
> on the other, unpacking the same
> squeeze bottles of Heinz, the same
> waxy beef patties and Salem potato chip bags.

Over the segregated picnickers floats the Goodyear company symbol—"a white foot / sprouting two small wings." Beulah's interior monologue, here as elsewhere, has the naturalness and accuracy of art concealing art. Dove has planed away unnecessary matter: pure shapes, her poems exhibit the thrift that Yeats called the sign of a perfected manner.

Helen Vendler, "In the Zoo of the New," *New York Review of Books,* 23 October 1986, pp. 51–52

ARNOLD RAMPERSAD   ⟨. . .⟩ with the consistently accomplished work of thirty-three year old Rita Dove, there is at least one clear sign if not of a coming renaissance of poetry, then at least of the emergence of an unusually strong new figure who might provide leadership by brilliant example. Thus far, Rita Dove has produced a remarkable record of publications in a wide range of respected poetry and other literary journals. Two books of verse, *The Yellow House on the Corner* (1980) and *Museum* (1983), have appeared from Carnegie-Mellon University Press. A third book-length manuscript of poetry, "Thomas and Beulah," is scheduled to be published early in 1986 by the same house. Clearly Rita Dove has both the energy and the sense of professionalism required to lead other writers. Most importantly—even a first reading of her two books makes it clear that she also possesses the talent to do so. Dove is surely one of the three or four most gifted young black American poets to appear since LeRoi Jones ambled with deceptive nonchalance onto the scene in the late nineteen fifties, and perhaps the most disciplined and technically accomplished black poet to arrive since Gwendolyn Brooks began her remarkable career in the nineteen forties.

These references to the sixties and early seventies are pointed. Rita Dove's work shows a keen awareness of this period—but mainly as a point of radical departure for her in the development of her own aesthetic. In many ways, her poems are exactly the opposite of those that have come to be considered quintessentially black verse in recent years. Instead of looseness of structure, one finds in her poems remarkably tight control; instead of a reliance on reckless inspiration, one recognizes discipline and practice, and long, taxing hours in competitive university poetry workshops and in her study; instead of a range of reference limited to personal confession, one finds personal reference disciplined by a measuring of distance and a prizing objectivity; instead of an obsession with the theme of race, one finds an eagerness, perhaps even an anxiety, to transcend—if not actually to repudiate—black cultural nationalism in the name of a more inclusive sensibility. Hers is a brilliant mind, reinforced by what appears to be very wide reading, that seeks for itself the widest possible play, an ever expanding range of reference, the most acute distinctions, and the most subtle shadings of meaning. ⟨. . .⟩

As a poet, Dove is well aware of black history. One of the five sections of *The Yellow House* is devoted entirely to poems on the theme of slavery and freedom. These pieces are inspired by nameless but strongly representative victims of the "peculiar institution," as well as by more famous heroic figures (who may be seen as fellow black writers, most of them) such as Solomon Northrup, abducted out of Northern freedom on a visit to Washington ("I remember how the windows rattled with each report. / Then the wine, like a pink lake, tipped. / I was lifted—the sky swivelled, clicked into place"), and the revolutionary David Walker ("Compass needles, / eloquent as tuning forks, shivered, pointing north. / Evenings, the ceiling fan sputtered like a second pulse. / *Oh Heaven! I am full!! I can hardly move my pen!!!*"). In these works and others such as "Banneker" in the later volume, *Museum*, Dove shows both a willingness and a fine ability to evoke, through deft vignettes, the psychological terror of slavery. She is certainly adept at recreating graphically the starched idioms of the eighteenth and early nineteenth centuries, at breathing life into the monumental or sometimes only arthritic rhythms of that vanished and yet still echoing age. Her poems in this style and area are hardly less moving than those of Robert Hayden, who made the period poem (the period being slavery) virtually his own invention among black poets. Dove's special empathy as a historical poet seems to be with the most sensitive, most eloquent blacks, individuals of ductile intelligence made neurotic by pain, especially the pain of not being understood and of not being able to express themselves.

Arnold Rampersad, "The Poems of Rita Dove," *Callaloo* 9, No. 1 (Winter 1986): 52–54

PETER HARRIS   Rita Dove's *Thomas and Beulah*, winner of the 1987 Pulitzer Prize, has a distinctive, ambitiously unified design. It traces the history of two blacks who separately move North, to Ohio, meet and get married in the 1920's, and go on to raise four girls, enduring many vicissitudes before their deaths in the 1960's. Arranged serially and accompanied by an almost essential chronology, the poems, we are told in a note beforehand, are meant to be read in order. Much as Michael Ondaatje has done in his poem-like novel, *Coming through Slaughter*, Dove reconstructs the past through a series of discontinuous vignettes which enter freely into the psyches of the two main characters.

It is important that the poems are arranged chronologically because we often need all the help we can get in clarifying many of the references. Even with chronology as a guide, the poems sometimes seem unnecessarily obscure and cryptic. More often, however, the difficulty of the work is justifiable because the insights are exactly as subtle as they are oblique. In exploiting the virtues of ellipsis, Dove evidently has faith we will have gumption enough to stare a hole in the page until our minds leap with hers across the gaps. For example, in the opening poem, "The Event," Thomas dares his drunken friend, Lem, to jump off a riverboat and swim to a nearby island. Lem jumps and drowns. Later in the volume, we find out that Thomas is haunted by Lem's death for the rest of his life. But in the opening poem, the aftershock goes unmentioned:

> Thomas, dry
> on deck, saw the green crown shake
> as the island slipped

under, dissolved
in the thickening stream.
At his feet

a stinking circle of rags,
the half-shell mandolin.
Where the wheel turned the water

gently shirred.

Given Dove's reticent lyricism, we can't be completely sure from this description that Lem had drowned; we can only guess. That leaves us uncertain
and, therefore, vulnerable, which is quite appropriate because the world we
are entering with Thomas is fraught with deceptive beauty and danger. Even
the shirring of roiled water can indicate death. ⟨. . .⟩

⟨. . .⟩ The psychic cost of suffering makes itself keenly felt in *Thomas and
Beulah*, a blues book that aims, through music and sympathy, to reach an
affirmative answer to the question posed by Melvin B. Tolson, which Dove
includes as the epigraph to the volume:

> Black Boy, O Black Boy,
> is the port worth the cruise?

Peter Harris, "Poetry Chronicle: Four Salvers Salvaging: New Work by Voigt, Olds,
Dove, and McHugh," *Virginia Quarterly Review* 64, No. 2 (Spring 1988): 270–73

STEVEN SCHNEIDER   SS: How does it feel to be the first black
woman poet since Gwendolyn Brooks to win the Pulitzer Prize?

RD: My first reaction was quite simply disbelief. Disbelief that first of all
there hasn't been another black person since Gwendolyn Brooks in 1950
to win the Pulitzer Prize in poetry, though there certainly have been some
outstanding black poets in that period. On a public level, it says something
about the nature of cultural politics of this country. It's a shame actually.
On a personal level, it's overwhelming.

SS: Did you feel you had written something special when you completed
Thomas and Beulah?

RD: I felt I had written something larger than myself, larger than what
I had hoped for it to be. I did not begin this sequence as a book; it began
as a poem. The book grew poem by poem, and it wasn't until I was about
a third of the way through that I realized it would have to be a book. So

I grew with it and I had to rise to it. I started with the Thomas poems because I wanted to understand my grandfather more—what he was like as a young man, how he grew up and became the man I knew. To do that though, I realized pretty early on that I could rely neither on my memories of him nor on the memories of my mother or her sisters or brothers, but I had to get to know the town he lived in. What was Akron, Ohio like in the '20s and '30s? It was different from the Akron I knew. That meant I had to go to the library and read a whole bunch of stuff I never counted on researching to try to get a sense of that period of time in the industrial Midwest. On other levels, I had to enter male consciousness in a way which was—well, I knew I could do it for one or two poems but this was an extended effort. I was really, at a certain point, very very driven to be as honest as I could possibly be. Also, I didn't want to impose my language or my sensibility upon their lives. And things got—

SS: Things got very complicated?

RD: That's right.

SS: Did you have a different kind of satisfaction about finishing this book than your other two books?

RD: It was different. I am not going to say I was more satisfied; I don't think I have a favorite book of mine. But there was a feeling of relief because I had made it through.

Steven Schneider, "Coming Home: An Interview with Rita Dove," *Iowa Review* 19, No. 3 (Fall 1989): 112–13

ROBERT McDOWELL   Rita Dove has always possessed a story-teller's instinct. In *The Yellow House on the Corner* (1980), *Museum* (1983), and *Thomas and Beulah* (1985), this instinct has found expression in a synthesis of striking imagery, myth, magic, fable, wit, humor, political comment, and a sure knowledge of history. Many contemporaries share Dove's mastery of some of these, but few succeed in bringing them together to create a point of view that, by its breadth and force, stands apart. She has not worked her way into this enviable position among poets without fierce commitment.

Passing through a graduate writing program (Iowa) in the mid-1970s, Dove and her peers were schooled in the importance of sensation and its representation through manipulation of The Image. The standard lesson plan, devised to reflect the ascendancy of Wallace Stevens and a corrupt revision of T. S. Eliot's objective correlative, instructed young writers to renounce realistic depiction and offer it up to the province of prose; it promoted subjectivity and imagination-as-image; it strangled a generation of poems.

How and why this came to pass is less important, really, than admitting that it is so. Literary magazines are gorged with poems devoid of shapeliness and scope. Imagistic, cramped, and confessional, they exist for the predictably surprising, climactic phrase. A historically conscious reader, aware of literary tradition, might understandably perceive an enormous cultural amnesia as the dubiously distinguishing feature of such poems. Such a reader will rue the fact that the writing and interpretation of poetry has diminished to a trivial pursuit, a pronouncement of personal instinct. If this is the dominant direction of a discouraging Moment, then Rita Dove distinguishes herself by resolutely heading the other way.

Unlike the dissembling spirit indicated above, Dove is an assembler who gathers the various facts of this life and presents them in ways that jar our lazy assumptions. She gives voice to many positions and many characters. Like the speaker/writer of classic argumentation, she shows again and again that she understands the opposing sides of conflicts she deals with. She tells all sides of the story. Consider the titles of her books, their symbolic weight. The personal turning point *House on the Corner* evolves, becoming the public Museum (symbol of preserved chronology); that, in turn, gives way to the names of two characters whose lives combine and illustrate the implicit meanings of the personal House·and the public Museum.

> Robert McDowell, "The Assembling Vision of Rita Dove," *Conversant Essays: Contemporary Poets on Poetry*, ed. James McCorkle (Detroit: Wayne State University Press, 1990), p. 294

JOHN SHOPTAW   At the beginning of Rita Dove's arresting new volume of poetry ⟨*Thomas and Beulah*⟩, we are given directions for reading that turn out to be true but impossible to follow: "These poems tell two sides of a story and are meant to be read in sequence." The impossibility is not physical, as in the instructions prefacing John Ashbery's long double-columned poem, *Litany*, which tell us that the columns "are meant to be read as simultaneous but independent monologues"; rather, the impossibility in reading the two sides of Rita Dove's book—Thomas's side (I. "Mandolin," 23 poems) followed by Beulah's side (II. "Canary in Bloom," 21 poems)— is biographical and historical. The lives of Thomas and Beulah, whether considered together or individually, lack what would integrate them into a single story. The events in *Thomas and Beulah* are narrated in strict chrono- logical order, which is detailed in the appended chronology. The subjection of story time to historical time, unusual in modern narratives, gives Dove's sequence a tragic linearity, a growing sense that what is done cannot be undone and that what is not done but only regretted or deferred cannot be redeemed in the telling. The narrative runs from Thomas's riverboat life (1919) to his arrival in Akron (1921) and marriage to Beulah (1924), to their children's births, his jobs at Goodyear, his stroke (1960) and death (1963). Then the narrative begins again with Beulah: her father's flirtations, Thomas's flirtations and courtship (1923), their marriage (1924), a preg- nancy (1931), her millinery work (1950), a family reunion (1964), and death (1969). In the background, the Depression and the March on Wash- ington mark respectively the trials of the couple's and their children's genera- tion.

The sequence of *Thomas and Beulah* resembles fiction more than it does poetic sequence—Faulkner's family chronicles in particular. Dove's modern- ist narrator stands back paring her fingernails like an unobtrusive master or God. The cover shows a snapshot, of Thomas and Beulah presumably, and the volume may be considered as a photo album, or two albums, with only the date and place printed underneath each picture. Thomas and Beulah are probably Rita Dove's grandparents; the book is dedicated to her mother, Elvira Elizabeth, and the third child born to Thomas and Beulah is identified in the chronology as Liza. But whether the couple is actually Rita Dove's grandparents is less important than the fact that all evidence of their relation has been removed. Any choice of genre involves an economy of gains and losses. Objective, dramatic narration—showing rather than telling—has the advantage of letting the events speak for themselves and the disadvantage of dispensing with the problematics of narrative distortion and a camera- eye or God's eye view. *Thomas and Beulah* tells it like it is and assumes it is like it tells us.

John Shoptaw, "Segregated Lives: Rita Dove's *Thomas and Beulah*," *Reading Black, Reading Feminist: A Critical Anthology*, ed. Henry Louis Gates, Jr. (New York: Meridian, 1990), pp. 374–75

BONNIE COSTELLO   The discipline of writing *Thomas and Beulah*, a family epic in lyric form, required Rita Dove to focus, as never before, her talent for compression. How to get years of her grandparents' joy and anguish into spare lines without presuming to sum up for them; how to telescope distances of place, background, dreams, without narrating—these were some of the problems she solved so brilliantly in that book. The past shed its patina as bits of voice and image shone through to bespeak whole epochs and regions. The book moved us by its understatement, the major ally of compression, and by its sympathetic imagination, that refused to make Thomas and Beulah stereotypes, the mere objects of our pity or nostalgia.

In *Grace Notes* Dove returns to the range of subjects and settings that characterized her first two books (she is remarkably broad in the scope of her references without ever being showy). All the features we have grown to appreciate in this poet arise here in their finest form: descriptive precision, tonal control, metaphoric reach within uncompromising realism. Moreover, she had brought these talents to bear upon a new intimacy and moral depth, served by memory and imagination working together.

The first poem of *Grace Notes*, set off as a kind of prologue, establishes the tone and terms of the volume. "Summit Beach, 1921" presents a girl of courtship age, refusing to join in the festive abandon of young dancers on the beach and choosing to sit by the fire instead. Within 25 lines we learn the history of this girl's stance and come to know her motives and desires even while we never know her name or her relation to the poet. A scar on her knee is the consequence of her childhood fantasy of flying off "Papa's shed." Yet she still "refused / to cut the wing," advised by her father to preserve angelic innocence ("you're all you've got") and waits, instead, for love's "music skittering up her calf." The dreams of this young woman, her "parasol and invisible wings" are in one sense betrayed by the reality around her, the limits imposed because of gender and race—this is a "Negro beach"—and more universally because of gravity and mortality. The winking scar on her knee is the constant reminder of the real world's pull. Yet the poet clearly admires the resilience of this dreamer and her spirit—scarred but winged—pervades the poems of *Grace Notes*. All of Dove's books have been marked by their thoughtful arrangement and *Grace Notes*, divided into five sections, marks out several distinctive areas of reflection, united by the dual images of wounds and wings, themes of pain and the will to resist one's limits, which she introduces in this first poem.

Bonnie Costello, "Scars and Wings: Rita Dove's *Grace Notes*," *Callaloo* 14, No. 2 (Spring 1991): 434–35

EKATERINI GEORGOUDAKI   Although conditions were more hospitable for black women writers after the Black Power/Black Arts Movement of the 1960s and the Feminist Movement of the 1970s, the ideologies of class, gender, and race still persisted in American society in the 1980s, when Rita Dove started publishing her work. She therefore shares certain dilemmas and concerns with previous Afro-American women poets, such as their feelings of displacement, fragmentation, and isolation, and their distaste for conventional stereotypes, hierarchies, divisions and boundaries. She also continues their search for wholeness, balance, connection, continuity, reconciliation with the self and the world, as well as their efforts to redefine the self and history, and to renew cultural values.

As a black person living in the predominantly white societies of the Old and New World, having entered an inter-racial and inter-cultural marriage (her husband is a German writer), and trying to forge an autonomous female poetic voice against the background of a male dominated Euro- and Afro-American literary tradition, Dove has often crossed social and literary boundaries, violated taboos, and experienced displacement, i.e. living "in two different worlds, seeing things with double vision," wherever she has stayed (USA, Germany, Israel). Talking to Judith Kitchen and Stan Sanvel Rubin about her European experiences which inspired her second book, *Museum* (1983), Dove admits that she had a sense of displacement while she was in Europe, and that she expressed this sense through various characters and situations in *Museum*. She remarks, however, that her stay in Europe broadened her world view and contributed to her personal growth as a person and an artist:

> When I went to Europe for the first time—that was in '74, way before I had thought of this book—it was mind boggling to see how blind I'd been in my own little world of America. It had never dawned on me that there was a world out there. It was really quite shocking to see that there was another way of looking at things. And when I went back in '80–81 to spend a lot of time, I got a different angle on the way things are, the way things happen in the world and the importance they take. Also as a *person* going to Europe I was treated differently because I was American. I was Black, but they treated me differently than people treat me here because I am Black. And in fact, I often felt a little like Fiammetta; I became an object. I was a Black American, and therefore I became a representative of all of that.

And I sometimes felt like a ghost, I mean, people would ask me questions, but I had a feeling that they weren't seeing *me*, but a shell. So there was that sense of being there and not being there, you know. Then because you are there you can see things a little clearer sometimes. That certainly was something, I think, that informed the spirit of *Museum*.

Dove's complex experiences in the USA and abroad (Europe, N. Africa, Israel) have affected both her vision and her poetic method. Although she deals with the problems of racism and sexism, she does not adopt the polemical voice of either a black nationalist or a feminist poet, and therefore she does not let indignation, anger, and protest control her verse. Although she focuses on the black experience in many of her works she goes beyond the definition of black literature which reflected the black ideal that prevailed since the late 1960s: "Black literature BY blacks, ABOUT blacks, directed TO blacks. ESSENTIAL black literature is the distillation of black life."

Ekaterini Georgoudaki, "Rita Dove: Crossing Boundaries," *Callaloo* 14, No. 2 (Spring 1991): 419–20

KIRKLAND C. JONES   In Dove's poems, dramatic monologue and compressed narrative are the primary contexts through which the language of the people is presented. In her short stories, though they are often very brief, the dialogues and musing of her characters are set forth in authentic speech patterns. Moreover, Dove has a keen sense of history. She links the past and the present through her characters' names and through the appropriateness of their speech, revealing Dove's brilliant cross-cultural perceptivity, as her characters' voices move in and out of the centuries, simultaneously transcending the local and the mundane. "Catecorner," an expression found in ⟨*Fifth Sunday's*⟩ title story, is a folksy way of describing the site of the church building, along with the phrase "let loose," meaning to set free. And the language of the black church adds enough flavoring to join the generations of worshippers with their inherited family and community traditions—"the junior ushers," "the junior choir," as they stand up to sing, "their blue silk robes swaying slightly as they rocked to the beat." The marching choir, the little-girl "gleaners," the fat officious women in white, all fit the story's "Fifth Sunday" language, modern enough to be Methodist and familiar enough to impart a quality of agedness and blackness.

Aunt Carrie, in the story that bears her name, speaks long dramatic monologues, and her speech is almost correct enough to match her assumed primness, allowing her to communicate with her young niece to whom she recounts more than one interesting story. Aunt Carrie is the type of matron who sprinkles her addresses with "dear." But she lapses occasionally into the remembered language of her parents and grandparents—"Don't go apologizing to me . . . makes me blush," she exclaims, and later in a much more relaxed, more confiding tone, she admits to her niece, "I didn't think about nothing at all." But on a whole, dialect is more subtle in the prose vignettes than in the author's most representative poems.

> Kirkland C. Jones, "Folk Idiom in the Literary Expression of Two African American Authors: Rita Dove and Yusef Komunyakaa," *Language and Literature in the African American Imagination*, ed. Carol Aisha Blackshire-Belay (Westport, CT: Greenwood Press, 1992), pp. 152–53

❖ Bibliography

Ten Poems. 1977.

The Only Dark Spot in the Sky. 1980.

The Yellow House on the Corner. 1980.

Mandolin. 1982.

Museum. 1983.

Fifth Sunday. 1985.

Thomas and Beulah. 1986.

The Other Side of the House (with Tamarra Kaida). 1988.

Grace Notes. 1989.

Through the Ivory Gate. 1992.

Selected Poems. 1993.

The Darker Face of the Earth: A Verse Play in Fourteen Scenes. 1994.

⬨ ⬨ ⬨

Ralph Ellison
1914–1994

RALPH WALDO ELLISON was born on March 1, 1914, in Oklahoma City, Oklahoma. His father, Lewis Ellison, was a construction worker and trades-man who died when Ellison was three. His mother, Ida Millsap, worked as a domestic servant but was active in radical politics for many years. Ellison thrived on the discarded magazines and phonograph records she brought home from the white households where she worked. He attended Douglass High School in Oklahoma City, where he learned the soprano saxophone, trumpet, and other instruments, playing both jazz and light classical music.

In 1933 Ellison began studying music at the Tuskegee Institute in Ala-bama. He remained there for three years before coming to New York in 1936, where he held a number of odd jobs while continuing to study music and sculpture. In New York he met Langston Hughes and Richard Wright, who gave him great encouragement in his writing. Ellison's short stories, essays, and reviews began appearing in the *Antioch Review*, the *New Masses*, and many other magazines and journals in the late 1930s. At this time his interest in social justice attracted him to the Communist party, although he would later repudiate it. Ellison gained a modicum of financial security in 1938 when he was hired by the Federal Writers' Project to gather folklore and present it in literary form. The four years he spent at this work enriched his own writing by providing source material that would be incorporated into his own fiction.

In 1943, wishing to help in the war effort, Ellison joined the merchant marine. The next year he received a Rosenwald Foundation Fellowship to write a novel; although he mapped out a plot, he failed to finish the work (one section was published as a short story, "Flying Home"). After the war he went to a friend's farm in Vermont to recuperate, and it was here that he conceived the novel that would establish him as a major writer—*Invisible Man*. He worked on the book for five years, and it was finally published in 1952. This long novel is both a historical biography of the black man in America and an allegory of man's quest for identity. *Invisible Man* received the National Book Award for fiction in 1953 and is now regarded as one of the most distinguished American novels of the century. *Shadow and Act* (1964), Ellison's second book, is a collection of personal essays about literature, folklore, jazz, and the author's life.

Even before finishing *Invisible Man*, Ellison had conceived the idea for another novel. Although he published several segments of it as short stories and read others on television and at lectures, the work remained unfinished at the time of his death; a large portion of it was destroyed by a fire at Ellison's summer home in Massachusetts in 1967. Because he did not advocate black separatism, Ellison fell out of sympathy with the black writers and thinkers of the 1960s; but over the last two decades he has again become a much sought-after lecturer on college campuses. A second collection of essays, *Going to the Territory*, was published in 1986.

Ralph Ellison held visiting professorships at Yale, Bard College, the University of Chicago, and elsewhere. From 1970 to 1979 he was Albert Schweitzer Professor in the Humanities at New York University, later becoming an emeritus professor there. He held a fellowship of the American Academy of Arts and Letters in Rome from 1955 to 1957, and received the United States Medal of Freedom in 1969. He was a charter member of the National Council of the Arts, has served as trustee of the John F. Kennedy Center for the Performing Arts, and was honorary consultant in American Letters at the Library of Congress. Ellison was married twice, but details of his first marriage are unavailable; in 1946 he married Fanny McConnell. Ralph Ellison died in New York City on April 16, 1994.

▓ *Critical Extracts*

SAUL BELLOW   I was keenly aware, as I read this book ⟨*Invisible Man*⟩, of a very significant kind of independence in the writing. For there is a "way" for Negro novelists to go at their problems, just as there are Jewish or Italian "ways." Mr. Ellison has not adopted a minority tone. If he had done so, he would have failed to establish a true middle-of-consciousness for everyone.

Negro Harlem is at once primitive and sophisticated; it exhibits the extremes of instinct and civilization as few other American communities do. If a writer dwells on the peculiarity of this, he ends with an exotic effect. And Mr. Ellison is not exotic. For him this balance of instinct and culture or civilization is not a Harlem matter; it is *the* matter, German, French, Russian, American, universal, a matter very little understood. It is thought that Negroes and other minority people, kept under in the great status battle, are in the instinct cellar of dark enjoyment. This imagined enjoyment provokes envious rage and murder; and then it is a large portion of human nature itself which becomes the fugitive murderously pursued. In our society Man—Himself—is idolized and publicly worshipped, but the single individual must hide himself underground and try to save his desires, his thoughts, his soul, in invisibility. He must return to himself, learning self-acceptance and rejecting all that threatens to deprive him of his manhood.

This is what I make of *Invisible Man*. It is not by any means faultless; I don't think the hero's experiences in the Communist party are as original in conception as other parts of the book, and his love affair with a white woman is all too brief, but it is an immensely moving novel and it has greatness.

Saul Bellow, "Man Underground," *Commentary* 13, No. 6 (June 1952): 609

EARL H. ROVIT   The most obvious comment one can make about Ralph Ellison's *Invisible Man* is that it is a profoundly comic work. But the obvious is not necessarily either simple or self-explanatory, and it seems to me that the comic implications of Ellison's novel are elusive and provocative enough to warrant careful examination both in relation to the total effect of the novel itself and the American cultural pattern from which it derives. ⟨. . .⟩

First it should be noted that Ellison's commitment to what Henry James has termed "the American joke" has been thoroughly deliberate and undisguised. Ellison once described penetratingly the ambiguous *locus* of conflicting forces within which the American artist has had always to work: "For the ex-colonials, the declaration of an American identity meant the assumption of a mask, and it imposed not only the discipline of national self-consciousness, it gave Americans an ironic awareness of the joke that always lies between appearance and reality, between the discontinuity of social tradition and that sense of the past which clings to the mind. And perhaps even an awareness of the joke that society is man's creation, not God's."

This kind of ironic awareness may contain bitterness and may even become susceptible to the heavy shadow of despair, but the art which it produces has been ultimately comic. It will inevitably probe the masks of identity and value searching relentlessly for some deeper buried reality, but it will do this while accepting the fundamental necessity for masks and the impossibility of ever discovering an essential face beneath a mask. That is to say, this comic stance will accept with the same triumphant gesture both the basic absurdity of all attempts to impose meaning on the chaos of life, and the necessary converse of this, the ultimate significance of absurdity itself.

Ellison's *Invisible Man* is comic in this sense almost in spite of its overtly satirical interests and its excursions into the broadly farcical. Humorous as many of its episodes are in themselves—the surreal hysteria of the scene at the Golden Day, the hero's employment at the Liberty Paint Company, or the expert dissection of political entanglements in Harlem—these are the materials which clothe Ellison's joke and which, in turn, suggest the shape by which the joke can be comprehended. The pith of Ellison's comedy reverberates on a level much deeper than these incidents, and as in all true humor, the joke affirms and denies simultaneously—accepts and rejects with the same uncompromising passion, leaving not a self-cancelling neutralization of momentum, but a sphere of moral conquest, a humanized cone of light at the very heart of the heart of darkness. *Invisible Man*, as Ellison has needlessly insisted in rebuttal to those critics who would treat the novel as fictionalized sociology or as a dramatization of archetypal images, is an artist's attempt to create a *form*. And fortunately Ellison has been quite explicit in describing what he means by *form*; in specific reference to the improvisation of the jazz-musician he suggests that form represents "a definition of his identity: as an individual, as a member of the collectivity, and as a link in the chain of tradition." But note that each of these definitions of identity must be individually exclusive and mutually contradictory on any logical terms. Because of its very pursuit after the uniqueness of individuality, the successful definition of an individual must define out the possibilities of generalization into "collectivity" or "tradition." But herein for Ellison in his embrace of a notion of fluid amorphous identity lies the real morality and humor in mankind's art and men's lives—neither of which have much respect for the laws of formal logic.

Earl H. Rovit, "Ralph Ellison and the American Comic Tradition," *Wisconsin Studies in Contemporary Literature* 1, No. 3 (Fall 1960): 34–35

JONATHAN BAUMBACH   I hesitate to call Ralph Ellison's *Invisible Man* (1952) a Negro novel, though of course it is written by a Negro and is centrally concerned with the experiences of a Negro. The appellation is not so much inaccurate as it is misleading. A novelist treating the invisibility and phantasmagoria of the Negro's life in this "democracy" is, if he tells the truth, necessarily writing a very special kind of book. Yet if his novel is interesting only because of its specialness, he has not violated the surface of his subject; he has not, after all, been serious. Despite the differences in their external concerns, Ellison has more in common as a novelist with Joyce, Melville, Camus, Kafka, West, and Faulkner than he does with other serious writers like James Baldwin and Richard Wright. To concentrate on the idiom of a serious novel, no matter how distinctive its peculiarities, is to depreciate it, to minimize the universality of its implications. Though the protagonist of *Invisible Man* is a southern Negro, he is, in Ellison's rendering, profoundly all of us.

Despite its obvious social implications, Ellison's novel is a modern gothic, a Candide-like picaresque set in a dimly familiar nightmare landscape called the United States. Like *The Catcher in the Rye*, *A Member of the Wedding*, and *The Adventures of Augie March*, Ellison's novel chronicles a series of initiatory experiences through which its naïve hero learns, to his disillusion and horror, the way of the world. However, unlike these other novels of passage, *Invisible Man* takes place, for the most part, in the uncharted spaces between the conscious and the unconscious, in the semilit darkness where nightmare verges on reality and the external world has all the aspects of a disturbing dream. Refracted by satire, at times, cartooned, Ellison's world is at once surreal and real, comic and tragic, grotesque and normal—our world viewed in its essentials rather than its externals.

The Negro's life in our white land and time is, as Ellison knows it, a relentless unreality, unreal in that the Negro as a group is loved, hated, persecuted, feared, and envied, while as an individual he is unfelt, unheard, unseen—to all intents and purposes invisible. The narrator, who is also the novel's central participant, never identifies himself by name. Though he experiences several changes of identity in the course of the novel, Ellison's hero exists to the reader as a man without an identity, an invisible "I." In taking on a succession of identities, the invisible hero undergoes an increasingly intense succession of disillusioning experiences, each one paralleling and anticipating the one following it. The hero's final loss of illusion forces

him underground into the coffin (and womb) of the earth to be either
finally buried or finally reborn.

Jonathan Baumbach, "Nightmare of a Native Son," *The Landscape of Nightmare:
Studies in the Contemporary American Novel* (New York: New York University Press,
1965), pp. 68–69

EDWARD MARGOLIES   Not surprisingly, Ellison's understanding
of his early life corresponds to his definition of Negro jazz. And ultimately
it is jazz, and blues especially, that becomes the aesthetic mainspring of his
writing. If literature serves as a ritualistic means of ordering experience, so
does music, as Ellison well understands. And it is more to the rites of the
jazz band than to the teachings of Kenneth Burke or the influences of
Hemingway, Stein, Eliot, Malraux, or Conrad (persons whom Ellison men-
tions as literary ancestors and preceptors) that Ellison owes the structure
and informing ideas of his novel. Particularly relevant is the attention Ellison
casts on the jazz soloist. Within and against a frame of chordal progressions
and rhythmic patterns, the soloist is free to explore a variety of ideas and
emotions. But this freedom is not absolute. The chordal background of the
other musicians demands a discipline that the soloist dare not breach. He
is as much a part of the whole as he is an individual, and he may well lose
himself in the whole before he recovers his individual identity. Finally,
music, however tragic its message, is an affirmation of life, a celebration of
the indomitable human spirit, in that it imposes order and form on the
chaos of experience. ⟨. . .⟩

Since the blues, according to Ellison, is by its very nature a record of
past wrongs, pains, and defeats, it serves to define the singer as one who
has suffered, and in so doing it has provided him with a history. As the
novel ⟨*Invisible Man*⟩ develops, the hero takes on the role of a Negro
Everyman, whose adventures and cries of woe and laughter become the
history of a people. As a high-school boy in the South, he is a "Tom"—
little better than a darky entertainer; in college, a Booker T. Washington
accommodationist. When he moves North, he works as a nonunion laborer
and then flirts for a while with Communism. Finally, he becomes a Rinehart,
Ellison's word for the unattached, alienated, urban Negro who deliberately
endeavors to manipulate the fantasies of whites and Negroes to his own
advantage. But besides being a kind of symbolic recapitulation of Negro

history, the blues structure of the novel suggests a philosophy of history as well—something outside racial determinism, progress, or various ideologies, something indefinably human, unexpected and perhaps nonrational.

> Edward Margolies, "History as Blues: Ralph Ellison's *Invisible Man*," *Native Sons: A Critical Study of Twentieth-Century Negro American Authors* (Philadelphia: J. B. Lippincott Co., 1968), pp. 130, 133

BARBARA CHRISTIAN   Unlike Wright and other notable black writers, Ellison is the spokesman for the "infinite possibilities" that he feels are inherent in the condition of being an artist rather than a Negro artist. He repeatedly states in his essays that his primary concern is not the social but rather the aesthetic responsibilities of the writer. ⟨. . .⟩

There is one word that crops up repeatedly in both the essays and *Invisible Man* and which is at the base of Ellison's aesthetic beliefs. That word is *myth*, the magical transformer of life. Influenced by T. S. Eliot whom he calls his literary ancestor, Ellison combines the literary past and the memory and culture of the individual with the present, thus placing the contemporary writer alongside the other men who have written in the English language. Baldwin stresses the fact that the writer creates out of his own experience. Ellison would add that one writes out of one's experience as understood through one's knowledge of self, culture, and literature. Self, in Ellison's case, refers to his own past and background, culture to the American culture and more specifically to Negro American culture, and literature to the entire range of works in European literature that help to make up Western sensibility.

Even Ellison's name itself is steeped in myth as he points out in the essay, "Hidden Names and Complex Fate." His father had named him after Ralph Waldo Emerson and Ellison recalls that "much later after I began to write and work with words, I came to suspect that my father had been aware of the suggestive powers of names and the magic involved in naming." The name *Ralph Waldo* indeed had magic for it enabled Ellison to see the power of the myth and to envision the role that myth could play in achieving his aim which was, as he put it, "to add to literature the wonderful American speech and idiom and to bring into range as fully as possible the complex reality of American experience as it shaped and was shaped by the lives of my own people." Myths in order to be preserved and appreciated must be written down and Ellison, in his comments on Hemingway and Faulkner, is constantly aware that one element of the American past is sorely missing from most American literature. As Ralph Waldo Emerson could merge the myths and attitudes of New England into his philosophy of Transcendentalism, Ralph Waldo Ellison would merge that essential element, the nature of black folklore and life style, into American literature—and myth could be the carrier.

> Barbara Christian, "Ralph Ellison: A Critical Study," *Black Expression: Essays by and about Black Americans in the Creative Arts*, ed. Addison Gayle, Jr. (New York: Weybright & Talley, 1969), pp. 354–55

TONY TANNER   In the introduction to his essays (*Shadow and Act*), Ralph Ellison, recalling the circumstances of his youth, stresses the significance of the fact that while Oklahoman jazz musicians were developing 'a freer, more complex and driving form of jazz, my friends and I were exploring an idea of human versatility and possibility which went against the barbs or over the palings of almost every fence which those who controlled social and political power had erected to restrict our roles in the life of the country.' The fact that these musicians working with 'tradition, imagination and the sounds and emotions around them', could create something new which was both free yet recognizably formed (this is the essence of improvisation) was clearly of the first importance for Ralph Ellison; the ideas of versatility and possibility which he and his friends were exploring provide the ultimate subject-matter, and nourish the style, of his one novel to date, *Invisible Man* (1952), a novel which in many ways is seminal for subsequent American fiction. His title may owe something to H. G. Wells's novel *The Invisible Man*, for the alienated Griffin in Wells's novel also comes to realize 'what a helpless absurdity an Invisible Man was—in a cold and dirty climate and a crowded, civilized city' and there is a very suggestive scene in which he tries to assemble an identity, which is at the same time a disguise, from the wigs, masks, artificial noses, and clothes of Omniums, the large London store. It would not be surprising if Wells's potentially very probing little novel about the ambiguity involved in achieving social 'identity' had stayed in Ellison's extremely literate memory. But if it did so it would be because Ellison's experience as a Negro had taught him a profounder sort of invisibility than any chemically induced vanishing trick.

As the narrator says in the opening paragraph, it is as though he lives surrounded by mirrors of distorting glass, so that other people do not see him but only his surroundings, or reflections of themselves, or their fantasies. It is an aspect of recent American fiction that work coming from members of so-called minority groups has proved to be relevant and applicable to the situation of people not sharing their immediate racial experience or, as it may be, sexual inclination; and *Invisible Man*, so far from being limited to an expression of an anguish and injustice experienced peculiarly by Negroes, is quite simply the most profound novel about American identity written since the war.

> Tony Tanner, *City of Words: American Fiction 1950–1970* (New York: Harper & Row, 1971), p. 50

ARTHUR P. DAVIS   Among Ellison's earliest publications was a short story which came out in 1944 called "Flying Home." In this short fiction we have an introduction to the techniques Ellison was later to use superbly in his novel. A narrative concerning an incident in the Air Force school for Negro pilots in the Deep South, the work makes use of realistic details, a flashback technique, the Greek myth of Icarus, a Negro folk story, and miscellaneous symbols of the modern world. Ellison makes the whole story an extended metaphor of the Negro's place in American society.

The simple story concerns Todd, a Negro pilot trainee in Alabama who flies upward too precipitously, and strikes a buzzard (Jim Crow), and crashes on the property of a white landowner. When Todd regains consciousness, the first persons he sees are Jefferson, an old Negro sharecropper, and a boy, whom Jefferson sends for a physician. In the interim the old man needles the pilot. Why you want to fly, Boy, he asks, in effect, you *could* get shot for a buzzard. Note the emphasis on *buzzard*, a bird symbolizing the past because it eats dead things. Note also the old stay-in-your-place attitude held not only by whites but by Negroes as well. In his way Jefferson is a buzzard, resenting this fancy new-type Negro.

Jefferson then tells Todd a folk story known to most Negroes: the story of his going to Heaven where he was given six-foot angels' wings. Jefferson, however, flew too fast and dangerously and was thrown out of Heaven. The implications of the story are obvious, and the old man's taunting laughter drives Todd into a screaming rage: "Can I help it because they won't actually let us fly? Maybe we are a bunch of buzzards feeding on a dead horse, but we can hope to be eagles, can't we?"

At the end of the story the white landowner brings in orderlies from a mental institution. "You all know you cain't let the Nigguh get up that high without going crazy. The Nigguh brain ain't built right for high altitudes."

Here is a brilliant mélange of realism, folk story, and symbolism, with a touch of surrealism at the end—the kind of fusion found on a grand scale in *Invisible Man*.

Arthur P. Davis, *From the Dark Tower: Afro-American Writers 1900 to 1960* (Washington, DC: Howard University Press, 1974), pp. 209–10

WILLI REAL   It is not uncommon to regard short stories as precursors of more comprehensive fictional works or even merely as by-products of a novelist's career. This view seems confirmed by some of Ralph Ellison's pieces of short fiction. His first story, "Slick Gonna Learn," is an excerpt from an unpublished novel, the famous "Battle Royal," first chapter of Ellison's *Invisible Man*, goes back to an earlier short story of that name, and his stories "Flying Home" and "King of the Bingo Game" are said to anticipate major themes of *Invisible Man* as well. Yet it is still difficult if not impossible to say whether Ellison will be remembered as a novelist or as a novelist *and* a short story writer. ⟨. . .⟩

The protagonist of "King of the Bingo Game" is neither an ideal hero nor an anti-hero. Like all other characters both black and white, he is unnamed (his wife Laura being the only exception in the story). He was reared in the South and, like so many other people during the Great Migration, he walked the traditional road to freedom: like the protagonist of *Invisible Man* and like Ellison himself, he left the rural South where black solidarity was greater but white domination also more rigid, for the more industrialized North. But instead of finding the Promised Land there, he has to experience the depersonalizing influence of Northern slums where human emotions are crippled and where folk ties are eroded. As he possesses no birth certificate which is called by Deutsch a petty, bureaucratic technicality, he is officially a non-person, a nobody unable to get a job. Thus his personal situation which is also that of the protagonist in "Slick Gonna Learn," is representative of that of so many people living in a slum. It means

being caught in a vicious circle which is characterized by poverty, denial
of individuality, denial of work, denial of medical care, death. ⟨. . .⟩

The aimlessness and senselessness of the protagonist's way of acting, the
cyclic structure of the story is enhanced by a literary device whose full effect
is only revealed by considering the context of this piece of short fiction as
a whole: irony.

> Willi Real, "Ralph Ellison: 'King of the Bingo Game,' " *The Black American Short
> Story in the 20th Century*, ed. Peter Bruck (Amsterdam: B. R. Grüner Publishing Co.,
> 1977), pp. 111, 115, 122

RICHARD FINHOLT   Ellison, after Poe, is the American writer
most self-consciously committed to the idea of the mind thinking, of the
mind, that is, as the ultimate source of transcendence or salvation. But he
is also the inheritor of a wellspring of emotional pain, the collective black
experience in America, that has received its traditional artistic expression
in the blues beat and lyric. ⟨. . .⟩

In fact, the novel ⟨*Invisible Man*⟩ amounts to a critique of both the
intellectual and the emotional dimensions of the American experience. The
Brotherhood (an obvious pseudonym for the Communist Party), which
prides itself on its "reasonable point of view" and "scientific approach to
society," represents the *head* of the social structure, as do also such characters
as Bledsoe, Norton, Emerson, and all who think without feeling; and characters like Trueblood, Emerson Jr., Lucius Brockway, Tarp, Tod Clifton, and
Ras, all those who feel without thinking, represent the *heart*. Given the
two dimensions, the invisible man's problem, as for the heroes of the other
writers studied here, is "How to Be!" And, as with the others, salvation is
the attainment of a balance, of a unification of mind and body, thought
and feeling, idea and action, that forms a pattern of existence with the
potential to transcend the "biological morality" (Audrey's term) imposed
from within and the social morality imposed from without.

Melville saw all men "enveloped in whale lines"; it is Ellison's vision
that all men, whether powerful or weak, are puppets controlled by invisible
strings ("the force that pulls your strings"), like Clifton's dancing Sambo
doll. Ellison's vision is of a complex chattering-monkey society composed
of blind, mindless puppets wearing the masks assigned to them, playing the
roles demanded of them, striking out blindly at the targets provided for

them. A metaphor for this society is the battle royal ("suddenly alive in the dark with the horror of the battle royal"), in which the young black boys are set plunging and swinging wildly about a boxing ring. Blindfolded, they fight "hysterically," in a "confused" state of "terror" and "hate," while not one blow reaches the southern whites who are the makers of their pain and confusion. Tatlock comes to believe in the game, as the vet doctor will later warn the invisible man not to do, comes to believe that by striking at his comrade, the youthful invisible man, he is striking at a representative of whites (by virtue of the invisible man's college scholarship). Ironically, one of the white men has to remind the invisible man that he is nothing but a "Sambo." ⟨. . .⟩

Ellison differs from the other writers ⟨. . .⟩ in that he envisions no unifying force at the center of the cosmos; where the others see a pattern of meaning on which to build what Ellison calls a "plan of living," Ellison sees only "chaos." The human problem then becomes how "to give pattern to the chaos which lives within the pattern" of the "certainties" upon which blind men have built their societies. In *Symbolism and American Literature* Charles Feidelson calls Poe's philosophy "materialistic idealism." Allowing for the same possibility of a contradiction in terms, Ellison's philosophy might be called existential transcendentalism.

Richard Finholt, "Ellison's Chattering-Monkey Blues," *American Visionary Fiction: Mad Metaphysics as Salvation Psychology* (Port Washington, NY: Kennikat Press, 1978), pp. 98–100

ROBERT G. O'MEALLY   Ellison's political and critical positions have won him considerable animosity from whites and blacks alike. He maintains that art has functions that embrace the political but that differ from the rhetoric and cant of most political testimony. Ellison's truth is that of the artist; he insists upon the variety, ambiguity, comedy, tragedy, and terror of human life—beyond all considerations of political platforms. As a writer, Ellison's challenge is to charge one's work with as much life and truth as possible. Art, he says, is fundamentally a celebration of human life; it is not a wailing complaint about social wrongs.

This loftiness has not meant that Ellison has lost sight of his beginnings. Quite the contrary. Since his first review was printed in 1937, he has called for precise, sympathetic writing about the true nature of Afro-American experience. Never having written any fiction in which blacks do not figure centrally, Ellison has sought to capture in fiction the language and lore, the rites and the values, the laughter and the sufferings, as well as the downright craziness, which characterize black life in America. Ellison knows that the only way to grasp universal values and patterns is by holding fast to particularities of time, place, culture, and race. The Invisible Man is an identifiably Afro-American creature whose experience, nonetheless, is so deeply *human* that readers throughout the world identify and sympathise with him. ⟨. . .⟩

Ralph Ellison is a progressive and accomplished writer and intellectual, an American "man of good hope" in the tradition of Emerson, Mark Twain, Du Bois, and James Weldon Johnson. His importance lies in his unsinkable optimism concerning his race, his nation, man's fate. Moreover, it lies in his insistence on literary craft under the pressure of inspiration as the best means of transforming everyday experience, talk, and lore into literature.

Robert G. O'Meally, *The Craft of Ralph Ellison* (Cambridge, MA: Harvard University Press, 1980), pp. 180–81

LOUIS MENAND   *Going to the Territory* is filled with the stories of men and women who personify the kind of cultural mobility Ellison takes to be definitive of the American experience—a kind of mobility unknown to the world of *Native Son*. Among the book's heroes are Duke Ellington, whose music moves one, says Ellison, "to wonder at the mysterious, unanalyzed character of the Negro American—and at the white American's inescapable Negro-ness"; Romare Bearden, who is admired for discovering a method of painting that allowed him "to express the tragic predicament of his people without violating his passionate dedication to art as a fundamental and transcendent agency for confronting and revealing the world"; Inman Page, the first black to graduate from Brown and the principal of Ellison's segregated high school in Oklahoma City, who carried the culture of the Ivy League to the frontier; a music teacher—Hazel Harrison—at Tuskegee Institute in the 1930s who kept a signed Prokofiev manuscript on the lid of her piano; a black custodian with the extraordinary name of Jefferson Davis Randolph, at the Oklahoma State Law Library, whose advice white legislators sought out when they needed information on some point of law; and Richard Wright himself, who is celebrated in a short memorial sketch.

And there is a large cast of anonymous characters: the slaves who imitated and transformed the European dance steps they saw being performed through the plantation house window; the black workingmen who became sophisticated critics of grand opera by moonlighting as spear-carriers at the Metropolitan Opera House in New York; middle-class white kids who try to sound like a Baptist choir; even "the white youngster who, with a transistor radio, screaming a Stevie Wonder tune, glued to his ear, shouts racial epithets at black youngsters trying to swim at a public beach." But the chief figure in these essays, as it is in virtually everything Ellison has written since *Invisible Man*, is the young man who began his literary education at an all-black college in Alabama by looking up the books listed in the footnotes to *The Waste Land* and who eventually became the author of a best-selling novel— the figure of Ralph Ellison himself.

It is difficult to think of another writer—Wordsworth is the sort of person who comes to mind—who makes his own experience the touchstone for everything in as explicit and consistent a fashion as Ellison does. He regards the details of his own life—details that might seem to others exceptional or fortuitous—as emblems of general significance. He has transformed his biography, through many retellings, into a kind of parable of cultural possibility. The parable is offered in all humility, for it is Ellison's great virtue that he is unable to imagine that other people might be less capable of achievement than himself. Some virtues have a way of turning into handicaps, though, and it is also possible to feel that an inability to imagine lives more severely deprived of opportunity and determination can be Ellison's most serious shortcoming.

Louis Menand, "Literature and Liberation," *New Republic*, 4 August 1986, pp. 37–38

KERRY McSWEENEY   The big questions for the American novelist, as Ellison eloquently phrased them in 1957, were these:

> How does one in the novel (the novel which is a work of art and not a disguised piece of sociology) persuade the American reader to identify that which is basic in man beyond all differences of class, race, wealth, or formal education? ... How does one persuade readers with the least knowledge of literature to recognize the broader values implicit in their lives? How, in a word, do we affirm that which *is* stable in human life beyond all

despite all processes of social change? How give the reader that which we do have in abundance, all the countless untold and wonderful variations on the themes of identity and freedom and necessity, love and death, and with all the mystery of personality undergoing its endless metamorphosis?

There is nothing new about these criteria for assessing a novel, nor about Ellison's ambitions as a writer of prose fiction. Both are squarely in the great moralizing tradition of the realistic novel. Ellison's claims, for example, are essentially the same as those made by George Eliot in England in the middle of the nineteenth century when she spoke of "the greatest benefit we owe the artist [being] the extension of our sympathies. Appeals founded on generalizations and statistics [i.e., on sociology] require a sympathy ready made, a moral sentiment already in activity; but a picture of human life such as a great artist can give, surprises [readers] into that attention to what is apart from themselves, which may be called the raw material of moral sentiment. [Art] is a mode of amplifying experience." In realizing their intentions, both the author of *Invisible Man* and the author of *Middlemarch* use the same general strategy of blending their directly expressed thematic concerns and moral propositions with a densely textured, solidly specified, and vividly presented social world. Many are the variations played in *Invisible Man* on the themes of identity, freedom, and the mystery of personality; but they are no less central to the novel than is the manifold of wonderfully rendered aural and visual particulars: for example, the voices of Trueblood recalling his sweet nights in Mobile, Peter Wheatstraw singing about his woman, and Ras exhorting a mob; or the descriptions of the types who frequent the lobby of the Men's House, of the crowd at Tod Clifton's funeral, and of the clutter of household objects of the dispossessed couple, including the paragraph-long description of the spilled contents of a single drawer that the narrator picks up from the snow.

While the mixture of moral concern and felt life in *Invisible Man* is traditional, the formal means employed to shape and organize the material are modernist. In the artistic elaboration and presentation of its subjects, and in the degree of formal control employed, Ellison's novel has more in common with Joyce's *Ulysses* than with Eliot's *Middlemarch*. These elaborations include the patterns formed by recurring images, symbols, and motifs; the polyphonic organization of chapters, some of which have a realistic or narrative level; the changes from chapter to chapter (and even within a single chapter) in style and presentational mode—from straightforwardly representational to expressionistic and surrealistic; and the intermittent use of techniques of defamiliarization (like the eruption of Jack's glass eye) and other devices that complicate the reader's engagement with the text. ⟨. . .⟩ one may say that one of the most striking and original features of *Invisible Man* is the counterpoint between a compelling story that is in its own right startlingly and sometimes horrifyingly eventful (there are no battle royals, police shootings, or race riots in *Ulysses*) and the high degree of artistic elaboration, which repeatedly invites the reader to reflect rather than to react.

Kerry McSweeney, *Invisible Man: Race and Identity* (Boston: Twayne, 1988), pp. 11–13

EDITH SCHOR   In discussing his work in progress with John Hersey, Ellison mentioned several problems he has had in writing this novel. He was satisfied with the parts but not with the connections between the parts, a problem that had also prolonged the writing of *Invisible Man*. In this novel, working the connections out is more complicated because the story is told by more than one main voice. Initially Ellison tried first-person narration, then third-person narration. His decision to stay out of the narrative and let the people speak for themselves stems from his long-held appreciation of American vernacular speech as one of the enrichments of literature.

Another difficulty Ellison spoke of is the need to determine what can be implied and what must be rendered for American sensibilities formed from so many different sources and social divisions. A writer must provide the reader "with as much detail as is possible in terms of the visual *and* the aural *and* rhythmic—to allow him to involve himself." Writing out of an individual sense of American life leaves the writer with an uncertainty about the social values that can be taken for granted by particular artifacts, symbols, or allusions. The writer can only evoke "what is already there, implicitly in the reader's head: his sense of life."

Another complication in writing this novel is that its dramatic incidents move back and forth in time. Time present in the novel is the mid-fifties, but the story goes back into earlier experiences too, even to some of the childhood experiences of Hickman who is an elderly man in time present. It's a matter of the past being active in the present—or of the characters becoming aware of the manner in which the past operates in their present lives. The sense of the past with its "systems of values, beliefs, customs, and hopes for the future that have evolved through the history of the Republic provides a further medium of communication" and allows for "that brooding, questioning stance that is necessary for fiction." Of course with one of the characters a senator, this gets into general history and even broader implications. 〈. . .〉

Since the novel remains a work in progress, further comment on it as an entity can only be conjecture. In contrast to the published fragments, which can be evaluated on their own, the novel they would comprise at present is the province of the creator, not the critic.

Edith Schor, *Visible Ellison: A Study of Ralph Ellison's Fiction* (Westport, CT: Greenwood Press, 1993), pp. 136–37

Bibliography

Invisible Man. 1952.
The Writer's Experience (with Karl Shapiro). 1964.
Shadow and Act. 1964.
The City in Crisis (with Whitney M. Young, Jr., and Herbert Gans). 1967.
Going to the Territory. 1986.

◈ ◈ ◈

Lorraine Hansberry
1930–1965

LORRAINE VIVIAN HANSBERRY was born on May 19, 1930, in Chicago, Illinois, the youngest of four children of a well-to-do family. Her father, Carl Augustus Hansberry, the founder of his own real estate business, was a prominent figure in the black community in Chicago, and in her youth Hansberry encountered such distinguished figures as Paul Robeson and Duke Ellington. In 1938 her father bought a house in a white neighborhood and fought his case all the way to the Supreme Court for the right to live there. Even after his death in 1946, prominent black artists and politicians continued to be frequent guests to the Hansberry house.

Hansberry graduated from Englewood High School in Chicago in 1947. She studied art, English, and stage design at the University of Wisconsin but left in 1950 without taking a degree. Nevertheless, her urge to write was stimulated at Wisconsin, especially when she saw a production of Sean O'Casey's *Juno and the Paycock*. Moving to New York later that year, she began to write full-time for *Freedom* magazine, which was founded by Paul Robeson. Her articles on Africa and on civil rights issues affecting blacks, women, and the poor, and her speeches to civil rights and other groups, made her a prominent young spokeswoman for progressive causes. In 1952 she attended the Intercontinental Peace Congress in Montevideo, Uruguay, in place of Paul Robeson, whose passport had been removed by the U.S. government. After marrying Robert Barron Nemiroff, a Jewish man, in 1953, she devoted herself to writing while working at a variety of odd jobs, including a brief teaching stint at the Jefferson School of Social Science. The couple's financial worries were relieved when a song cowritten by Nemiroff became a hit, allowing Hansberry to quit her jobs and write full-time.

Hansberry's first play, *A Raisin in the Sun*, was begun in 1956 and completed in 1958. It is a starkly realistic play about the life of several generations of a black family on the South Side of Chicago, perhaps inspired in part by Arthur Miller's *Death of a Salesman*, although the title is taken from

Langston Hughes's celebrated poem "Harlem" ("What happens to a dream deferred . . . Does it dry up like a raisin in the sun . . . Or does it explode?"). It received tryouts in New Haven, Philadelphia, and Chicago before opening on Broadway in March 1959, starring Sidney Poitier, Ruby Dee, Lou Gossett, and others. The play received 530 performances in a nineteen-month run, and Hansberry became the first black American writer to win the New York Drama Critics Circle Award. In the screenplay she wrote for the film version, Hansberry added several scenes, but these were not filmed; nevertheless, the film was both a critical and popular success when it opened in 1961. Nemiroff's 1973 adaptation of *A Raisin in the Sun* as a musical won a Tony award. A made-for-television version of the play, which restored the omissions from the film version, aired in 1989. Hansberry's screenplay was published in 1992.

In 1960 Hansberry was commissioned by NBC to write a television play on slavery; the result was *The Drinking Gourd*, but NBC executives felt the play was too controversial and it was not produced. Her next play, *The Sign in Sidney Brustein's Window*, opened in October 1964, and in spite of mixed reviews was kept running by friends and admirers until the playwright's death of cancer at the age of thirty-four on January 12, 1965.

In spite of their divorce in 1964, Hansberry named Nemiroff her literary executor. His collection of excerpts from her plays, journals, speeches, and letters, *To Be Young, Gifted and Black: Lorraine Hansberry in Her Own Words*, was presented off-Broadway in 1969. He produced *Les Blancs*, a play set in Africa, in 1970. His edition of *Les Blancs: The Collected Last Plays of Lorraine Hansberry*, which includes *The Drinking Gourd* and *What Use Are Flowers?* as well as the title play, was published in 1972.

▩ *Critical Extracts*

HAROLD CLURMAN   *A Raisin in the Sun* is authentic: it is a portrait of the aspirations, anxieties, ambitions and contradictory pressures affecting humble Negro folk in an American big city—in this instance Chicago. It is not intended as an appeal to whites or as a preachment for Negroes. It is an honestly felt response to a situation that has been lived through, clearly understood and therefore simply and impressively stated.

Most important of all: having been written from a definite point of view (that of a participant) with no eye toward meretricious possibilities in showmanship and public relations, the play throws light on aspects of American life quite outside the area of race.

The importance of the production transcends its script. The play is organic theatre: cast, text, direction are homogeneous in social orientation and in quality of talent. Without the aid of an aesthetic program or bias of any kind but through cultural and emotional consanguinity—a kind of spontaneous combustion which occurs when individuals who share a common need find each other under the proper circumstances—a genuine ensemble has been achieved.

Harold Clurman, "Theatre," *Nation*, 4 April 1959, pp. 301–2

GERALD WEALES   Despite an incredible number of imperfections, *Raisin* is a good play. Its basic strength lies in the character and the problem of Walter Lee, which transcends his being a Negro. If the play were only the Negro-white conflict that crops up when the family's proposed move is about to take place, it would be an editorial, momentarily effective, and nothing more. Walter Lee's difficulty, however, is that he has accepted the American myth of success at its face value, that he is trapped, as Willy Loman was trapped, by a false dream. In planting so indigenous an American image at the center of her play, Miss Hansberry has come as close as possible to what she intended—a play about Negroes which is not simply a Negro play.

The play has other virtues. There are genuinely funny and touching scenes throughout. Many of these catch believably the chatter of a family—the resentments and the shared jokes—and the words have the ring of truth that one found in Odets or Chayefsky before they began to sound like parodies of themselves. In print, I suspect, the defects of *Raisin* will show up more sharply, but on stage—where, after all, a play is supposed to be—the impressive performances of the three leads (Poitier, Ruby Dee, and Claudia McNeil) draw attention to the play's virtues.

Gerald Weales, "Thoughts on *A Raisin in the Sun:* A Critical Review," *Commentary* 27, No. 6 (June 1959): 529

ARNA BONTEMPS   Lorraine Hansberry, the exciting author of *Raisin in the Sun*, is in some very fundamental literary ways related to the sturdy author of *Native Son*, *Black Boy* and *Uncle Tom's Children*. Even the Hansberry-Wright link, however, which is by no means limited to the way in which they have drawn upon their common Chicago background for subject matter, is marked by notable differences. Miss Hansberry's star came up unheralded. Nothing from her typewriter had been published or produced prior to *Raisin in the Sun*. The critical and popular approval which followed this event made her famous, and the rejoicing this occasioned can only be compared to the kudos which followed Richard Wright's sunburst a little more than a decade earlier. But her recognition was based on a play. *Native Son* was a novel, *Black Boy* an autobiography, *Uncle Tom's Children* a collection of stories. And the two authors, though they had both spent crucial years of their lives in the Chicago jungle, if that's the word for the South Side of those days, were separated by more than just a span of time in their development.

Richard Wright's young manhood in Chicago was poverty ridden. Lorraine Hansberry's family was well-to-do by South Side standards. Her father was in the real estate business. He could, in a manner of speaking, have owned or managed the rental property in which Bigger Thomas killed the rat with the frying pan. How his perceptive daughter came to see the human turmoil in those substandard quarters through eyes of sympathy and deep understanding has not been told. Miss Hansberry's subsequent writing has consisted mainly of articles in periodicals. It has not tended toward autobiography.

A lesser writer, one imagines, particularly a lesser Negro writer in the United States, might have been in a hurry, given her talents and background, to give the world a picture of debutants' balls and gracious living to compensate for the ugliness Richard Wright had forced before the eyes of millions of readers, to the embarrassment of our favored few. She also avoided the equally unwise assumption that more of the same material that Wright had presented would prove to be equally arresting when presented by her, equally instructive. But it doesn't work that way without the addition of new elements, and the new Hansberry ingredient was *technique*.

In the theatre, a medium that demands a maximum of know-how, usually attained only after long and painful apprenticeship, years of heartbreaking trial and error, she showed up at first bow with complete control of her tools and her craft. This was little short of startling. Self-educated Richard

Wright had been a toiling, sometimes almost awkward manipulator of the devices of composition. He had won over this disadvantage by sheer power. In Lorraine Hansberry's case this particular shoe seemed to be on the other foot.

Arna Bontemps, "New Black Renaissance," *Negro Digest* 11, No. 1 (November 1961): 53–54

HAROLD CRUSE   *A Raisin in the Sun* demonstrated that the Negro playwright has lost the intellectual and, therefore, technical and creative, ability to deal with his own special ethnic group materials in dramatic form. The most glaring manifestation of this conceptual weakness is the constant slurring over, the blurring, and evasion of the internal facts of Negro ethnic life in terms of class and social caste divisions, institutional and psychological variations, political divisions, acculturation variables, clique variations, religious divisious, and so forth. Negro playwrights have never gone past their own subjectivity to explore the severe stress and strain of class conflict within the Negro group. Such class and clique rivalries and prejudices can be just as damaging, demoralizing and retarding as white prejudice. Negro playwrights have sedulously avoided dealing with the Negro middle class in all its varieties of social expression, basically because the Negro playwright has adopted the Negro middle-class morality. Therefore, art itself, especially the art of playwriting, has become a stepping stone to middle-class social status. As long as the morality of the Negro middle class must be upheld, defended, and emulated in social life *outside* the theater it can never be portrayed or criticized *inside* the theater à la Ibsen, or satirized à la Shaw. In this regard it becomes the better part of social and creative valor to do what Hansberry did—"Let us portay only the good, simple ordinary folk because this is what the audiences want, especially the white audiences; but let us give the whites the Negro middle-class ball to carry towards the goal of integration. Beyond that very functional use of the Negro in the theater, of what other value is this thing, the so-called Negro play? None at all, so let us banish it along with that other parochial idea 'The Negro Theater.' We don't like this 'Negro play' category in the American theater anyhow, and we don't like to be told that we must write it, but we'll *use* it (as a starter) and then we'll go on to better things; that is, we'll become what they call human and universal, which in the white folks' lexicon and cultural philosophy means 'universally white.' "

⟨. . .⟩ A Raisin in the Sun expressed through the medium of theatrical art that current, forced symbiosis in American interracial affairs wherein the Negro working class has been roped in and tied to the chariot of racial integration driven by the Negro middle class. In this drive for integration the Negro working class is being told in a thousand ways that it must give up its ethnicity and become human, universal, full-fledged American. Within the context of this forced alliance of class aims there is no room for Negro art (except when it pays off) or Negro art institutions (We middle-class Negroes ain't about to pay for that!), because all of this is self-segregation which hangs up "our" drive for integration. From all of this it can be seen how right E. Franklin Frazier was when he observed: "The new Negro middle class that has none of the spirit of service . . . attempts to dissociate itself as much as possible from identification with the Negro masses. . . . The lip service which they give to solidarity with the masses very often disguises their exploitation of the masses."

Harold Cruse, The Crisis of the Negro Intellectual (New York: William Morrow, 1967), pp. 281–83

JAMES BALDWIN   We really met ⟨. . .⟩ in Philadelphia, in 1959, when A Raisin in the Sun was at the beginning of its amazing career. Much has been written about this play; I personally feel that it will demand a far less guilty and constricted people than the present-day Americans to be able to assess it at all; as an historical achievement, anyway, no one can gainsay its importance. What is relevant here is that I had never in my life seen so many black people in the theatre. And the reason was that never in the history of the American theatre had so much of the truth of black people's lives been seen on the stage. Black people ignored the theatre because the theatre had always ignored them.

But, in Raisin, black people recognized that house and all the people in it— the mother, the son, the daughter and the daughter-in-law—and supplied the play with an interpretative element which could not be present in the minds of white people: a kind of claustrophobic terror, created not only by their knowledge of the house but by their knowledge of the streets. And when the curtain came down, Lorraine and I found ourselves in the backstage alley, where she was immediately mobbed. I produced a pen and Lorraine handed me her handbag and began signing autographs. "It only happens once," she said. I stood there and watched. I watched the people, who loved Lorraine for what she had brought to them; and watched Lorraine, who loved the people for what they brought to *her*. It was not, for her, a matter of being admired. She was being corroborated and confirmed. She was wise enough and honest enough to recognize that black American artists are in a very special case. One is not merely an artist and one is not judged merely as an artist: the black people crowding around Lorraine, whether or not they considered her an artist, assuredly considered her a witness. This country's concept of art and artists has the effect, scarcely worth mentioning by now, of isolating the artist from the people. One can see the effect of this in the irrelevance of so much of the work produced by celebrated white artists; but the effect of this isolation on a black artist is absolutely fatal. He *is*, already, as a black American citizen, isolated from most of his white countrymen. At the crucial hour, he can hardly look to his artistic peers for help, for they do not know enough about him to be able to correct him. To continue to grow, to remain in touch with himself, he needs the support of that community from which, however, all of the pressures of American life incessantly conspire to remove him. And when he is effectively removed, he falls silent—and the people have lost another hope.

Much of the strain under which Lorraine worked was produced by her knowledge of this reality, and her determined refusal to be destroyed by it.

James Baldwin, "Sweet Lorraine," *Esquire* 72, No. 5 (November 1969): 139

LLOYD W. BROWN   Ever since the sixties the reputation and significance of several established Black American writers have become issues in the running ethnopolitical debates on Black American literature. James Baldwin, Ralph Ellison, and LeRoi Jones, for example, have been at the center of confrontations between "militants" and "moderates," Black "extremists" and white "liberals," integrationists and Black nationalists, and so on. And it is increasingly evident that Lorraine Hansberry has joined this list of controversial writers, especially on the basis of her first play, *A Raisin in the Sun* (1959). On the anti-integrationist side, Harold Cruse ⟨in *The Crisis of the Negro Intellectual*, 1967⟩ deplores *Raisin* as "the artistic, aesthetic and class-inspired culmination of the efforts of the Harlem leftwing literary and cultural in-group to achieve integration of the Negro in the arts." In other words, it is a "most cleverly written piece of glorified soap opera," a "second-rate" play about working-class Blacks who "mouth middle class ideology." Moreover, the alleged shortcomings of Lorraine Hansberry's integrationist philosophy are linked, somehow, with her supposed inferiority as a dramatic artist: "*A Raisin in the Sun* demonstrated that the Negro playwright has lost the intellectual and, therefore, technical and creative, ability to deal with his own special ethnic group materials in dramatic form."

On the other side of the debate, both C. W. E. Bigsby ⟨in *Confrontation and Commitment: A Study of Contemporary American Drama 1959–1966*, 1967⟩ and Richard A. Duprey ⟨in "Today's Dramatists," *American Theatre*, 1967⟩ have praised Hansberry precisely because, in their view, she transcends those "special ethnic group materials." Thus, according to Duprey, *Raisin* is full of human insights that transcend any racial "concerns," and Bigsby praises her compassion and her understanding of the need to "transcend" history. In short, Hansberry's work has been caught up in the continuing conflict between the ethnic criteria of social protesters and the pro-integrationist's ethos of love and reconciliation. And when a critic such as Jordan Miller ⟨in "Lorraine Hansberry," *The Black American Writer*, Vol. 2, ed. C. W. E. Bigsby, 1971⟩ is confronted with this kind of debate he responds with the art-for-art's-sake thesis. He refuses to discuss Hansberry's work "on the basis of any form of racial consciousness" or "in any niche of social significance," and insists instead on the critic's "obligation" to judge the dramatist's work as "dramatic literature quite apart from other factors."

These three representative viewpoints need to be emphasized here because, taken together, they demonstrate a continuing problem in the study of Black literature: the tendency, for one reason or another, to isolate questions of structure or technique from those of social, or racial, significance.

Lloyd W. Brown, "Lorraine Hansberry as Ironist," *Journal of Black Studies* 4, No. 3 (March 1974): 237–38

ELLEN SCHIFF   A notably sensitive concept of the Jewish experience as archetypal furnishes the subtext of Lorraine Hansberry's *The Sign in Sidney Brustein's Window* (1965), at the same time illuminating one of the most successful characterizations of the Jew on the post-1945 stage. Brustein is the literary heir to the lineage established by Galsworthy's Ferdinand de Levis (*Loyalties*, 1922). He is the Jew who has found his niche in society and occupies it with the same aplomb with which he wears his identity.

In making Brustein the axis of her play and the magnet that attracts its other outsiders, Hansberry draws on the historical experience of the Jew. Her protagonist personifies an alien factor that has earned a degree of acceptance in society. Having accomplished that, he tends to regard race, creed and previous conditions of servitude largely as bothersome clichés and to devote himself to other pressing concerns. Hence Sidney, not unkindly, dismisses his black friend Alton's preoccupation with making a cause of his blackness: "Be a Martian if you wanna." He admonishes the homosexual David:

> If somebody insults you—sock 'em in the jaw. If you don't like
> the sex laws, attack 'em. I think they're silly. You wanna get up a
> petition? I'll sign one. Love little fishes if you want. *But*, David,
> please get over the notion that your particular sexuality is
> something that only the deepest, saddest, the most nobly tortured
> can know about. It ain't . . . it's just one kind of sex—that's all.
> And in my opinion . . . the universe turns regardless.

There is no question of Sidney Brustein's *becoming* assimilated. Married to "the only Greco-Gaelic-Indian hillbilly in captivity," preferring his bohemian life in Greenwich Village to the conventional security of his brother Manny's uptown office, removed enough to laugh with genuine amusement at his mother's carping, "*Not* that I have anything against the goyim, Sidney, she's a nice girl, but . . . ," he justifiably feels entitled to his past participle: "I'm assimilated," he declares.

Although he attributes his need for periodic retreats to an imaginary mountain top to a Jewish psyche "less discriminating than most," Brustein manifests distinctly Jewish traits. He loves life with the love of an idealist who prides himself on being true to his moral principles. An incurable optimist, at thirty-seven he refuses to be daunted by bad luck. For instance, the failure of his cabaret and his consequent indebtedness do not discourage him from investing in a small weekly newspaper. Even though he has sworn to put an end to his long career in the service of "every committee To Save, To Abolish, Prohibit, Preserve, Reserve and Conserve that ever was," Sidney is easily persuaded to support ward politician Wally O'Hara's campaign to clean up city government. Sidney is an incorrigible insurgent. "I *care!''* he explains to his gay friend David who writes plays about meaning-lessness and alienation, "I care about it all. It takes too much energy *not* to care."

Ellen Schiff, *From Stereotype to Metaphor: The Jew in Contemporary Drama* (Albany: State University of New York Press, 1982), pp. 156–57

ANNE CHENEY   Paul Robeson's influence on Lorraine Hansberry is difficult to assess. They constantly crossed paths in her lifetime. She loved his voice and the songs he sang. He was her first employer, at *Freedom*. Indirectly she learned through him and *Freedom* of the dire condition in which most blacks lived, and of the dangers of being an artist. He was an inspiration and, to some extent, a warning.

Langston Hughes's influence is much more obvious. He did not allow himself—especially in the McCarthy era—to become primarily involved in the political struggle for racial equality. His poetry reflects the lives of black people, frequently with humor, but he understates his sense of personal frustration or anger, or of impending danger to those who do not understand his poetry. Rather, he explains himself and others of his race. He did not hate those who chose to misunderstand; rather, he found them absurd. Of course, in "A Dream Deferred" Hughes does warn those who would thwart the lives of others, but it is a detached warning, an offering from a wise observer who is above all an artist.

Hansberry did not get her social consciousness primarily from Hughes. What she got from him instead was a consciousness of the poetic possibilities of her own race, an appreciation of the black American culture, and—because of Hughes himself—an awareness that, in spite of all obstacles, black people remain a dynamic, powerfully creative force in American society whose achievements must be celebrated in art.

From W. E. B. Du Bois she gained an admiration for the black intellectual, socialism, and black leadership. He spent most of his long life trying, with mixed success, to get a hearing for racial equality in America. Ironically, when the black population raised its collective voice and white people began to show signs of listening at last, he moved to Ghana, where he began to edit a multivolumed *Encyclopedia Africana*.

From Frederick Douglass, Hansberry learned about slavery and its psychology. This knowledge she would put to use in *The Drinking Gourd*, a play too outspoken to be broadcast on commercial television. From Douglass, too, she learned the invaluable lesson that the sufferings of a people may be presented truthfully in ways that rise above propaganda to the level of art. This lesson, perhaps, was the key to the synthesis of action and language toward which, in her own very different kind of writing, she was working.

These four men, among many people, particularly influenced Hansberry. But they could not, finally, answer the question she asked herself. Du Bois— even though he founded *Phylon* and edited *Crisis* to promote black art— and Douglass were not as deeply devoted to art for its own sake as were Robeson and Hughes. Rather, Du Bois and Douglass used their considerable rhetorical skills to illuminate and investigate the black conditions. They left behind books now considered works of art, but the creation of art was not their primary intention. Robeson sacrificed his musical career to pursue justice for members of his race and to become a revolutionary. Hughes pursued his art and—when forced to choose—left the struggle to others.

One month after she questioned her commitment to revolutionary activity, Hansberry wrote in her journal: "Have the feeling I should throw myself back into the movement. . . . But that very impulse is immediately flushed with a thousand vacillations and forbidding images. . . . *comfort* has come to be its own corruption. . . . *Comfort*. Apparently I have sold my soul for it. I think when I get my health back I shall go into the South to find out what kind of revolutionary I am. . . ." Hansberry died six months after writing of her intention to go South, where militants were being murdered, and as a result never answered her question. She died with her dilemma unresolved.

Anne Cheney, *Lorraine Hansberry* (Boston: Twayne, 1984), pp. 53–54

AMIRI BARAKA   *Raisin* first appeared in 1959, in the earlier stages of the civil rights movement. As a document reflecting the essence of those struggles, *Raisin* is unexcelled. For many of us it was—and remains—the quintessential civil rights play. It is probably also the most widely appreciated black play (particularly by Afro-Americans).

But Hansberry has done more than *document*, which is the most limited form of realism. She is a "critical realist," the way that Langston Hughes, Richard Wright and Margaret Walker are. That is, she analyzes and assesses reality and shapes her statement as an esthetically powerful and politically advanced work of art.

George Thompson in *Poetry and Marxism* points out that drama is the most expressive artistic form to emerge from great social transformation. Shakespeare is the artist of the destruction of feudalism—and the emergence of capitalism. The mad Macbeths, bestial Richard IIIs and other feudal worthies are shown, like the whole class, as degenerating. This is why Shakespeare deals with race (*Othello*), anti-Semitism (*The Merchant of Venice*) and feminism (*The Taming of the Shrew*).

Hansberry's play, too, was political agitation. It dealt with the same issues of democratic rights and equality that were being aired in the streets, but it dealt with them realistically, not as political abstraction. ⟨. . .⟩

We thought Hansberry's play belonged to the "passive resistance" part of the movement, which ended the minute Malcolm's penetrating eyes and words began to charge through the media with deadly force. We thought her play "middle class" in that its focus seemed to be on "moving in white folks' neighborhoods," when most blacks were just trying to pay their rent in ghetto shacks.

We missed the essence of the work: that Hansberry had created a family engaged in the same class and ideological struggles as existed in the movement—and within individuals. What is most telling about our ignorance is that Hansberry's play remains overwhelmingly popular and evocative of black and white reality; and the masses of black people saw it was true.

The next two explosions in black drama, Baldwin's *Blues for Mr. Charlie* and my own *Dutchman* (both 1964), raise up the militance and self-defense clamor of the movement as it evolved into the Malcolm era. But neither play is as much a statement from the majority of blacks as is *Raisin*. For one thing, both (regardless of their "power") are too concerned with white people.

Lorraine Hansberry's play, though it seems "conservative" in form and content to the radical petite bourgeoisie, is the accurate telling and stunning vision of the real struggle. The concerns I once dismissed as "middle class"—of buying a house and moving into "white folks' neighborhood"—actually reflect the essence of black will to defeat segregation, discrimination and oppression. The Younger family is our common ghetto Fanny Lou Hammers, Malcolm X's and Angela Davises, etc. And their burden surely will be lifted or one day it certainly will explode.

Amiri Baraka, *"Raisin in the Sun's* Enduring Passion," *Washington Post,* 16 November 1986, pp. F1, 3

STEVEN R. CARTER   Hansberry's extensive use of parallels to *Hamlet* in *Les Blancs* is highly creative and she gained many advantages by it. First, it permitted her to make an indirect but glowing tribute to one of the finest products of English and European culture, thus indicating her keen awareness that Europe has created far more than colonialism and that much of what Europe has done remains immensely valuable to the whole world, including Africa. This appreciation is even stated explicitly in the play by Tshembe: "Europe—in spite of all her crimes—has been a great and glorious star in the night. Other stars shone before it—and will again with it." Tshembe also attests to the continuing relevance of *Hamlet* and other great European works when, upon being summoned to a meeting of resistance fighters, he explains that "it's an old problem, really . . . Orestes . . . Hamlet . . . the rest of them . . . We've really got so many things we'd rather be doing."

Second, having praised the highest ideals and achievements of European civilization, Hansberry could—so easily—point to the multitude of ways in which the European colonial powers and their offshoot, the United States, were currently failing to adhere to them. When Charlie Morris, an American journalist who has been seeking a dialogue with Tshembe, exposes his failure to understand the African's reference to the fierce woman spirit summoning him to fight for his people, Tshembe reminds this representative of Western culture that "when you knew her you called her Joan of Arc! Queen Esther! La Passionara! And you did know her once, you did know her! But now you call her nothing, because she is dead for you! She does not exist for you!" As Tshembe rightly implies, one of the great tragic ironies of history is that so many of the countries that had fought hard, bloody battles to establish the principles of liberty, equality and fraternity within their own boundaries then fought hard, bloody battles to suppress these principles in other countries solely to satisfy their greed and lust for power. An African nationalist upholding these values may thus be judged a truer heir to the mantle of Hamlet than European colonizers of their American counterparts. However, as Hansberry knew full well, this mantle does not belong only to the more idealistic African revolutionaries but may be donned by anyone who finds the strength and commitment to wear it. At the end, Charlie Morris himself, after many mistakes and vacillations, seems prepared to defy established authority at home and abroad for what he now knows to be the truth about the fight against colonialism in Zatembe. On the other hand, as the speaker of the truth about Tshembe and the resistance movement, perhaps Charlie qualifies more as Horatio, but Horatio too deserves respect.

Third, by paralleling the European drama of Hamlet with the African fable of the thinking hyena, Hansberry affirms that wisdom and folly are not the exclusive properties of any culture and that African culture is one of the "stars that shone before" European culture "and will again with it." Margaret B. Wilkerson, in her introduction to the New American Library edition of *Lorraine Hansberry: The Collected Last Plays*, has argued that while "the parallels to Hamlet are obvious . . . Hansberry, instinctively recognizing the inappropriateness of relying only on a Western literary reference point, provides Tshembe with another metaphor—from African lore—Modingo, the wise hyena who lived between the lands of the elephants and the hyenas." While Wilkerson's point is in general well taken, it seems more likely that what Hansberry did was deliberate rather than instinctive. In an interview with Patricia Marks for Radio Station WNYC in New York, Hansberry suggested that "perhaps we must take a more respectful view of the fact that African leaders today say that with regard to Europe and European traditions in the world we will take the best of what Europe has produced and the best of what we have produced and try to create a superior civilization out of the synthesis. I agree with them and I think that it commands respect for what will be inherently African in that contribution." Hansberry's *Les Blancs* provides an excellent example of how such a synthesis might be formed.

Steven R. Carter, "Colonialism and Culture in Lorraine Hansberry's *Les Blancs*," *MELUS* 15, No. 1 (Spring 1988): 30–31

J. CHARLES WASHINGTON   Viewers of *A Raisin in the Sun* can be moved by a tragic hero who is elevated by his growth from ignorance to knowledge, and deeply affected by a realistic hero whose transcendence involves a tremendous sacrifice—at the play's end, Walter and his family are as poor and powerless as they were before. The new house provides a "pinch of dignity" that allows them a bit more breathing and living space, but their lives are essentially unchanged. Without the greater financial rewards the business could have produced, they must all continue working at the same menial jobs in order to survive and pay for the house. In fact, they may be even worse off, since the birth of Ruth's second child will mean an extra mouth to feed. Walter and Ruth have made no substantive economic progress; their current life is a modern version of the life of Lena and Big Walter. The principal hope that Ruth and Walter have is the one Lena and Big Walter had and which people everywhere have always had—that some day in the future their children will be able to make their parents' dreams come true.

Considering that this sobering reality should provide a cause for despair would involve a serious misunderstanding of the author's intention and a grievous contradiction of her faith in the perfectibility of humanity based on her conviction that humankind will "do what the apes never will—*impose* the reason for life on life." Moreover, this small but significant hope, as well as the characters who embody it, offers perhaps the best example of the universal materials the play abounds in, giving Hansberry's art its distinguishing mark and enduring value. Illustrating her ability to see synthesis where others could only see dichotomy, Hansberry discovered the basis of this universal hope, indeed of her faith in humanity, in the Black experience: ". . . if blackness brought pain, it was also a source of strength, renewal and inspiration, a window on the potentials of the human race. For if Negroes could survive America, then there was hope for the human race indeed."

J. Charles Washington, "A *Raisin in the Sun* Revisited," *Black American Literature Forum* 22, No. 1 (Spring 1988): 123–24

MARGARET B. WILKERSON   Lorraine Hansberry, despite her bourgeois upbringing, had seen the fruit of racism and segregation in the struggles of her neighbors who came from all classes, since all blacks were confined to the Black Metropolis, Bronzeville, of Chicago. She had seen the personal toll on her father, and herself had been the near-victim of a mob protesting her family's move into a white neighborhood. Exactly when and how her sexual radicalization developed is less clear at this point, but what is obvious is that the usual generalizations about the black middle class simply were not borne out by a study of her early life. She was attracted to the theatre as a laboratory for manipulating and interpreting human experience, especially as it related to race, class, and gender; theatre as a persuasive and visible art form that allowed her to comment on the contradictions within the human personality; and the drama as the most attractive medium for, as she said, talking to people and sharing her vision of human potential. She found confirmation in the progressive left of Harlem—which she immediately joined upon moving to New York City—because it gave theatre and other cultural activities high priority, including them as a necessary extension and expression of ideas. Part of Hansberry's achievement in A Raisin in the Sun was to embody progressive ideas in the life and struggle of a black family (without resorting to the jargon of the left), and to build that family into a metaphor that whites and blacks, liberals, radicals, and even some conservatives could affirm, while winning one of the most prized awards of the theatre establishment. She managed it so well that the two FBI agents who saw the Broadway production and reported on its political import to the Bureau saw no revolutionary danger in the play. They, of course, did not realize that Walter Lee's sons and Mama's daughters would stride the boards in the next two decades, changing for good the image of blacks in the theatre and creating the artistic arm of the black nationalist movement. The line of Hansberry's influence stretches into and beyond the 1960s, but it begins in the 1930s and 1940s as she grew up in the peculiar crucible of segregation known as Chicago.

> Margaret B. Wilkerson, "Excavating Our History: The Importance of Biographies of Women of Color," Black American Literature Forum 24, No. 1 (Spring 1990): 80–81

STEVEN R. CARTER   Hansberry's goal in all her work was realism—the truthful depiction, as she said, of "not only what is but what is possible . . . because that is part of reality too." A realism rooted, she hoped, in characters so truthfully and powerfully rendered that an audience could not but identify with them. But she did not think of realism as a specific form or genre, and strongly disagreed with those critics who saw it as limiting. As she told Studs Terkel, "I think that imagination has no bounds in realism—you can do anything which is permissible in terms of the truth of the characters. That's all you have to care about." She had a flair for significant, eye-and-mind-catching spectacle, as in Walter's imaginary spear-wielding table-top oratory and Iris Brustein's dance. Les Blancs in particular is filled with such spectacle, from the initial appearance of the woman warrior spirit with "cheeks painted for war," to Tshembe's elaborate ritual donning of ceremonial robes, to the gesture-filled oral storytelling of Peter/ Ntali, to the explosion and gunshot-packed climax. Her use of spectacle,

moreover, was almost always symbolic, as in Tshembe's construction of a
wall of cloth between Charlie Morris and himself representing the spiritual
wall between them at the moment. Her "realistic" drama in such instances
differed little from expressionism or poetic fantasy; she always chose the
best means to express the whole truth about her characters, no matter
whether critics would have deemed it appropriate to her form or not.

As a politically and socially committed writer, Hansberry strove to present
a host of unpleasant and challenging truths in her work, although often
with such wit and dramatic force that they no longer seemed unpalatable
but inevitable. She was unquestionably a Marxist but in the largest sense
of this frequently narrowed and abused term, as unhindered by doctrine and
as open to new ideas as was Marx himself, and as complicated, wide-ranging,
open-minded, and even at times ambivalent in her approach to esthetics
as Henri Arvon has shown Marx to be. Keeping faith with her myriad
commitments never precluded the portrayal of the full complexity of life
as Hansberry saw it. Few writers in any genre have delineated so completely
and strikingly the social dilemmas of our time, and none have surpassed—
or are likely to surpass—her ability to point out the heights toward which
we should soar.

Steven R. Carter, Hansberry's Drama: Commitment amid Complexity (Urbana: University of Illinois Press, 1991), pp. 190–91

Bibliography

A Raisin in the Sun. 1959.
The Movement: Documentary of a Struggle for Equality. 1964.
The Sign in Sidney Brustein's Window. 1965.
To Be Young, Gifted and Black: Lorraine Hansberry in Her Own Words. Adapted
        by Robert Nemiroff. 1969.
Les Blancs. Adapted by Robert Nemiroff. 1972.
Les Blancs: The Collected Last Plays of Lorraine Hansberry. Ed. Robert Nemiroff.
        1972.
A Raisin in the Sun: The Unfilmed Original Screenplay. Ed. Robert Nemiroff.
        1992.

⬥ ⬥ ⬥

Toni Morrison
b. 1931

TONI MORRISON was born Chloe Anthony Wofford in Lorain, Ohio, on February 18, 1931, the second of four children of George Wofford, a shipyard welder, and his wife Ramah Willis Wofford. After attending Lorain High School, she went to Howard University, where she earned a B.A. in 1953, with a major in English and a minor in classics. She joined the Howard University Players and in the summer toured the South with a student-faculty repertory troupe.

After securing an M.A. at Cornell in 1955, Morrison taught for two years at Texas Southern University, then in 1957 returned to Howard, where she became an instructor of English and married Harold Morrison, a Jamaican architect. In 1964 she divorced Morrison and returned with her two sons to Lorain; a year and a half later she became an editor for a textbook subsidiary of Random House in Syracuse. By 1970 she had moved to an editorial position at Random House in New York, where she eventually became senior editor. In this capacity she anonymously edited *The Black Book* (1974), a collection of documents relating to the history of black Americans. Morrison has taught black American literature and creative writing at two branches of the State University of New York (Purchase and Albany), as well as at Yale University, Bard College, and Trinity College, Cambridge. She is currently Robert F. Goheen Professor in the Council of the Humanities at Princeton University.

Toni Morrison began to write when she returned to Howard in 1957, and since then she has published several novels in which the problems of black women in the Midwest are a major theme. Her first novel, *The Bluest Eye* (1970), draws upon her childhood in Lorain by depicting the lives of several young women, one of whom, Pecola, comes to believe that blue eyes are a symbol of whiteness and, therefore, of superiority. *Sula* (1973), set in the mythical town of Medallion, Ohio, has an even tougher edge, addressing issues of both racial and gender equality in its portrayal of the contrasting lives of two young women, one of whom settles down to middle-class conformity and the other of whom, Sula, attempts to achieve freedom by flaunting these conventions.

Morrison's third novel, *Song of Solomon* (1977), is a rich evocation of history in its chronicle of a black family over nearly a century; it was both a popular and critical success, winning the National Book Critics Circle Award and the American Academy and Institute of Arts and Letters Award. *Tar Baby* (1981), set on an imaginary Caribbean island, was less well received. But with her fifth novel, *Beloved* (1987), Morrison came to be recognized as perhaps the leading black American writer of her generation. This dense historical novel about a fugitive slave, Sethe, and her descendents not only achieved best-seller status but won the Pulitzer Prize for fiction. *Jazz* (1992) is a less ambitious work but is nonetheless a poignant depiction of the lives of black Americans in a mythical "City" in the 1920s.

Morrison has also written a small body of nonfiction. In the 1970s she wrote several pieces on black American women for the *New York Times Magazine*. Simultaneously with the release of *Jazz* appeared a challenging monograph, *Playing in the Dark: Whiteness and the Literary Imagination* (1992), probing the role of black Americans as symbols of the "other" in white American literature. In 1993 Morrison was awarded the Nobel Prize for literature. She is currently at work on a revision of *The Bluest Eye* and a new novel, tentatively entitled *Paradise*.

◈ *Critical Extracts*

L. E. SISSMAN   *The Bluest Eye* is not flawless. Miss Morrison's touching and disturbing picture of the doomed youth of her race is marred by an occasional error of fact or judgment. She places the story in a frame of the bland white words of a conventional school "reader"—surely an unnecessary and unsubtle irony. She writes an occasional false or bombastic line: "They were through with lust and lactation, beyond tears and terror." She permits herself some inconsistencies: the real name of Soaphead Church is given as both Elihue Micah Whitcomb and Micah Elihue Whitcomb. None of this matters, though, beside her real and greatly promising achievement: to write truly (and sometimes very beautifully) of every generation

of blacks—the young, their parents, their rural grandparents—in this country
thirty years ago, and, I'm afraid, today.
L. E. Sissman, "Beginner's Luck," *New Yorker*, 23 January 1971, p. 94

JERRY H. BRYANT   Sula, Ms. Morrison's protagonist, has qualities
I have seen in a fictional black female only recently. When she is 11 years
old, she cuts off the tip of her finger to demonstrate to a gang of threatening
boys what she can do to them if she can do that to herself. She swings a
child around by the wrists and half intentionally lets him slip out of her
grasp into the river, where he drowns. In the shadows of her porch, she
watches in an "interested" way while her mother burns to death.
     Most of us have been conditioned to expect something else in black
characters—guiltless victims of brutal white men, yearning for a respectable
life of middle-class security; whores driven to their profession by impossible
conditions; housekeepers exhausted by their work for lazy white women.
We do not expect to see a fierceness bordering on the demonic. ⟨. . .⟩
     ⟨. . .⟩ Morrison at first seems to combine the aims of the Black Freedom
Movement and women's liberation. Sula and Nel discover when they are
11 years old "that they were neither white nor male, and that all freedom
and triumph was forbidden to them." When they grow up, Nel slips on the
collar of convention. She marries, has two children, becomes tied to her
"nest," a slave to racism and sexism. Sula goes to the big city, gets herself
an education, and returns a "liberated" woman with a strange mixture of
cynicism and innocence: "She lived out her days exploring her own thoughts
and emotions, giving them full rein, feeling no obligation to please anybody
unless their pleasure pleased her . . . hers was an experimental life." ⟨. . .⟩
     Morrison does not accept—nor does she expect us to accept—the unquali-
fied tenets of either of the two current freedom movements. There is more
to both society and the individual, and she subjects each of these to a
merciless analysis. The result is that neither lends itself to a clear moral
judgment. For all her selfishness and cruelty, Sula's presence elicits the best
in people, diluting their usual meanness and small-spiritedness. Indeed, with
Sula's death the "Bottom" dies, its black people rushing headlessly in a
comi-tragedy of communal suicide.
     Jerry H. Bryant, "Something Ominous Here," *Nation*, 6 July 1974, pp. 23–24

JOAN BISCHOFF   Henry James delineated one of the earliest and most memorable precocious female protagonists in depicting the title character in *What Maisie Knew*. The extent of little Maisie's understanding of the adult world has remained tantalizingly elusive for several generations of readers, while her innocent suffering has shone with terrible poignance. Now, it seems, a new American novelist is offering some contemporary twists of the Jamesian type. With the publication of *The Bluest Eye* in 1970 and *Sula* in 1974, Toni Morrison has laid claim to modern portrayal of the preternaturally sensitive but rudely thwarted black girl in today's society. *Sula* is more fully dominated by the title character, and Sula's characterization is the more complex; in both novels, however, the protagonist is forced into premature adulthood by the *donnée* of her life. Pecola's comprehension of her world is never articulated for either the other characters or the reader; Sula, too, remains a partial enigma both in and out of her narrative. But the pain that each experiences is made vivid and plain. Taken together, the two novels can—and I think must—be read as offering different answers to a single question: What is to become of a finely attuned child who is offered no healthy outlet for her aspirations and yearnings? Pecola escapes in madness; Sula rejects society for amoral self-reliance. For both, sensitivity is a curse rather than a blessing. Morrison's second novel, though richer in many ways, is essentially a reworking of the material of the first with an alternative ending. Though her characters' problems are conditioned by the black milieu of which she writes, her concerns are broader, universal ones. Her fiction is a study of thwarted sensitivity. ⟨. . .⟩

Both Morrison's novels find beauty in sensitive response and show its inevitable doom in a world in which only the hard, the cagey, and the self-interested can triumph. Although both Pecola and Sula fill essential roles in their communities, it is not the admirable in their characters that has an influence. Pecola serves as the bottom-most societal rung whose lowliness raises the self-esteem of everyone else, while Sula's acknowledged "evil" encourages others' righteous sense of comparative superiority. Sensitivity is lovely, but impractical, says Morrison. It is a pragmatic outlook, if not a particularly happy one.

Joan Bischoff, "The Novels of Toni Morrison: Studies in Thwarted Sensitivity," *Studies in Black Literature* 6, No. 3 (Fall 1975): 21, 23

REYNOLDS PRICE   Toni Morrison's first two books—*The Bluest Eye* with the purity of its terrors and *Sula* with its dense poetry and the depth of its probing into a small circle of lives—were strong novels. Yet, firm as they both were in achievement and promise, they didn't fully forecast her new book, *Song of Solomon*. Here the depths of the younger work are still evident, but now they thrust outward, into wider fields, for longer intervals, encompassing many more lives. The result is a long prose tale that surveys nearly a century of American history as it impinges upon a single family. In short, this is a full novel—rich, slow enough to impress itself upon us like a love affair or a sickness—not the two-hour penny dreadful which is again in vogue nor one of the airless cat's cradles custom-woven for the delight and job-assistance of graduate students of all ages.

Song of Solomon isn't, however, cast in the basically realistic mode of most family novels. In fact, its negotiations with fantasy, fable, song and allegory are so organic, continuous and unpredictable as to make any summary of its plot sound absurd; but absurdity is neither Morrison's strategy nor purpose. The purpose seems to be communication of painfully discovered and powerfully held convictions about the possibility of transcendence within human life, on the time-scale of a single life.

Reynolds Price, "Black Family Chronicle," *New York Times Book Review*, 11 September 1977, p. 1

SUSAN L. BLAKE   The "Song of Solomon" that provides the title of Toni Morrison's third novel is a variant of a well-known Gullah folktale about a group of African-born slaves who rose up one day from the field where they were working and flew back to Africa. In the novel, this tale becomes both the end of, and a metaphor for, the protagonist's identity quest: Macon Dead III, known as Milkman, finds himself when he learns the story of his great-granddaddy Solomon who could fly. From this story he himself learns to fly, metaphorically: "For now he knew what Shalimar [Solomon] knew: if you surrendered to the air, you could *ride* it."

In basing Milkman's identity quest on a folktale, Morrison calls attention to one of the central themes in all her fiction, the relationship between individual identity and community, for folklore is by definition the expression of community—of the common experiences, beliefs, and values that identify a folk as a group. The use of the folktale of the flying Africans in this quest seems to establish equivalence between Milkman's discovery of community and his achievement of identity, but paradoxes in the use of the folktale suggest a more complex relationship and help to define just what Morrison means by the concept of community, a concept which she vigorously endorses.

The flight of the transplanted Africans dramatizes the communal identity of Afro-Americans in several ways. It establishes "home" as the place of common origin and dissociates the Africans from the American plantation where their identity is violated. It dissociates them as well from American-born slaves, for only the African-born have the power to fly. At the same time, as the ability to fly distinguishes the Africans from their descendants, it represents an identity that the African-descended tellers of the tale believe they would have if they had not had another identity forced upon them by slavery. The tale thus represents a common dream, a common disappointment, and a group identity. As the object of Milkman's quest, it suggests a multi-leveled equivalence between individual identity and community. Simply as folktale, it is an artifact of Afro-American history; its content links Afro-American to pan-African history; it is localized to represent Milkman's family history. His discovery of the tale thus represents Milkman's discovery of his membership in ever more inclusive communities; his family, Afro-Americans, all blacks. ⟨. . .⟩

The multiple ways of seeing Milkman's discovery as a discovery of community suggest that *Song of Solomon* is an elaborate, and entertaining, expansion of the equation between identity and community. In fact, however, the end of Milkman's quest is not the discovery of community, but a solitary leap into the void. And its mythical foundation is not the typical tale of the Africans flying as a group to their common home, but a highly individualistic variant. Milkman's discovery does not result in any of the conventional indications of community. Although Milkman is reconciled with Pilate and the two of them return to Shalimar to bury the bones of her father, Pilate dies (as she has lived, protecting Milkman's life) as soon as the burial is accomplished.

> Susan L. Blake, "Folklore and Community in *Song of Solomon*," MELUS 7, No. 3 (Fall 1980): 77–79

DARRYL PINCKNEY   The setting ⟨of *Tar Baby*⟩ is exotic—an imagined tropical island called Isle des Chevaliers, privately owned, found off Dominique. But, like the small towns in ⟨Morrison's⟩ previous books, it also has its allegorical lore. ⟨. . .⟩

The story is not entirely confined to this mysterious island. The characters in *Tar Baby* recall the mansions of Philadelphia, trailers in Maine, the cream-colored streets of Paris of their past lives. There are heated moments in Manhattan. A hamlet in northern Florida, an all black town called Eloe, turns out to be very much like Eatonville, Zora Neale Hurston's celebrated birthplace in the same region. Travel, in Morrison's earlier novels, tended to mean crossing the country. Here, there are frequent and anxious escapes to the reservations counter at Air France.

Something else has changed. The laboring poor of *The Bluest Eye*, the self-sufficient women and drifting men of *Sula*, the avaricious middle class and defiantly marginal citizens of *Song of Solomon*—they are gone, replaced, in *Tar Baby*, by the rich, their servants, their dependents, and the sans culottes who threaten their security. Though much is made of money, fashion, commodities as consciousness, and the experiences open to the privileged, the cultured, and those clever enough to hustle a piece of the action, the people living on Isle des Chevaliers, voluntary exiles all, seem to inhabit a world that is oppressively parochial and provincial. ⟨. . .⟩

Many of Morrison's previous concerns are here—having to do with the inner life of black women and especially the offhand, domestic violence and conjugal brutality that burn out daily life. Much of the recent fiction by Afro-American women contains these themes. Their message is new and arresting, as if, in the past, the worries of the kitchen or the bedroom were not sufficiently large to encompass the intense lives of black people in a racist society. But *Tar Baby*'s sense of such experience is inchoate, muffled. One wishes for the fierce concentration, the radical economy of the novels of Gayl Jones as they describe the inner world of black women in language that is harsh, disturbing, and utterly unsentimental.

Darryl Pinckney, "Every Which Way," *New York Review of Books*, 30 April 1981, pp. 24–25

GLORIA NAYLOR and TONI MORRISON   TM: ⟨. . .⟩ I

remember after *The Bluest Eye* having an extremely sad six or eight months. And I didn't know what it was because that was the first time I had ever written a novel. And I wasn't thinking about being a novelist then. I just wrote *that* and I thought that would be *that* and that would be the end of *that* 'cause I liked to read it and that was enough. But then I moved from one town to another, for one thing, and I was feeling, for this very sustained period, what can only be described now as missing something, missing the company I had been keeping all those years when I wrote *The Bluest Eye*, and I couldn't just write because I was able to write. I had to write with the same feeling that I had when I did *The Bluest Eye*, which was that there was this exciting collection of people that only I knew about. I had the direct line and I was the receiver of all this information. And then when I began to think about *Sula*, everything changed, I mean, all the colors of the world changed, the sounds and so on. I recognized what that period was when I finished *Sula*, and I had another idea which was *Song of Solomon*. When I finished *Song of Solomon*, I didn't have another idea for *Tar Baby* but then I knew that it arrives or it doesn't arrive and I'm not terrified of a block, of what people call a block. I think when you hit a place where you can't write, you probably should be still for a while because it's not there yet.

GN: Even a block with an idea itself? That doesn't frighten you?

TM: It doesn't bother me. And that brings me to the book that I'm writing now called *Beloved*. I had an idea that I didn't know was a book idea, but I do remember being obsessed by two or three little fragments of stories that I heard from different places. One was a newspaper clipping about a woman named Margaret Garner in 1851. It said that the Abolitionists made a great deal out of her case because she had escaped from Kentucky, I think, with her four children. She lived in a little neighborhood just outside of Cincinnati and she had killed her children. She succeeded in killing one; she tried to kill two others. She hit them in the head with a shovel and they were wounded but they didn't die. And there was a smaller one that she had at her breast. The interesting thing, in addition to that, was the interviews that she gave. She was a young woman. In the inked pictures of her she seemed a very quiet, very serene-looking woman and everyone who interviewed her remarked about her serenity and tranquility. She said, "I will not let those children live how I have lived." She had run off into a little woodshed right outside her house to kill them because she had been caught as a fugitive. And she had made up her mind that they would not suffer the way that she had and it was better for them to die. And her mother-in-law was in the house at the same time and she said, "I watched her and I neither encouraged her nor discouraged her." They put her in jail for a little while and I'm not even sure what the denouement is of her story. But that moment, that decision was a piece, a tail of something that was always around ⟨. . .⟩

Gloria Naylor and Toni Morrison, "Gloria Naylor and Toni Morrison: A Conversation," *Southern Review* 21, No. 3 (July 1985): 583–84

STANLEY CROUCH   *Beloved* ⟨. . .⟩ explains black behavior in terms of social conditioning, as if listing atrocities solves the mystery of human motive and behavior. It is designed to placate sentimental feminist ideology, and to make sure that the vision of black woman as the most scorned and rebuked of the victims doesn't weaken. Yet perhaps it is best understood by its italicized inscription: *"Sixty Million and more."* Morrison recently told *Newsweek* that the reference was to all the captured Africans, who died coming across the Atlantic. But sixty is ten times six, of course. That is very important to remember. For *Beloved*, above all else, is a blackface holocaust novel. It seems to have been written in order to enter American slavery into the big-time martyr contest, a contest usually won by references to, and works about, the experience of Jews at the hands of Nazis. As a holocaust novel, it includes disfranchisement, brutal transport, sadistic guards, failed and successful escapes, murder, liberals among the oppressors, a big war, underground cells, separation of family members, losses of loved ones to the violence of the mad order, and characters who, like the Jew in *The Pawnbroker*, have been made emotionally catatonic by the past.

That Morrison chose to set the Afro-American experience in the framework of collective tragedy is fine, of course. But she lacks a true sense of the tragic. Such a sense is stark, but it is never simpleminded. For all the memory within this book, including recollections of the trip across the Atlantic and the slave trading in the Caribbean, no one ever recalls how the Africans were captured. That would complicate matters. It would have demanded that the Africans who raided the villages of their enemies to sell them for guns, drink, and trinkets be included in the equation of injustice, something far too many Afro-Americans are loath to do—including Toni Morrison. In *Beloved* Morrison only asks that her readers tally up the sins committed against the darker people and feel sorry for them, not experience the horrors of slavery as they do. ⟨. . .⟩

But Morrison ⟨. . .⟩ can't resist the temptation of the trite or the sentimental. There is the usual scene in which the black woman is assaulted by white
men while her man looks on; Halle, Sethe's husband, goes mad at the sight.
Sixo, a slave who is captured trying to escape, is burned alive but doesn't
scream: he sings "Seven-o" over and over, because his woman has escaped
and is pregnant. But nothing is more contrived than the figure of Beloved
herself, who is the reincarnated force of the malevolent ghost that was
chased from the house. Beloved's revenge—she takes over the house, turns
her mother into a servant manipulated by guilt, and becomes more and
more vicious—unfolds as portentous melodrama. Whan Beloved finally
threatens to kill Sethe, 30 black women come to the rescue. At the fence
of the haunted property, one of them shouts, and we are given this: "Instantly
the kneelers and the standers joined her. They stopped praying and took a
step back to the beginning. In the beginning there were no words. In the
beginning was the sound, and they all knew what that sound sounded like."
    Too many such attempts at biblical grandeur, run through by Negro folk
rhythms, stymie a book that might have been important. Had Morrison
higher intentions when she appropriated the conventions of a holocaust
tale, Beloved might stand next to, or outdistance, Ernest Gaines's The Autobiography of Miss Jane Pittman and Charles Johnson's Oxherding Tale, neither
of which submits to the contrived, post-Baldwin vision of Afro-American
experience. Clearly the subject is far from exhausted, the epic intricacies
apparently unlimited. Yet to render slavery with aesthetic authority demands
not only talent, but the courage to face the ambiguities of the human soul,
which transcend the race. Had Toni Morrison that kind of courage, had
she the passion necessary to liberate her work from the failure of feeling
that is sentimentality, there is much that she could achieve. But why should
she try to achieve anything? The position of literary conjure woman has
paid off quite well. At last year's PEN Congress she announced that she
had never considered herself American, but with Beloved she proves that
she is as American as P. T. Barnum.

        Stanley Crouch, "Aunt Medea," New Republic, 19 October 1987, pp. 41–43

SUSAN WILLIS   There is a sense of urgency in Morrison's writing,
produced by the realization that a great deal is at stake. The novels may
focus on individual characters like Milkman and Jadine, but the salvation

of individuals is not the point. Rather, these individuals, struggling to reclaim or redefine themselves, are portrayed as epiphenomenal to community and culture, and it is the strength and continuity of the black cultural heritage as a whole that is at stake and being tested.

As Morrison sees it, the most serious threat to black culture is the obliterating influence of social change. The opening line from *Sula* might well have been the novel's conclusion, so complete is the destruction it records: "In that place, where they tore the night shade and blackberry patches from their roots to make room for the Medallion City Golf Course, there was once a neighborhood." This is the community Morrison is writing to reclaim. Its history, terminated and dramatically obliterated, is condensed into a single sentence whose content spans from rural South to urban development. Here, as throughout Morrison's writing, natural imagery refers to the past, the rural South, the reservoir of culture that has been uprooted— like the blackberry bushes—to make way for modernization. In contrast, the future is perceived of as an amorphous, institutionalized power embodied in the notion of "Medallion City," which suggests neither nature nor a people. Joining the past to the future is the neighborhood, which occupies a very different temporal moment (which history has shown to be transitional), and defines a very different social mode, as distinct from its rural origins as it is from the amorphous urban future.

It is impossible to read Morrison's four novels without coming to see the neighborhood as a concept crucial to her understanding of history. The neighborhood defines a Northern social mode rather than a Southern one, for it describes the relationship of an economic satellite, contiguous to a larger metropolis rather than separate subsistence economics like the Southern rural towns of Shalimar and Eloe. It is a Midwestern phenomenon rather than a Northeastern big-city category, because it defines the birth of principally first-generation, Northern, working-class black communities. It is a mode of the forties rather than the sixties or the eighties, and it evokes the many locally specific black populations in the North before these became assimilated to a larger, more generalized, and less regionally specific sense of black culture that we today refer to as the "black community."

Susan Willis, "Eruptions of Funk: Historicizing Toni Morrison," *Specifying: Black Women Writing the American Experience* (Madison: University of Wisconsin Press, 1987), pp. 93–95

TERRY OTTEN   In Toni Morrison's fiction characters one way or another enact the historical plight of blacks in American society. She offers no apology for her black female perspective. Though the black experience frames and informs her fictional narratives, it in no way reduces their universality. For all their complexity and diversity, the novels are woven together by common themes: the passage from innocence to experience, the quest for identity, the ambiguity of good and evil, the nature of the divided self, and especially, the concept of a fortunate fall. Morrison works the gray areas, avoiding simpleminded absolutes. Guitar tells Milkman at one point that "there are no innocent white people," but Milkman knows that there are no innocent blacks, either, least of all himself. Blacks as frequently as whites inflict extreme physical and psychological violence on blacks: the Breedloves torment each other, and Cholly rapes his daughter; Eva Peace burns her son, and Nel and Sula betray the other self; Milkman callously rejects Hagar, and Guitar kills Pilate; Son takes revenge on the childlike Cheyenne, and Jadine abandons Son; Sethe murders her daughter, and Beloved demands uncompromising payment—and of course much more. There is no doubt, though, that underlying all these manifestations of cruelty is the pernicious racism of American culture which wields its power to pervert and distort the moral center. Clearly, Morrison wants us to see the most insidious form of evil in the malevolent ability of racism to misshape the human spirit.

Terry Otten, *The Crime of Innocence in the Fiction of Toni Morrison* (Columbia: University of Missouri Press, 1989), p. 95

HAROLD BLOOM   Morrison, like any potentially strong novelist, battles against being subsumed by the traditions of narrative fiction. As a leader of African-American literary culture, Morrison is particularly intense in resisting critical characterizations that she believes misrepresent her own loyalties, her social and political fealties to the complex cause of her people. If one is a student of literary influence as such, and I am, then one's own allegiances as a critic are aesthetic, as I insist mine are. One is aware that the aesthetic has been a mask for those who would deny vital differences in gender, race, social class, and yet it need not be an instrument for the prolongation of exploiting forces. The aesthetic stance, as taught by Ruskin, Pater, and Wilde, enhances a reader's apprehension of perception and sensation. Such a mode of knowing literature seems to me inescapable, despite times like our own, in which societal and historical resentments, all with their own validity, tend to crowd out aesthetic considerations. Yet, as an artist, Morrison has few affinities with Zora Neale Hurston or Ralph Ellison, or with other masters of African-American fiction. Her curious resemblance to certain aspects of D. H. Lawrence does not ensue from the actual influence of Lawrence, but comes out of the two dominant precursors who have shaped her narrative sensibility, William Faulkner and Virginia Woolf. Faulkner and Woolf have little in common, but if you mixed them potently enough you might get Lawrence, or Toni Morrison.

Lest this seem a remote matter to a passionate reader of Morrison, I would observe mildly that one function of literary study is to help us make choices, because choice is inescapable, this late in Western cultural history. I do not believe that Morrison writes fiction of a kind I am not yet competent to read and judge, because I attend to her work with pleasure and enlighten-ment, amply rewarded by the perception and sensation that her art generates. Reading Alice Walker or Ishmael Reed, I cannot trust my own aesthetic reactions, and decide that their mode of writing must be left to critics more responsive than myself. But then I reflect that every reader must choose for herself or himself. Does one read and reread the novels of Alice Walker, or of Toni Morrison? I reread Morrison because her imagination, whatever her social purposes, transcends ideology and polemics, and enters again into the literary space occupied only by fantasy and romance of authentic aes-thetic dignity. Extraliterary purposes, however valid or momentous they may be for a time, ebb away, and we are left with story, characters, and style, that is to say, with literature or the lack of literature. Morrison's five novels to date leave us with literature, and not with a manifesto for social change, however necessary and admirable such change would be in our America of Chairman Atwater, Senator Helms, President Bush, and the other luminaries of what we ought to go on calling the Willie Horton election of 1988.

Harold Bloom, "Introduction," *Toni Morrison*, ed. Harold Bloom (New York: Chelsea House, 1990), pp. 1–2

WILFRED   D.   SAMUELS and   **CLENORA   HUDSON-WEEMS**   ⟨. . .⟩ Morrison writes to and for blacks. She has no problems stating this fact. "When I view the world, perceive it and write it, it is the world of black people. It is not that I won't write about white people. I just know that when I'm trying to develop the various themes I write about, the people who best manifest these for me are the black people whom I invent. It is not deliberate or calculated or self-consciously black, because I recognize and despise the artificial black writing some writers do." As Morrison told Walter Clemons, however, this does not mean that whites cannot adequately respond to her works. "When I write, I don't try to translate for white readers . . . Dostoevski wrote for a Russian audience, but we're able to read him. If I'm specific, and I don't overexplain, then anybody can overhear me."

It is clear, then, that Morrison sees her work as speaking to a specific audience but as reaching beyond the bounds of that audience to the rest of humankind. ⟨. . .⟩ Morrison uses the black slave experience in America as a metaphor for the human condition, which is necessarily all-inclusive.

Wilfred D. Samuels and Clenora Hudson-Weems, Toni Morrison (Boston: Twayne, 1990), p. 140

DOROTHEA DRUMMOND MBALIA   *Tar Baby* is an assimilation and advancement of the primary theme of her three earlier novels. For the first time, Morrison frees her work from the narrow geographical boundaries of American society. Recognizing that people of African descent, no matter where they live, share a common identity, a common history, and a common oppression, she uses an island in the Caribbean as the dominant and pivotal setting for her novel. In doing so, Morrison reflects her own maturing consciousness of the fact that African people must seek a common solution to their plight. She herself states that "Black culture survives everywhere pretty much the same" and that "Black people take their culture wherever they go."

Furthermore, in *Tar Baby* Morrison creates a revolutionary protagonist, Son, who realizes that he cannot run away and leave a body. Having discovered first the importance of knowing one's history and one's relationship to his people, Son commits himself to sharing this knowledge with other Africans. Thus, by struggling to politically educate Therese, Gideon, Sydney, Ondine, and, in particular, Jadine—symbols of the larger Pan-African society—Son becomes a disciple for African people, a modern-day revolutionary. 〈. . . But〉 what Son fails to realize is that there are some Africans, like Jadine, who—because they share the aspirations of the ruling class and receive handouts from it—will refuse to struggle against capitalism even though they are conscious of the fact that it is the primary enemy of African people.

Despite its weaknesses, the novel's theme and narrative structure reflect Morrison's heightened class consciousness. Structurally, she has embraced the traditional African concept of collectivism, for each of the major characters, as well as the omniscient narrator, contributes to the organic world of the novel. The story is told, in effect, by taking individual threads and sewing them into a whole, a wholeness that she so ardently wishes for African people.

> Dorothea Drummond Mbalia, *Toni Morrison's Developing Class Consciousness* (Selinsgrove, PA: Susquehanna University Press, 1991), pp. 26–27

JANE MILLER   Within the first half-page of Toni Morrison's novel 〈*Jazz*〉, an 18-year-old girl has been shot dead by her middle-aged lover, and his wife has been manhandled from the funeral after attempting to cut the dead girl's face with a knife. Both events are witnessed and kept secret by a community which has reason to distrust the police and to look kindly upon a hitherto gentle, childless couple, whose sudden, violent sorrows they recognise and are able to forgive. And as the spring of that year, 1926, bursts a month or two later upon the 'City' of this extraordinary novel, its all-seeing gossip of a narrator is moved to declare—if only provisionally— that 'history is over, you all, and everything's ahead at last.'

The novel's theme tune is spun out from these contrasts and whirled through a series of playful improvisations by a storyteller who admits to being—and, as it turns out, expects the reader to be—'curious, inventive and well-informed'. It is impossible to resist the seductions of this particular narrative voice as it announces its own fallibilities, mourns its distance from some of the events it will therefore need to invent, boldly revises its own speculations, even as it recalls, replays, retrieves them for us before our very eyes and with our assumed complicity. For, of course, this voice also undertakes to guarantee both tale and telling as truth, history, music known and shared by all who have roots in the black urban communities of America in the Twenties. And for readers with quite other roots? Well, the voice is no more prepared than Morrison is herself to 'footnote the black experience for white readers'. As she put it in a recent interview: 'I wouldn't try to explain what a reader like me already knew.' ⟨. . .⟩

Jazz is a love story, indeed a romance. And romance and its high-risk seductions for young women come with special health warnings when it is poor young black women who might succumb to it. For romance has always been white, popular, capitalistic in its account of love as transactions voluntarily undertaken between class and beauty and money. But the romance which is a snare and a delusion has also spelled out a future for young women, a destiny, significance and pleasure—and particularly when there was little enough of those possibilities for them or for the men they knew. The older women of Morrison's novels know that sex can be a woman's undoing, that men, 'ridiculous and delicious and terrible', are always trouble. The narrator in *Jazz* is generous with warnings: 'The girls have red lips and their legs whisper to each other through silk stockings. The red lips and the silk flash power. A power they will exchange for the right to be overcome, penetrated.'

Morrison's writing of a black romance pays its debt to blues music, the rhythms and the melancholy pleasures of which she has so magically transformed into a novel. More than that, she has claimed new sources and new kinds of reading as the inspiration for a thriving literature.

Jane Miller, "New Romance," *London Review of Books*, 14 May 1992, p. 12

DENISE HEINZE   As an artist, Morrison negotiates a very complex matrix of reality in which she is both despised and revered, absent and present, ignored and sought after. The result is a double-visionary canon, a symbiosis of novel-writing in which Morrison has complete mastery over the fictive reality she creates. And by her creative mediation between the real and fictive worlds, she generates possibilities rather than records continued frustration and oppression. Morrison may not write from a stance of art as life, but she may be a psychological and spiritual Wizard of Oz for life as art. ⟨. . .⟩

By combining political consciousness with aesthetic sensibility, Morrison achieves a very delicate balance: without directly denouncing white society, she illustrates the demise of blacks who have adopted the corrupting influence of the white community. By indirection Morrison avoids the polarization of black and white humanity—one as inherently good, the other irrevocably corrupt—and thus allows all people to vicariously experience a rebirth through the black community. While her intent may be to valorize the black community and ignite both blacks and whites into political action, what she also wishes is to elevate through art the beautiful—and hence reclaimable—in the human condition.

Perhaps therein lies her appeal, for in denouncing the dominant culture she presents to an aging America alternatives that have always existed and are now emerging, but which have long been suppressed by the rhetoric of an entrenched ideology. Morrison's success as a great American writer is perhaps a function of two factors: (1) her ability to manipulate her insider/outsider status, for she both subverts and maintains, is exploited by and exploits the literary establishment, and (2) her recognition that her double-consciousness can never be, perhaps never should be, integrated into a single vision. Indeed, she is in the truly remarkable position of being able to articulate with near impunity two cultures—one black, the other white American. By orchestrating this sense of connectedness between cultures rather than attempting to dissolve the differences, Morrison's successful career appears to have transcended the "permanent condition" of double-consciousness that afflicts her fictional characters.

Denise Heinze, *The Dilemma of "Double Consciousness": Toni Morrison's Novels* (Athens: University of Georgia Press, 1993), pp. 8–10

Bibliography

The Bluest Eye. 1970.
Sula. 1973.
The Black Book (editor). 1974.
Song of Solomon. 1977.
Tar Baby. 1981.
Beloved. 1987.
Race-ing Justice, En-gendering Power: Essays on Anita Hill, Clarence Thomas, and the Construction of Social Reality (editor). 1992.
Jazz. 1992.
Playing in the Dark: Whiteness and the Literary Imagination. 1992.

Lecture and Speech of Acceptance, upon the Award of the Nobel Prize for Literature.
      1994.
Conversations with Toni Morrison. Ed. Danille Taylor-Guthrie. 1994.

Ishmael Reed
b. 1938

ISHMAEL REED was born on February 22, 1938, in Chattanooga, Tennessee, the son of Henry Lenoir, a fundraiser for the YMCA, and Thelma Coleman; he took his name from his stepfather, Bennie Stephen Reed, an autoworker. The family moved to Buffalo in 1942, where Reed spent a few years at Buffalo Technical High School before graduating from East High School in 1956. He then attended the State University of New York at Buffalo, but had to withdraw in 1960 for lack of funds. At this time he married Priscilla Rose, with whom he would have two children before separating in 1963; they divorced in 1970.

Reed began working at the Talbert Mall Project, a black housing project in Buffalo. This experience led to a period of social activism, which included work on a newspaper, the *Empire Star Weekly*, and a controversial radio station, WVFO. In 1962 Reed moved to New York City, where he edited an underground magazine, the *Advance*, in Newark, New Jersey; he also participated in the Umbra Workshop, a black writers' group, and, in 1965, organized the American Festival of Negro Art.

Reed had begun writing satirical sketches in college. In 1967, the year he moved to Berkeley, California, his first novel, *The Free-Lance Pallbearers*, was published. This wide-ranging satire set the tone for Reed's other novels, whose only unifying themes are outrageousness and a refusal to toe a party line: *Yellow Back Radio Broke-Down* (1969), a vicious attack on Christianity; *Mumbo Jumbo* (1972) and *The Last Days of Louisiana Red* (1974), parodies of the detective novel in which a black detective uses HooDoo to probe African-American cultural history; *Flight to Canada* (1976), an ironic imitation of the slave narrative; *The Terrible Twos* (1982) and its sequel, *The Terrible Threes* (1989), satires on conservative politics and religion; *Reckless Eyeballing* (1986), a send-up of black feminism; and *Japanese by Spring* (1993), an attack on academic life.

Reed has also distinguished himself as a poet. His first volume of poetry was *catechism of d neoamerican hoodoo church* (1970), and it was followed by

Conjure: Selected Poems 1963–1970 (1972; nominated for the National Book Award and the Pulitzer Prize in poetry), *Chattanooga* (1973), *A Secretary to the Spirits* (1978), and *New and Collected Poems* (1988).

In 1970 Reed married Carla Blank, a dancer, with whom he had one child. The next year, with Steve Cannon and Al Young, he founded the Yardbird Publishing Company, which published an annual *Yardbird Reader* from 1972 to 1976; Reed has also won acclaim for his anthologies, *19 Necromancers from Now* (1970) and *Calafia: The California Poetry* (1979). In 1976 he formed the Before Columbus Foundation to promote the work of ethnic writers.

As an essayist Reed is as outspoken as he is as a novelist and poet. Four collections of his essays have appeared: *Shrovetide in Old New Orleans* (1978), *God Made Alaska for the Indians* (1982), *Writin' Is Fightin'* (1988), and *Airing Dirty Laundry* (1993). In much of his work, especially his novels and essays, Reed has faced accusations of misogyny and of being more successful at attacking his perceived enemies than advocating his own beliefs. But Reed was a pioneer of multiculturalism as opposed to the "monoculturalism" that he sees as still dominant in the United States.

In spite of his hostility to the academy, Reed has been a guest lecturer at many universities, including Yale, Harvard, Columbia, and Dartmouth. He has been the recipient of many awards, including a Guggenheim award for fiction, an American Civil Liberties Award, and a Pushcart Prize.

GEORGE LAMMING   Ishmael Reed is a prolific writer who also works in more than one medium. His novels (*Free-Lance Pall Bearers, Yellow Back Radio Broke-Down, Mumbo Jumbo*) have already consolidated his reputation as one of those black writers who refuse to be categorized according to the revelance of his theme. He asks no favors of any orthodoxy, but lets his imagination make its bid for the creation of new forms. Yet one cannot fail to notice the craft and discipline with which he controls the natural swing and bounce of his verse.

In his latest collection, *Conjure*, Reed offers us a sharp and provocative contrast in style. If ⟨Derek⟩ Walcott's echoes are those of the classical humanist, grave and formal, Reed's tone and rhythm derive from the militant tradition of the black underground. But his is an unusual brand of militancy; it is much concerned with the politics of language. He argues for a clean, free struggle between the liberating anarchism of the black tongue and the frozen esthetic of a conventional White Power. "May the best church win/ shake hands now and come out conjuring." His verse is distinguished by a fine critical intelligence, and his stance before the wide variety of American life is supremely confident. He can evoke with poetic realism the savagery which shaped the pioneering spirit as well as crystallize the fraudulence at the heart of the "civilizing" mission.

> George Lamming, [Review of *Conjure*], *New York Times Book Review*, 6 May 1973, p. 37

NEIL SCHMITZ   In the "Neo-HooDoo Manifesto," which first appeared in the Los Angeles *Free Press* (September 18–24, 1970), Reed devises a myth that divides history into a war between two churches, two communities of consciousness: the "Cop Religion" of Christianity and the transformed Osirian rite, Voodoo. Sounding at once like ⟨William⟩ Burroughs and Davy Crockett, he then declares the contest: "Neo-HooDoos are detectives of the metaphysical about to make a pinch. We have issued warrants for a god arrest." ⟨. . .⟩

If only in theory, then, Neo-HooDoo represents a new direction (so Reed argues) for the Black writer, an escape from the decadence of Anglo-American literature that reverses the path historically taken by Black writers and intellectuals in the United States. In *The Narrative of the Life of Frederick Douglass*, just before Douglass' epical fight with the "nigger-breaker," Edward Covey, another slave gives Douglass "a certain *root*, which if I would take some of it with me, *carrying it always on my right side*, would render it impossible for Mr. Covey, or any other white man, to whip me." Douglass keeps this *"root"* italicised in his discussion of the event—it is Black magic—and what Douglass is striving to assert in his narrative is his possession of White magic, the word. Neo-HooDoo in effect stresses the power of that *"root"* and contends that the word is without value unless suffused and transformed by its occult force. It is this piece of Africa given to Douglass, and then forgotten by Douglass, that Reed strives to redeem.

But where are the "original folk tales" and native idioms in Reed's fiction? How far indeed does Neo-HooDoo (both as myth and mode) take him from established literary canons? His discourse in *Yellow Back Radio* and *Mumbo Jumbo* curves in and around colloquial Black English, which serves him as a stylistic device, not as a language. It is withal a learned and allusive discourse as mixed in its diction as Mark Twain's. His forms are not narrative legends taken from an oral tradition, but rather the popular forms of the Western and the Gangster Novel. As A. B. Spellman observes in *Black Fire*, this frustrated search for indigenous forms "is not the exclusive predicament of the Afro-American artist—the exponents of negritude in Africa and the Indies have spent years dealing with it. Novelist Edouard Glissant of Martinique had an extremely difficult time reorienting his style to develop a fictional form that conformed more to the oral folk tale than to the French novel. Glissant's compatriot, Aimé Césaire, feeling trapped in a European language, went back into Surrealism to find an anti-French, which would, in a sense, punish the colonialists for forcing him to write in a European language." Césaire's fate, writing anti-French, resembles Reed's in *Yellow Back Radio* and *Mumbo Jumbo*. Reed is driven to Burroughs for an anti-English as Césaire was to André Breton. *Yellow Back Radio* is a Black version of the Western Burroughs has been writing in fragments and promising in full since the fifties. Not only is the content of the fiction eclectic in its composition, but Loop's performance as a *houngan* in it has a good deal of Burroughs' "Honest Bill." For the core of his narrative, Reed borrows almost intact the sociological drama Norman Mailer describes in *The White Negro*— that migration of White middle-class youth in revolt against the values of their own culture toward the counter-culture of Black America—and then weaves into this phenomenon a barely disguised account of the student uprisings at Berkeley and other campuses. The shooting at Kent State comes after the publication of *Yellow Back Radio*, but it is accurately prefigured in the book.

Neil Schmitz, "Neo-HooDoo: The Experimental Fiction of Ishmael Reed," *Twentieth Century Literature* 20, No. 2 (April 1974): 132–33

DARWIN TURNER   Who or what is the poet Ishmael? An intellectual anti-intellectual. A religious opponent of religion. A duelling pacifist. A black antagonist champion of blacks. A poet influenced by Yeats, Pound, Blake, and the Umbra poets. A Black Arts poet who attacks Black Arts critics and poets. A satirical creator of myths. An ideologue who derides ideologies. A poet who ranges in allusion from Nixon to Wotan and Osiris. A poet of the topical and the ancient. A poet ignored in Stephen Henderson's trenchant analysis of the blackness of contemporary black poetry (*Understanding the New Black Poetry*, 1973), but whose poetry offers a point-by-point illustration of Henderson's analysis. Stir these contradictions together slowly in a vat of satire; whirl yourself wildly until dizzy; then pour slowly. The brew is the poetry of Ishmael Reed, to be sipped as delicately as one might sip a poison of 2 parts bourbon, 1 part vodka, and a dash of coke. There is no guarantee that every drinker will like the concoction. Occasionally, the sip is flat. Most often, however, it is quickly intoxicating. ⟨. . .⟩

Reed vitriolically attacks the corrupt values and venal slogans slavishly venerated by "proper" Americans: pep pills (competitive drive), the artificially induced fetish for cleanliness and unblemished pale skin, antiseptic sexuality, etiquette, and other superficial paraphernalia of an "elegant" culture. His two-line insert of polite phrases is a mocking transition and prologue to the conversion of these values into a food that can be eaten only by indestructible people: an explosive stew "topped with kegs . . . of whipped dynamite and cheery smithereens." Evoking the images of blacks and black culture that whites have used pejoratively, the African-American god-narrator prophesies that blacks will pass through the baptism of fire and dance with the sun.

Reed's showmanship and conjuring can be spellbinding. Like T. S. Eliot, he demands that his readers comprehend his allusions; but unlike Eliot, he presumes that many who approach with child-like innocence will understand, or be fascinated by the sounds.

Darwin Turner, "A Spectrum of Blackness," *Parnassus: Poetry in Review* 4, No. 2 (Spring–Summer 1976): 209–10, 217–18

ISHMAEL REED   ⟨. . .⟩ I think, probably, my material is more within the classical Afro-American tradition than some critics who accuse my characters of being pathological—like this person, Addison Gayle, Jr., whom the liberal establishment has made the black aesthetic czar. You see, there was a fight there in the sixties where somebody said that he didn't feel he was qualified to judge Eldridge Cleaver's work. I don't feel that I'm qualified to listen to Duke Ellington, you know—it's just absurd. They had been intimidated by these fascist types, you know. ⟨. . .⟩ And they felt that they wanted to bow out. So then these black opportunists in the English departments, who really didn't care that much about Afro-American culture—as a matter of fact, had contempt for it—people like Houston Baker, Jr. and

Addison Gayle, Jr.—both juniors, incidentally—were the ones that they set up to arbitrate taste. Not Gayle as much as Baker. Baker and I had an exchange where it got really personal. It's always been that kind of attack which people have made.

There was a nonaggression pact signed where liberal whites said, "Well, you guys do it. You be the guardians of the Afro-American experience. Check them, you know." They had a lot in common. They both were against any kind of experimentation in form or content. So they wanted to keep Afro-American writers in their place. To the novel of nightmare and pain that Roger Rosenblatt and Irving Howe. . . . They are all together; they all publish in the same magazines. I was naughty enough to call Harold Courlander a tourist for the *Washington Post,* because his material on Afro-American culture was not substantial. For example, he did a book on the Afro-American culture, Afro-American folklore, in which he didn't use many of the writings of the Afro-Americans and natives, not many Haitian writers, not any writers from the country. They used white nineteenth-century tourists to describe the kind of dances that the Africans were doing in New Orleans, which is not very accurate when there were a lot of other sources they could have used. So I said that. So the next thing I know, they're jumping on *Flight to Canada.* It's predictable.

Rosenblatt and Irving Howe, I understand they have some kind of relationship with *The New Republic.* I had *The New Republic* in the book, you know. And then McPherson is connected with *The New Republic.* I guess white writers have the same problem, but it just seems like some kind of assassination thing: "You don't fit in." If you're not giving them some kind of decorative prose—what they call elegance and eloquence—then you're a bad boy; you're a heathen, you know. When it comes between heathens and the kind of writers they promote—the tokens they got back East, dependent upon them—I'd rather be on the side of the heathens. That's why I've been more around Alaska among Eskimos and the Indians in the Southwest. I get along with people like that; I'm influenced by their cultures. But this is a transition. I think some of the people I'm working with and I have to take credit for this, we have changed the whole way of Afro-American writing in that there's been a revolt. We came to the West Coast instead of going to Europe, as was the practice in the forties and fifties, and others went South and to the Midwest. And so this machine that they tried to create has crumbled.

Ishmael Reed, cited in Cameron Northouse, "Ishmael Reed," *Conversations with Writers II* (Detroit: Gale Research Co., 1978), pp. 219–20

STANLEY CROUCH   The trouble with *The Terrible Twos* is that he's said it all before and said it much better. This time out, he's picked another genre to tear apart with his imposition of varied forms and combinations of perspective. Just as he used *Antigone* in *The Last Days of Louisiana Red* to create a brilliant satire that collapsed under the strain of its near-misogyny, and just as he used the western for *Yellow Back Radio Broke-Down*, the detective story for *Mumbo Jumbo*, the slave narrative and *Uncle Tom's Cabin* for *Flight to Canada*, Reed weaves Rastafarianism and a reverse of the Todd Clifton dummy sequence from *Invisible Man* together with Dickens's *A Christmas Carol* in *The Terrible Twos*. Again we get the self-obsessed harpies, the mission Indians, the black hero who takes over the white form (unlike Todd Clifton, Black Peter is not controlled by whites who speak through his mouth—he speaks through theirs), the dumb black street hustlers who get into a game too complicated for them to understand, the corruption of Christianity, the secret society of powerful white bosses, the argument that preliterate custom and belief are just as good as modern civilization (if not better) and the beleaguered black hero who has woman problems (Reed touches on the sexual provincialism of black women, which didn't begin to change until the late 1960s when they had to compete with liberated and liberal white women for the affections of black men, but he doesn't do anything with that proverbial hot potato).

I'm not saying that Reed should abandon his concerns, but I am saying that for all the literary appropriations in *The Terrible Twos*, it hasn't the level of invention that made his best work succeed. There is too much predictability, too much dependence on revelation through conversation and interior monologue. Most of the mysteries must be explained by the characters, and what we do discover through their narratives isn't very interesting. ⟨. . .⟩ There are some funny passages along the way, however. There is even an attempt to infuse his surreal puppet show with realistic relationships, especially on an erotic level, and this brings what freshness there is to the novel. It also suggests that Reed may soon examine the range of sexual and social attractions that a multiracial society makes so possible, especially since the passage from Europe to the Third World can sometimes take place within only a few city blocks. If that is what he intends for his sequels—*The Terrible Threes* and *The Terrible Fours*—then the world he has developed, one quilted with endless allusions, mythology, improvisation and concentric circles of time and culture, could give birth to the potential so basic to the social contract and to the diversity of this country—Ishmael

Reed's All-American Novel. *The Terrible Twos*, unfortunately, is mostly a shadow of his former work, and a shadow that tells us little we don't already know.

Stanley Crouch, "Kinships and Aginships," *Nation*, 22 May 1982, pp. 618–19

ROBERT MURRAY DAVIS   Ishmael Reed's political and esthetic intransigence might well be responsible for his relative neglect by all critical schools, for in all of his work he has gone out of his way to reject, among others, the New York literary establishment; Jewish critics of Black literature; other Black writers and critics of differing political, esthetic, and even physical hue; and the whole idea of English departments, which, he argues with a logic even more irritating than his ad hominem attacks, should be made part of ethnic studies programs. Certainly it would be easier to ignore Reed than to argue with him, but academic critics are masochistic enough to overlook everything except the lack of viable critical approach to Reed's work, especially to his novels. While it is possible that all of us should seek training in voodoo mythology and ritual, though even this might annoy Reed, perhaps it would be more immediately useful to look at some conventional approaches to his fiction: comparative myth and genre, defined in terms both of literary theory and popular cultural. And while none of Reed's six novels can be regarded as typical, *Yellow Back Radio Broke-Down* illustrates most spectacularly Reed's "main job": "to humble Judeo-Christian culture."

As everyone familiar with Eliot, Joyce, and other modernists will see at once, the fact that Reed uses mythologies from various times and cultures offers nothing new in itself. There are, however, at least four major differences between the use of myth by the modernists and by Reed: shape; sources; cultural authority; and formal authority. Of course, he does all of these things in the context of specific works, not in a programmatic fashion, and in any case one should not subject him to a rigid format. ⟨. . .⟩

In his movement towards kinetic art as well as other aspects of his theory, Reed has departed as far from the spirit and method of the Modernists as he can. Whether or not in practice it is possible to use myth at all and not be in some sense bound by and to it, theoretically it is possible, and obviously it is possible to loosen the bonds and play with them, even to do rope tricks like Loop or Reed in *Radio*. Whether or not the method works, and it is difficult to make any method work in or out of literature, depends upon its embodiment in the individual work. Just as some Charlie Parker solos are better than others, depending in part on the complementary interaction between underlying received structure and the soloist's melodic inventiveness, so Reed can be more or less successful. I believe that he works best where he has firm structure against which to play his variations, and a structure, like the Western or the mystery, which is part of his lived experience rather than, like the Antigone and St. Nicholas stories, the product of research. In either case, there is no virtue per se in the method Reed has adopted, and he seems to be in danger of repeating method if not mythologies. On the other hand, the method is none the worse for being repeated if it is being refined and perfected. Since Reed will be only forty-five when this essay is published (no great age for a novelist or satirist), he and his audience should have plenty of time to discover whether "a way of thinking that's considered 'way-out' or even 'crazy' " will come to seem commonplace or ho-hum.

Robert Murray Davis, "Scatting the Myths: Ishmael Reed," *Arizona Quarterly* 39, No. 4 (Winter 1983): 406–7, 420

JEROME KLINKOWITZ   Those dour guardians of official culture Ishmael Reed calls "high-ass Anglo critics" have always had trouble with his work, especially when they try to segregate facts from fiction. Even his partisans have rough going from time to time as they try to pigeonhole this writer who's built much of his career on the flamboyant eclipse of stereotypes. Take a friend who's been wondering if he should zap poor Ishmael for being a "grant-hoarder" (the term is Reed's and he isn't one). This investigator's crowning argument is that among the contributors' notes to *Yardbird Lives!* (coedited with Al Young for Grove Press in 1978), Reed simply lists himself as "a businessman," as if admitting he's in league with the folks who run America's acronymic corporations and grants establishments.

"Hey wait," I beg my friend and cite Reed's disclaimer from the first page of his funniest novel, *The Last Days of Louisiana Red* (Random House, 1974), a note which warns that "in order to avoid detection by powerful enemies and industrial spies, nineteenth-century HooDoo people referred to their Work as 'The Business.' " The inspired grant-getting hustle my friend rightly condemns is hardly The Business our novelist describes, for if you read into *Louisiana Red* you'll find the HooDoo Businessmen have their own name for such shenanigans every decent person would deplore: Moochism, as in Cab Calloway's "Minnie the Moocher." But for the victims of a monocultural education, artists like Calloway don't exist. ⟨. . .⟩

Syncretism is one of the few formally abstract words in Reed's critical vocabulary, and he feels it is the key to a true national American literature reflecting the uniquely multicultural art which has evolved here. "Anglo" culture, as he calls it, then becomes one element among many, and the only loss is that of a dominant intellectual academy sworn to upholding the beliefs of a long-dead order. Gabriel García Márquez says much the same about his own multicultural, coastal Caribbean background where, as opposed to the rigidly colonial Spanish cultural of the highlands capital in Bogotá, history and fiction were allowed to blend, making truth "one more illusion, just one more version of many possible vantage points" where "people change their reality by changing their perception of it." Within this aesthetic, fact and imagination become one. And as our present age has been shaped by this union, so Reed creates a common method for writing novels and essays by using the best of it while warning of its dangers when abused.

Jerome Klinkowitz, "Ishmael Reed's Multicultural Aesthetic," *Literary Subversions* (Carbondale: Southern Illinois University Press, 1985), pp. 18–19, 21

ROBERT ELLIOT FOX   *Mumbo Jumbo* is an historico-aesthetic textbook, complete with illustrations, bibliography, and footnotes. It is Reed's dissertation on the metaphysics of consciousness and, simultaneously, a filmscript: though taking place primarily in New York, it opens with a prologue in New Orleans, following which Reed "rolls" the title and credits before plunging back into the story. The cinematic aspect is played up from the beginning: the first reference to Jew Grew as "a Creeping Thing" immediately brings to mind a Hollywood horror film, and the people dancing on hospital carts while the doctor is "slipping dipping gliding" is like a Marx Brothers comedy. (In fact, monster movies, slapstick, and detective films—*Mumbo Jumbo*, after all, is a "mystery"—all are significant influences on Reed's fiction which await more detailed analysis.)

The "heterophany of elements" found in Reed's work, which *Mumbo Junbo* exploits with particular brilliance, derives not only from modernist collage and postmodernist bricolage techniques, it is found as well in jazz, which, it is important to recognize, was the first mode of both black American modernism and postmodernism. This "heterophany of elements" is also a feature of Jew Grew and is analogous to the syncretization of the worship of African and other deities in Voodoo, the many varieties of gumbo, and such, which are found in Afro-American experience. Impromptu variations, based on individual refinement of collective knowledge, are crucial. There is a common saying among Yoruba masqueraders: "There is no house where supper is not prepared / But one stew tastes better than another." This is a form of artistic criticism used to distinguish one oral performer from another in terms of excellence, employing the same idea of recipe as Reed's poem "The Neo-Hoodoo Aesthetic," where everything depends upon the "cook."

However, the polyglot quality of Mumbo Jumbo may have another source: the slave narratives. Citing their "extremely mixed nature," James Olney offers the following description of what might be included:

> an engraved portrait or photograph of the subject of the narrative; authenticity testimonials, prefixed or postfixed; poetic epigraphs, snatches of poetry in the text, poems appended; illustrations . . .; interruptions of the narrative by way of declamatory addresses to the reader . . .; a bewildering variety of documents—letters to and from the narrator, bills of sale, newspaper clippings, notices of slave auctions and of escaped slaves . . .; and sermons and anti-slavery speeches and essays tacked on at the end to demonstrate the post-narrative activities of the narrative.

Many of these elements are to be found in Mumbo Jumbo and in Flight to Canada (Reed's fifth novel, a deliberate parody of slave narratives). It is further proof of the correctness of Reed's position when he denies that his work is derived from white models. Black literature and black art have their own lineage, their own heritage of experimentation and innovation. The uprooted (Africans in the Diaspora) have proven to be masters of rootwork, and, indeed, the concern with roots is a form of spiritual ecology, the preservation of the signs and symbols of a culture.

Robert Elliot Fox, "Ishmael Reed: Gathering the Limbs of Osiris," Conscientious Sorcerers: The Black Postmodernist Fiction of LeRoi Jones/Amiri Baraka, Ishmael Reed, and Samuel R. Delany (New York: Greenwood Press, 1987), pp. 50–51

REGINALD MARTIN   What is the position of Ishmael Reed within and external to the new black aesthetic? It is my assertion that Reed's work fails to meet the demanded criteria from the major aestheticians such as Addison Gayle, Houston Baker, and Amiri Baraka on these points:

(1) Reed uses humour, especially satire (in all his works, but especially *Mumbo Jumbo*) in dealing with subjects only entertained with seriousness before. Humour was an early insertion in the tenets of the original black aesthetic, but the tenor of the times in the 1960s, when the new black aesthetic was solidifying, demanded a direct confronting of social issues, and this was most often done in serious prose. For example, critics still have a difficult time handling Reed's *The Freelance Pallbearers* (1967), which was extreme satire containing negative black characterizations. Some critics have seen Reed's use of humour as a shirking of responsibility on his part; that is, he should be responsible (read serious) toward the serious problems which face black Americans.

(2) On the surface, Reed's protagonists are good role models only in that they are extremely intelligent and witty. Unlike the often totally serious and unflippant characters of other writers, Reed's main characters use wit and humour when faced with an oppressive society, as in *The Freelance Pallbearers* and *Yellow Back Radio Broke-Down* (1969), and not weapons, steadfastness, or religious dedication. Though his characters must be examined closely to see the positiveness they really convey, critics such as Baker and Baraka have denigrated Reed's humorous characterizations with the labels 'spurious' and 'unfocused'.

(3) Reed's work is often surreal. He opposes hate with humour, often synchronically presented, as in *Yellow Back Radio Broke-Down* and *The Terrible Twos* (1982), to achieve a textual structure that is not easily identifiable on the 'plain surface'. Critics have said that this is an attempt to escape discussing critical social issues.

(4) Reed's microcosms, being surreal, do not easily lend themselves to an identifiable social macrocosm; it is sometimes difficult for the reader to find a common experience to which to relate. Thus, that part of the new black aesthetic which insists on its own version of 'universality' is disappointed and repelled by Reed.

(5) Reed refuses to accommodate the demands of the adherents and leading aestheticians of the new black aesthetic, and confronts them, by name, in print; further, he refuses to accommodate the tastes of the general public, black or white, which has limited expectations and boundaries for the American writer who is black, as in *The Last Days of Louisiana Red* (1974) and *Flight to Canada* (1976).

Reed's battle with the new black aesthetic critics began early in his career. From the very start, he has disliked being categorized and seems to find it impossible to play the literary game by the rules of others.

Reginald Martin, *Ishmael Reed and the New Black Aesthetic Critics* (New York: St. Martin's Press, 1988), pp. 41–43

RICHARD WALSH   The direct source for Reed's aesthetic is actually HooDoo, the Afro-American version of the Haitian original. The importation of Voodoo into America not only provided it with the Afro-American pedigree that allows Reed to advance it in the name of both his own culture *and* the principle of multiculturalism; it also involved a process of distillation and accommodation to the existing cultural conditions, which accentuated exactly the qualities Reed values and makes the foundation of his aesthetic. ⟨. . .⟩

By way of Neo-HooDooism, then, Reed is able to return in *Flight to Canada* to the slave narrative he had earlier disowned. The fundamental condition of this return is a transformation of style: he defies the norms of the genre in almost every aspect of his novel. The objectives of the slave narrative were primarily to bear witness to the realities of slavery and to affirm the humanity of the slave against the brutal conditions that enslaved him. The realization of these priorities depended upon the accumulation of detail to give force to the testimony. Reed, however, proclaims himself a cartoonist. The slave narrative is constrained by its moral seriousness, while Reed cultivates irreverent humour: the slave-owner Swille tells Lincoln to "stop putting your fingers in your lapels like that. You ought to at least try to polish yourself, man. Go to the theatre. Get some culture." This disrespect for Lincoln in particular and his nonfictional characters generally is symptomatic of another of Reed's heresies, his abuse of historical veracity. His manipulation of these characters is not an intellectual exploitation of lacunae in the historical record, as it might be in the hands of E. L. Doctorow, but a flagrantly unhistorical farce. His abuses are always grounded to some degree in an assumed familiarity with the received text of history, and feed satirically or humorously upon it: their main function is to effect a transformation of the reverent tone handed down in this text by subverting the dignity of its icons.

Implicit in all this is Reed's complete lack of concern with the criterion of realism upon which the slave narratives depended. His artistic concerns place a lower value on the surface coherence of his narrative than on imperatives of his fictional argument, or the opportunistic satirical points to which he continually sacrifices narrative continuity. As a result of these priorities, the novel unselfconsciously displays its inconsistencies of character and motivation, illogical narrative developments, loose ends and mis-matched plotlines. There is little point in objecting that Reed does not reconcile his perspectives on Lincoln as player and fool, nor provide ade-quately for the swings in the relationship between Quickskill and the pirate Yankee Jack; that he refers back to Quickskill's dream as an event, and has Yankee Jack and his wife Quaw Quaw united at the opening of the novel, chronologically *after* her discovery that he uses her father's skull as an ashtray. The rationale for these aberrations lies on another plane: Reed refuses to be a slave to his narrative.

Reed's aesthetic decisions are motivated by his concern to affirm the multiculture in the *form* of his novel, a function for which the form of the original slave narratives is inadequate because of their appropriation as documents for the Abolitionist cause: "The political use to which the abolitionists put black literacy demanded a painstaking verisimilitude—a concern with even the most minute concrete detail" (Henry Louis Gates, Jr.). As such the slave narratives were denied the freedom of form through which their authors could have expressed *their* culture. And Reed insists that this co-opting of black literature by white liberals is a contemporary problem: "In fact, our worst enemies are radical liberals because they have so much influence on how we look in the media and in American culture. . . . They are only interested in the social realist, the 'experience' of black people. And this treatment limits and enslaves us."

Reed's revisionary interest in the slave narrative arises from his belief that the forms of slavery still exist in modern America, under the guise of the monoculture's institutionalized subordination of all other cultures: the institutional structure of slavery remains in sublimated form, as the machin-ery of a state of oppression he regards as *cultural* slavery. The material of the slave narrative therefore allows Reed to practise his necromancy, explor-ing the analogies it generates in the relative positions taken by the various factions of contemporary culture. But, more than just providing a metaphori-cal map of the system of cultural slavery he sees in modern America, he is also arguing for a direct continuity between the two levels, for an evolutionary transformation of actual into cultural slavery. In doing so, he is also engaging in the struggle "to get to our aesthetic Canada" by asserting in the novel's form his emancipation from the dictates of the dominant monoculture.

Richard Walsh, " 'A Man's Story Is His Gris-Gris': Cultural Slavery, Literary Emancipation and Ishmael Reed's *Flight to Canada*," *Journal of American Studies* 27, No. 1 (April 1993): 61–63

Bibliography

The Free-Lance Pallbearers. 1967.

Yellow Back Radio Broke-Down. 1969.

19 Necromancers from Now (editor). 1970.

catechism of d neoamerican hoodoo church. 1970.

Yardbird Reader (editor; with Al Young). 1972–76. 5 vols.

Mumbo Jumbo. 1972.

Conjure: Selected Poems 1963–1970. 1972.

Chattanooga. 1973.

The Last Days of Louisiana Red. 1974.

Flight to Canada. 1976.

Poetry Makes Rhythm in Philosophy. 1976.

Shrovetide in Old New Orleans. 1978.

Yardbird Lives! (editor; with Al Young). 1978.

A Secretary to the Spirits. 1978.

Calafia: The California Poetry (editor). 1979.

The Terrible Twos. 1982.

God Made Alaska for the Indians: Selected Essays. 1982.

Reckless Eyeballing. 1986.

Cab Calloway Stands In for the Moon. 1986.

New and Collected Poems. 1988.

Writin' Is Fightin': Thirty-seven Years of Boxing on Paper. 1988.

The Terrible Threes. 1989.

The Before Columbus Foundation Fiction Anthology: Selections from the American Book Awards 1980–1990 (editor; with Kathryn Trueblood and Shawn Wong). 1992.

Airing Dirty Laundry. 1993.

Ishmael Reed: An Interview (with Cameron Northouse). 1993.

Japanese by Spring. 1993.

◈ ◈ ◈

Ntozake Shange
b. 1948

NTOZAKE SHANGE was born Paulette Williams on October 18, 1948, in Trenton, New Jersey, the oldest child of a surgeon and a social worker. With her two younger brothers and sister she grew up in Trenton, at an air force base in upstate New York, and in St. Louis, Missouri. Her father painted and played percussion in addition to his duties as a physician, and she met many leading black figures in sports and the arts. She read widely as a child, and in her teens began to rebel against her privileged life. A turning point occurred when she was bussed to an all-white school for the gifted in St. Louis; she was, she says, unprepared for the hostility and harassment of white students.

Paulette Williams went on the Barnard College, where she majored in American studies, specializing in black American music and poetry. At Barnard she became active in the civil rights movement. After graduation in 1970 she went to the University of Southern California, teaching while earning a master's degree in American studies; the following year she changed her name, after consulting friends from the Xhosa tribe, who baptized her in the Pacific Ocean with her new African name. *Ntozake* means "she who comes with her own things"; *Shange* means "who walks like a lion."

Shange went on to teach in the women's studies program at Sonoma State College and began writing poetry intensively. Soon she was reading it at women's bars, accompanied by friends who were musicians and dancers. Out of these performances grew her first theatrical production, or "choreopoem," *For Colored Girls Who Have Considered Suicide/When the Rainbow Is Enuf*, a celebration of the survival and triumph of black women. Shange and her friend, choreographer Paula Moss, moved to New York City in the mid-1970s and first performed *For Colored Girls* in a jazz loft in SoHo in July 1975. The show evolved through a series of highly successful Off-Broadway productions, then opened uptown at the Booth Theatre in the fall of 1976; it was published in book form the next year. Shange, who had been in the show's cast since its first performance, remained in the Broadway production for one month. *For Colored Girls* played on Broadway for two years, then was taken by touring companies to Canada, the Caribbean, and other cities in the United States.

Shange's second major work to be staged in New York was *A Photograph: A Study of Cruelty*, termed a "poemplay" by its author. The production, which explores the relationship between a black woman dancer and her talented but unsuccessful photographer lover, ran at the Public Theatre during the 1977–78 season but received mixed reviews; it was published in a revised version as *A Photograph: Lovers in Motion* (1981). Shange did not appear in this play, having formed a three-woman ensemble called the Satin Sisters, who read their poetry against a background of jazz at the Public Theatre Cabaret.

Shange has written and performed in several theatrical pieces in New York in recent years, including *From Okra to Greens* (1978; published 1985). Her adaptation of Bertolt Brecht's play *Mother Courage and Her Children* was presented at the Public Theatre in 1980. Of her other plays, only *Spell #7* (1981) has been published. Her published books of verse include *Nappy Edges* (1978), *A Daughter's Geography* (1983), *Ridin' the Moon in Texas* (1987), and *The Love Space Demands* (1991). Shange has issued the novels *Sassafrass, Cypress & Indigo* (1982) and *Betsey Brown* (1985) as well as a volume of essays, *See No Evil* (1984).

▨ *Critical Extracts*

HAROLD CLURMAN   In a number of respects this work ⟨*For Colored Girls Who Have Considered Suicide/When the Rainbow Is Enuf*⟩ is unique. Its stress is on the experience of black women—their passionate outcry, as women, within the black community. There is no badmouthing the whites: feelings on that score are summed up in the humorously scornful lines addressed to a black man which begin: "ever since I realized there was someone callt a colored girl, a evil woman, a bitch or a nag, I been tryin' not to be that and leave bitterness in somebody elses cup. . . . I finally bein real no longer symmetrical and inervious to pain . . . so why don't we be white then and make everythin' dry and abstract wid no rhythm and no feelin' for sheer sensual pleasure. . . ." The woman who utters these words, like all the others, speaks not so much in apology or explanation of her black condition but in essential human protest against her black lover whose connection with her is the ordinary (white or black) callousness toward women. Thus she asserts "I've lost it / touch with reality / I know who's doin' it. . . . I should be unsure, if I'm still alive. . . . I survive on intimacy and to-morrow. . . . But bein' alive and bein' a woman and bein' colored is a metaphysical dilemma."

This gives only a pitifully partial notion of the pain and power, as well as the acrid wit—"so redundant in the modern world"—which much of the writing communicates. The thematic emphasis is constantly directed at the stupid crudity and downright brutality of their own men, which, whatever the causes, wound and very nearly destroy their women. These women have been driven to the very limits of their endurance (or "rainbow") and are desperately tired of hearing their men snivel that they're "sorry." Part of the joy in the performance lay in the ecstatic response of the women in the audience!

Harold Clurman, "Theatre," *Nation*, 1 May 1976, p. 542

JANET BROWN   Although *For Colored Girls* has many protagonists rather than one, its pattern of symbolic action is clearly a search for autonomy opposed by an unjust socio-sexual hierarchy. The search for autonomy in *For Colored Girls* succeeds, however, more thoroughly than in any of the other plays studied. Thus, it is the most idealistic of the plays examined as well.

The successful resolution to the search for autonomy is attributable first to the communal nature of the struggle. *For Colored Girls* has many agents who share in the same struggle, but just as significantly, none of these agents is able to transcend the unjust hierarchy alone. Rather the play's pattern of symbolic action shows a progression of sympathetic sharing and support among women culminating in the communal recitation and singing that ends the play.

Secondly, the play's optimistic resolution results from the agents' affirmations of self building through the play. The colored girl who at the beginning of the play "doesn't know the sound of her own voice: her infinite beauty," affirms by the end of the play that she has found God in herself. These two elements in the achievement of autonomy, sisterhood and self-realization, are symbolically united in the final song which affirms the holiness of self and which is sung by the whole community of women on stage.

Finally, the achievement of autonomy in *For Colored Girls* is not only socio-sexual or psychological but spiritual as well. The spirituality of the play's resolution, reflected in images of blessing hands, the spirits of women of the past haunting present-day women and the female god women find in themselves suggests the spiritual transcendence of sexism described by Mary Daly in *Beyond God the Father*. Such a transcendence, Daly says, will be "an ontological, spiritual revolution, pointing beyond the idolatries of sexist society and sparking creative action in and toward transcendence."

Just as Daly describes, the agents in *For Colored Girls* confront their own "non-being" in the fact of their "non-existence" as persons in the unjust hierarchy. Sechita has learned to disbelieve the grotesque distortion which is society's reflected image of her. The lady in sequins and feathers understands that without her costume she is nothing to the men who court her. The woman who lives in Harlem knows that she has no right to live and move freely in the world. ⟨. . .⟩

Thus, *For Colored Girls* is among the most idealistic of the plays studied, reflecting the feminist philosophy outlined by Daly more fully than any of the other plays studied. As Daly does, the play goes beyond denunciation of the unjust *status quo* to evoke an alternative, non-hierarchical order based on sororal community and a recognition of the worth of each individual. In *For Colored Girls* the agents' affirmation of individuality and community transcends the socio-sexual hierarchy, making the play an idealistic statement of the feminist impulse.

Janet Brown, *Feminist Drama: Definition and Critical Analysis* (Metuchen, NJ: Scarecrow Press, 1979), pp. 129–31

SANDRA HOLLIN FLOWERS   ⟨. . .⟩ there is definitely a crisis. Individually we have known this for some time, and lately black women as well as black men are showing growing concern about the steady deterioration of their relationships. Black literature, however, has lagged somewhat behind. The works which usually comprise Afro-American literature curricula and become part of general reading materials, for instance, show the position of the black man in America; but generally we see the black woman only peripherally as the protagonist's lover, wife, mother, or in some other supporting (or detracting) role. Certainly black women can identify with the predicament of black men. Black women can identify, for example, with the problems articulated in Ellison's *Invisible Man* because they share the same predicaments. But for black women the predicament of the black male protagonist is compounded by concerns which affect them on yet another level. This, then, is what makes *Colored Girls* an important work which ranks with Ellison's *Invisible Man*, Wright's *Native Son*, and the handful of other black classics—it is an artistically successful female perspective on a long-standing issue among black people. If, however, black men fail to acknowledge the significance of *Colored Girls*, if they resent it or insist that it does not speak to their concerns or is not important because it deals with "women's issues," then the crisis is more severe than any thought it to be.

Colored Girls is certainly woman's art but is also black art, or Third World art, as Shange probably would prefer to have it designated. Its language and dialect, its geography, its music, and the numerous allusions to Third World personalities make it an intensely cultural work. Many of these characteristics, however, are peculiar to Shange's upbringing, education, and experiences, with the result that the piece loses universality at points, as in the poem "Now I Love Somebody More Than." But even here, black audiences are sure to know which lady loved gardenias; they will know the Flamingoes and Archie Shepp and Imamu. Then there is the poem "Sechita" in which the dancer is linked to Nefertiti, hence to Africa and Olduvai Gorge, the "cradle of civilization"—all of which puts into perspective the cheapening of Sechita by the carnival audience. While "Sechita" speaks to the degradation of black womanhood, "Toussaint" speaks, with subtle irony, of the black woman's awakening to the black man.

Sandra Hollin Flowers, "*Colored Girls*: Textbook for the Eighties," *Black American Literature Forum* 15, No. 2 (Summer 1981): 51–52

SANDRA L. RICHARDS   Although the epistemology of experience within an African world view is inseparably cognitive *and* intuitive, Shange's protagonists, who are African people raised within the Western perspective, tend to feel that they must opt for one mode of knowledge over the other. Their Western heritage teaches them to see experience as fragmented rather than holistic and to value rational over emotional systems—hence, the dialectic of combat breath vs. will to divinity.

In *Spell #7*, subtitled a "quick magic trance manual for technologically stressed third world people," Shange tackles the iconography of "the nigger." Underneath a huge blackface minstrel mask, a master of ceremonies promises to perform a different kind of magic designed to reveal aspects of Black life authentically. The minstrel performers move through the pain of dance steps and memories associated with Black entertainment for white America on to the release of more private, improvisational party styles. In doing so, they banish the hideous mask along with their stage personae, thereby creating a safe space in which to expose secret hopes, fears, or dreams. 〈. . .〉

Shange draws upon two distinct traditions in contemporary Western theatre. In her commitment to combat breath, she achieves some of the effects described in Bertolt Brecht's dramatic theories. Chief among the German dramatist's tenets is the view that theatre must be an analytical forum which exposes bourgeois illusions and stimulates audiences to think objectively about the causes of social and personal ills. By constructing most of her plays as a series of poetic monologues, occasionally interrupted by conventional dialogue, she takes advantage of the telegraphic, elusive quality of poetry to encourage audiences to listen with close, critical attention; the resultant episodic structure diminishes the audiences' empathetic tendencies by denying them the opportunity to gain a more rounded sense of character. Additionally, the women's contrariness can function like Brecht's *Verfremdung* effect as an alienation device which keeps observers at a more objective, thinking distance from the characters. But because this contrariness also emotionally engages spectators, after a performance they are apt to demand answers to questions like, "Why are these women so strange; what does it mean? Is Shange describing reality accurately? How do I feel about what she describes?" Most importantly, in debating their responses to Shange's views, they can initiate a process of change in the world outside the theatre.

Sandra L. Richards, "Conflicting Impulses in the Plays of Ntozake Shange," *Black American Literature Forum* 17, No. 2 (Summer 1983): 74–75

CLAUDIA TATE   C.T.: When did you first know you were a writer?

SHANGE: I wrote when I was a child. I wrote stories. Then it became very difficult for me to get through school because somebody told me that "Negroes"—we weren't "black" then—didn't write. Some racial incident blocked my writing, and I just stopped. I can't remember exactly when it was. I started writing again in high school. I wrote some poetry, and it was published in a high-school magazine. That same year I'd been writing a lot of essays in English class, and I would always write about black people. Then I was told that I was beating a dead horse, so I stopped writing again. I started back at it when I was nineteen.

C.T.: Do you intend to include white people in your work?

SHANGE: I would never have a white person in a story I wrote with the possibile exception of "the white girl" [*Spell #7*] piece. I have no reason to do it. I was writing this real funny thing last night in my head. It was about my putting a story in a time capsule so that people in the year 20,000 could find it. It was a conversation with a white director: "Yes, I think it's wonderful that you think it's so good that you think it should be all white. Yes, I think it's fine that you think, even though the character is black, a white actress could do it so much better because you know black people really can't talk, although I remember that when my mother was speaking to me in my house, I never heard her talk like the white girl you're going to hire is going to talk like a black person. Then again, I'm only black, so how would I know how best to do it? Yes, I think it's wonderful that you think that because it's a black character you absolutely have to have this white actress play her because she's so good. And where in the world could you find a black person who could play her? I mean, after all it is a black character, and you know a black actress isn't perfectly trained to do this. So, yes, I think you should take my name off it and give me my money. Yes, it's perfectly all right if you use the story as is, but remember nobody in the world will believe that these people were really white. I mean, after all, they sweat."

This business is very sick. The theater is very sick. I feel really badly about it, though I'm compelled to keep working in this medium. What keeps me in the theater has nothing to do with an audience. It has to do with the adventure that's available in that little, three-dimensional stage. I can see a character who exists for me in one way become a real human body. That's a great adventure for me. I don't care. Theater gives my stuff what I cannot give it. Actors spend as many years learning how to act as I've spent learning how to write. Actors spend many years trying to give me something that I don't have. They make the piece come alive in a new way. For example, writers think they know how their characters sit. But if you give a piece to Avery Brooks or Laurie Carlos or Judy Brown or Mary Alice, how they sit can change everything. The timbre of their voices, how they walk, what they do, become available as a communal experience. You cannot read a book with somebody. Whereas, when you have a character there in front of you, that's somebody you know and anybody else sitting there with you would know also. Theater helps me, as a writer, known where I didn't give a character enough stuff, or where I told a lie. It's just a glorious thing to see actors make my characters come alive. But I don't like it when my artist-self has to be confined so that other people can understand. In the theater you have to do this; otherwise, they call your work "performance pieces," which means that you should be a white person and live downtown. Obviously, I can't do that.

Claudia Tate, "Ntozake Shange," *Black Women Writers at Work* (New York: Continuum, 1983), pp. 171–73

MAUREEN HONEY   Ntozake Shange dedicates her latest book of poems ⟨A *Daughter's Geography*⟩ to her family, most especially to her daughter; and it opens with an epigraph consisting of a poem written by a woman in revolutionary Cuba. Both the dedication and the epigraph anticipate the major theme of the book, which is that Third-World peoples are united by a long history and current oppression: that all of them are members of the same family with a common enemy. This theme is rendered by a voice more fierce than angry, more determined than defiant. It is a revolutionary volume, informed by a sensibility of struggle and hope. ⟨. . .⟩

This volume delights, inspires, and enlightens. Shange's political astuteness, ear for the street, and earthiness are a rare combination and one to be savored.

Maureen Honey, "A Sensibility of Struggle and Hope," *Prairie Schooner* 58, No. 4 (Winter 1984): 111–12

ELIZABETH BROWN-GUILLORY   Shange's theater pieces, beyond the commercially successful *For Colored Girls Who Have Considered Suicide/When the Rainbow Is Enuf*, have gone virtually unnoticed in critical studies. One case in point is Shange's *A Photograph: Lovers in Motion*, a drama that "comes closest to play form in that there is a logical progression of action and dialogue, with some detectable growth in at least one of the five characters." Though the stages of growth are not as readily detected as in plays by ⟨Alice⟩ Childress and ⟨Lorraine⟩ Hansberry, Michael in *A Photograph: Lovers in Motion* does embark on a journey that results in her wholeness. Shange's integrity as a dramatist who seeks to "transcend or bypass through music and dance the limitations of social and human existence" is not compromised in this theater piece, but rather is enhanced by the depth of these characters. Not only is *A Photograph: Lovers in Motion* an exploration of lives, but it is a drama that answers some of the whys of human behavior as the heroine grows and becomes a catalyst for the growth of her lover. ⟨. . .⟩

Blacks have traditionally turned to singing and dancing as coping strategies because those areas were open to blacks in white America. Shange's dramatic structure is exciting and innovative and, in at least one play, *A Photograph: Lovers in Motion*, the poet/playwright merges traditional dramatic structure with identifiable African American self-expression.

> Elizabeth Brown-Guillory, *Their Place on the Stage: Black Women Playwrights in America* (Westport, CT: Greenwood Press, 1988), pp. 97, 100

MARY K. DeSHAZER   *Spell #7* ⟨. . .⟩ focuses partly on sexist oppression but mainly on issues of color and class. The grotesque minstrel-show parody that begins the play jolts the audience with that familiar, insidious brand of racism once labeled comedy; and the magician's opening speech reveals the impact of internalized oppression on Black children who wanted desperately to be made white. "What cd any self-respectin colored american magician / do wit such an outlandish request," lou wonders as he recounts this story, besides put away his magic tools altogether, for "colored chirren believin in magic / waz becomin politically dangerous for the race." But now lou is back with his magic, he tells us, and "it's very colored / very now you see it / now you / dont mess wit me." The play quickly becomes an angry reclamation of those physical and psychic territories appropriated from Black Americans by racist terrorists: school kids, police, lynch mobs. "This is the borderline," one character, alec, claims in identifying himself and his dreams, "this is our space / we are not movin." The only safe territory, the characters reveal, is segregated space where magic rules and masks come off. But even a protected haven from which to speak cannot offset the daily horrors these unemployed performers face. Lily wishes for just one decent part, like lady macbeth or mother courage, only to be reminded by eli that she can't play lady macbeth when "macbeth's a white dude." Bettina's show remains open, "but if that director asks me to play it any blacker / i'm gonna have to do it in a mammy dress." What white audiences want is what they get, the actors bitterly remind us, and even selling out to racist taste doesn't pay the bills. Near the end of the play, alec offers one powerful suggestion that would make him less tired. A gong would sound for three minutes, all over the world, while "all the white people / immigrants & invaders / conquistadors & relatives of london debtors from georgia / kneel & apologize to us." This is not impossible, he insists; this is Black magic.

Mary K. DeShazer, "Rejecting Necrophilia: Ntozake Shange and the Warrior Revisioned," *Making a Spectacle: Feminist Essays on Contemporary Women's Theatre*, ed. Lynda Hart (Ann Arbor: University of Michigan Press, 1989), pp. 93–94

DEBORAH R. GEIS   Ntozake Shange's works defy generic classification: just as her poems (published in *Nappy Edges* and *A Daughter's Geography*) are also performance pieces, her works for the theater defy the boundaries of drama and merge into the region of poetry. Her most famous work, *for colored girls who have considered suicide/when the rainbow is enuf*, is subtitled "a choreopoem." Similarly, she has written *Betsey Brown* as a novel and then again (with Emily Mann) in play form, and her first work of fiction, *Sassafrass, Cypress & Indigo*, is as free with its narrative modes—including recipes, spells, letters—as Joyce was in *Ulysses*. Perhaps more so than any other practicing playwright, Shange has created a poetic voice that is uniquely her own—a voice which is deeply rooted in her experience of being female and black, but also one which, again, refuses and transcends categorization. Her works articulate the connection between the doubly "marginalized" social position of the black woman and the need to invent and appropriate a language with which to articulate a self.

In their revelation of such language, Shange's theatrical narratives move subtly and forcefully between the comic and the tragic. A brief passage from *for colored girls* underscores the precarious path between laughter and pain which Shange's characters discover they are forced to tread:

> distraught laughter fallin
> over a black girl's shoulder

it's funny/it's hysterical
the melody-less-ness of her dance
don't tell nobody, don't tell a soul
she's dancing on beer cans & shingles

These images associated with the word *hysterical* in this passage show the multilayered and interdependent qualities of the "black girl's" experience: *hysterical* connotes a laughter which has gone out of control, a madness historically—if not accurately—connected with femaleness. Moreover, the admonition "don't tell nobody, don't tell a soul" suggests the call to silence, the fear that to speak of her pain will be to violate a law of submission. The onlooker will aestheticize the dance or call attention to its comic qualities rather than realize the extent to which the dance and the laughter are a reaction against—and are even motivated by—the uncovering of pain.

The key here is the complexity, for Shange, of the performative experience. In her plays, especially *for colored girls* and *spell #7*, Shange develops her narration primarily through monologues because monologic speech inevitably places the narrative weight of a play upon its spoken language and upon the performances of the individual actors. But she does not use this device to develop "character" in the same fashion as Maria Irene Fornes and other Method-inspired playwrights who turn toward monologic language in order more expresssively to define and "embody" their characters both as women and as individuals. Rather, Shange draws upon the uniquely "performative" qualities of monologue to allow her actors to take on *multiple* roles and therefore to emphasize the centrality of *storytelling* to her work. This emphasis is crucial to Shange's articulation of a black feminist aesthetic (and to the call to humanity to accept that "black women are inherently valuable") on two counts. First, the incorporation of role-playing reflects the ways that blacks (as "minstrels," "servants," "athletes," etc.) are expected to fulfill such roles on a constant basis in Western society. Second, the space between our enjoyment of the "spectacle" of Shange's theater pieces (through the recitation of the monologues and through the dancing and singing which often accompany them), and our awareness of the urgency of her call for blacks/women to be allowed "selves" free of stereotypes, serves as a "rupturing" of the performance moment; it is the uncomfortableness of that space, that rupture, which moves and disturbs us.

Deborah R. Geis, "Distraught Laughter: Monologue in Ntozake Shange's Theater Pieces," *Feminine Focus: The New Women Playwrights*, ed. Enoch Brater (New York: Oxford University Press, 1989), pp. 210–11

PINKIE GORDON LANE   This collection of prose and poetry
⟨*Ridin' the Moon in Texas*⟩ calls forth so many images that the reader will
see him/herself in every page. It becomes an exposé of the reader's psyche.
Now that's saying a lot for a slender volume that takes "old wine and puts
it into new bottles." That is, Shange has employed the technique of using
visual art as a takeoff for creating the substance of her verbal images. Thus,
the book also contains color reproductions of exciting contemporary art in
various media: painting, sculpture, and photography. ⟨. . .⟩

These short, disconnected pieces (unlike ⟨Shange's⟩ earlier, loosely joined
narrative) contain lyricism, metaphor, and verbal subtleties (even elitism)
that range from the vernacular to the linguistically sophisticated. The book's
subjects range from a eulogy for a friend to social criticism. "Somewhere in
soweto there's a small girl / she's grown thin & frightened." These lines
from "Who Needs a Heart" allow us to experience what it is like living
under apartheid in South Africa as seen from the perspective of a black
child. ⟨. . .⟩

The book rocks, it rolls; but it also soars ethereally, shifting gears with
dizzying speed. Breathless in its Joycean stream of consciousness, it just as
quickly plummets to mother earth, its choice of style being adapted to the
mood and subject.

Pinkie Gordon Lane, [Review of *Ridin' the Moon in Texas*], *Black American Literature Forum* 24, No. 3 (Fall 1990): 578–79

EILEEN MYLES   All of the poems in *The Love Space Demands* take
up with the world. The riveting "crack annie" takes on the news. A crack
mother sacrifices her seven-year-old's pussy to her dealer, and the lead poem
of the book, "irrepressibly bronze, beautiful & mine," was written to work
with ⟨Robert⟩ Mapplethorpe's *Black Book*. It dives in unabashedly: "all my
life they've been near me / these men / some for a while like the / friend
of my father's who drove / each summer from denver to / st. louis / with
some different / white woman." The abandonment of the black woman by
the black man is the bold angle from which Shange broaches Mapplethorpe's
portraits. She looks at these men with admiration and lust. "look at me
pretty niggah," she says. Is it whiteness *and* homosexuality he's leaving her
for? Is that what she's saying? She moves on to "even tho' yr sampler broke

down on you," a poem that mumbles in your ear as its eye grazes the rushing landscape: "(you know where my beauty marks are / all / over / HARLEM)." In "intermittent celibacy" she rears up with "all i wanted / was to be / revealed." "abstinence / is not / celibacy," she explains, "cuz / when you filled with the Holy Ghost / every man / in the world / can smell it." "if I go all the way without you where would i go?" is as formidably persuasive on sexual abstinence as it is wildly Whitmanesque about its opposite. "i open / deep brown moist & black / cobalt sparklin everywhere." In "chastening with honey," she further expounds wiseguy spirituality: "like the Passion of Christ / which brought us Lent & we give up meat." Who are we? Whose poetry is it, so supremely confident, that its "I" or "we" can finally vanish into the nightmares of the urban landscape, from there smiting the reader's sensibility with simple reportage. Ultimately, she's taken on the work the media won't do. And she's written an unconditionally sex-positive book which suggests that having control of both the yes and the no switch constitutes real power.

Eileen Myles, "The Art of the Real," *Voice Literary Supplement* No. 98 (September 1991): 13

GETA LeSEUR   Ntozake Shange strives to fill a void in the female literary canon. With novels such as *sassafrass, cypress and indigo* in 1982 and *Betsey Brown* in 1985, and her dramatic choreopoem *For Colored Girls Who Have Considered Suicide/When the Rainbow Is Enuf* in 1977, she has joined the ranks of prominent black women who are giving a voice to their sisters. Through her works, the audience is exposed to the issues facing black women as they develop into adulthood. Issues of racism and sexism must be addressed in order for her characters to grow. Although each of her characters finds a definition of herself as a black woman, the paths taken are unique to the individual. Each woman fulfills herself with a particular interest from which she derives power, be that interest music, dancing, or weaving cloth. These women must also learn to relate to and separate themselves from the men in their lives. With strength of character, Shange's women imprint themselves permanently in our memories. Shange wrote in *sassafrass, cypress and indigo* that the novel is dedicated to "all women in struggle." Within that statement lies the power of her writing. Her works are about black women, but they are indeed for ALL women.

She uses Ebonics in a manner that does not exclude any gender, class or culture. Rather it invites all readers to enjoy as well as understand and confront issues facing us.

Shange said in a 1987 interview with Barbara Lyons for the *Massachusetts Review* that "unless black women are writing the pieces we're being left out in the same way we used to be left out of literature. We don't appear in things unless we write them ourselves." This oppression of black women is addressed by the characters in her writings. Black women are often deprived of their sense of childhood because they must immediately begin striving for recognition in the home and community. In *For Colored Girls . . .* one of the dancers, a lady in brown, sings solemnly "dark phrases of womanhood / of never havin been a girl" and continues with the realization that the invisibility of black women is like death. ⟨. . .⟩ As the choreopoem continues and with the heroines of her novels, Shange sings the black girl's song. Betsey, Sassafrass, Cypress, and Indigo tackle the invisibility of black women and carve their own places in society along with the nameless women dressed in the varied rainbow colors of *For Colored Girls. . . .* This play also explores the never-ending experiences of women—rape, abortion, abuse, love/hate relationships, mothering, death, formulating philosophies of life, third world concerns, what it means to be an Egyptian goddess, and "being colored and sorry at the same time."

Geta LeSeur, "From Nice Colored Girl to Womanist: An Exploration of Development in Ntozake Shange's Writings," *Language and Literature in the African American Imagination*, ed. Carol Aisha Blackshire-Belay (Westport, CT: Greenwood Press, 1992), pp. 167–68

▦ *Bibliography*

Melissa & Smith. 1976.

Sassafrass. 1976.

For Colored Girls Who Have Considered Suicide/When the Rainbow Is Enuf: A Choreopoem. 1977.

Nappy Edges (Love's a Lil Rough/Sometimes). 1978.

Three Pieces. 1981.

Some Men. 1981.

Spell #7. 1981.

A *Photograph: Lovers in Motion*. 1981.

Take the A Train. c. 1981.

Sassafrass, Cypress & Indigo. 1982.

A *Daughter's Geography*. 1983.

From Okra to Greens: A Different Love Story: Poems. 1984.

See No Evil: Prefaces, Essays & Accounts 1974–1983. 1984.

From Okra to Greens: A Different Kinda Love Story: A Play with Music and Dance. 1985.

Betsey Brown. 1985.

Ridin' the Moon in Texas: Word Paintings. 1987.

For Colored Girls Who Have Considered Suicide/When the Rainbow Is Enuf: A Choreopoem; and Spell #7. 1990.

The Love Space Demands: A Continuing Saga. 1991.

Plays: One. 1992.

I Live in Music. 1994.

Liliane. 1994.

◈ ◈ ◈

Alice Walker
b. 1944

ALICE MALSENIOR WALKER was born on February 9, 1944, in Eatonton, Georgia, the eighth child of sharecroppers Willie Lee and Minnie Tallulah (Grant) Walker. When she was eight she was blinded in her right eye after being accidentally shot with a BB gun by one of her brothers. She attended Spelman College from 1961 to 1963, then left to travel in Africa. She transferred to Sarah Lawrence College, where she received a B.A. in 1965. About this time she underwent a severe trauma in which she aborted a pregnancy and came close to suicide. In response to these events she took to writing, producing her first published short story, "To Hell with Dying," and the poems that would form her first collection of poetry. She married civil rights lawyer Melvyn Rosenman Leventhal in 1967; they had one child before their divorce in 1976.

During the late 1960s Walker participated in the civil rights movement in Mississippi. She wrote an essay, "The Civil Rights Movement: What Good Was It?," that won an *American Scholar* essay contest. She worked with Head Start programs in Mississippi and later served as writer in residence at Tougaloo College and Jackson State University.

Alice Walker has written several volumes of poetry, including *Once* (1968), *Revolutionary Petunias and Other Poems* (1973), *Good Night, Willie Lee, I'll See You in the Morning* (1979), *Horses Make a Landscape More Beautiful* (1984), and, most recently, *Her Blue Body Everything We Know: Earthling Poems 1965–1990 Complete* (1991). They have received considerable praise, particularly from the black and feminist communities.

Walker is, however, primarily known as a novelist. Her first novel, *The Third Life of Grange Copeland* (1970), depicts three generations in the life of a poor farm family. It was praised for the sensitivity with which the characters were drawn, but it received little attention from either popular or academic circles. In 1970 Walker discovered the work of Zora Neale Hurston, whom she would be instrumental in raising to the status of a major American author. Hurston's influence can be seen in many of the short stories Walker was writing in this period. Her second novel, *Meridian* (1976), is considered by many to be the best novel of the civil rights era. *The Color Purple* (1982), an epistolary novel concerning the growth to maturity of a poor black woman in an oppressive, brutish society, launched Walker to mainstream critical success and best-seller popularity. It received the 1983 Pulitzer Prize and the American Book Award, and was made into an Academy Award–nominated film by Steven Spielberg.

In 1989 Alice Walker published her fourth novel, *The Temple of My Familiar*, a work that resurrects some characters from *The Color Purple* but whose major action takes place in Africa. This novel was on the whole poorly received for its implausibility (a goddess informs the characters of the origin of women) and the stridency of its ideological message. Her fifth novel, *Possessing the Secret of Joy* (1992), however, fared better with reviewers. It deals with female circumcision and genital mutilation, the subject of a nonfiction book Walker published the next year in collaboration with Pratibha Parmar, *Warrior Masks*.

In addition to poetry and novels, Walker has written two volumes of short stories, *In Love and Trouble: Stories of Black Women* (1973) and *You Can't Keep a Good Woman Down* (1981); a biography of Langston Hughes for children; and a book of criticism and social commentary, *In Search of Our Mothers' Gardens: Womanist Prose* (1983). A selection of her essays, *Living by the Word*, appeared in 1988.

Walker has been a lecturer at Wellesley College and the University of Massachusetts, a writer in residence at the University of California at Berkeley, and the Fannie Hurst Professor of Literature at Brandeis University. She has also served as a contributing editor of *Ms.* magazine. Since 1978 she has lived in San Francisco.

◈ Critical Extracts

ALICE WALKER   Perhaps my Northern brothers will not believe me when I say there is a great deal of positive material I can draw from my "underprivileged" background. But they have never lived, as I have, at the end of a long road in a house that was faced by the edge of the world on one side and nobody for miles on the other. They have never experienced the magnificent quiet of a summer day when the heat is intense and one is so very thirsty, as one moves across the dusty cotton fields, that one learns forever that water is the essence of all life. In the cities it cannot be so clear to one that he is a creature of the earth, feeling the soil between the toes, smelling the dust thrown up by the rain, loving the earth so much that one longs to taste it and sometimes does.

Nor do I intend to romanticize the Southern black country life. I can recall that I hated it, generally. The hard work in the fields, the shabby houses, the evil greedy men who worked my father to death and almost broke the courage of that strong woman, my mother. No, I am simply saying that Southern black writers, like most writers, have a heritage of love and hate, but that they also have enormous richness and beauty to draw from. And, having been placed, as Camus says, "halfway between misery and the sun," they, too, know that "though all is not well under the sun, history is not everything."

No one could wish for a more advantageous heritage than that bequeathed to the black writer in the South: a compassion for the earth, a trust in humanity beyond our knowledge of evil, and an abiding love of justice. We inherit a great responsibility as well, for we must give voice to centuries not only of silent bitterness and hate but also of neighborly kindness and sustaining love.

> Alice Walker, "The Black Writer and the Southern Experience" (1970), *In Search of Our Mothers' Gardens: Womanist Prose* (San Diego: Harcourt Brace Jovanovich, 1983), pp. 20–21

MARK SCHORER   She is not a finished novelist. She has much to learn. Fortunately, what she has to learn are the unimportant lessons, that is, those that *can* be learned: some economy, formal shaping, stylistic tightening, deletion of points too repetitiously insisted upon, the handling of time, above all development rather than mere reversal of character. The important fictional qualities that she commands, those that she was born with, she has supremely.

> Mark Schorer, "Novels and Nothingness," *American Scholar* 40, No. 1 (Winter 1970–71): 172

JERRY H. BRYANT   My initial reaction to the first several stories of *In Love & Trouble* was negative. Miss Walker's search for ways to be new and different struck me as too willful and strained. I felt the same way about her earlier novel, *The Third Life of Grange Copeland*, whose style seemed too fine for the rough subject—the way two black men, a son and a father, try to degrade and destroy each other. But as I read on through these thirteen stories, I was soon absorbed by the density of reality they convey. They contain the familiar themes and situations of conventional black political and sociological fiction. There are black revolutionaries who read books and meet in small study groups, radical lady poets who read before black student audiences shouting "Right on!," and sharecroppers victimized by white landlords. But we see all these from genuinely new angles, from the point of view of the black woman or man totally absorbed in the pains of their inner life rather than the point of view of the protester or the newspaper headline. ⟨. . .⟩

But what I like most about these stories is what Miss Walker seems to like most about her people, the ones who are themselves, naturally and unself-consciously, and live by putting what they have to "everyday use," the title of one of her stories. She is best, therefore, not when she is depicting revolutionary consciousness or sophisticated awareness of the most recent rules of race relations, but when she is getting inside the minds of the confused, the ignorant, the inward-turning character, when she lets stand the mysterious and the ambiguous, and gives up explaining by doctrine the nature of her characters' lives. She can put a lump in the reader's throat even when she is a little sentimental. But what she can do most powerfully is make me feel the heat of her characters' lives, smell their singed bodies going up in literal and figurative flames of their own making. That is when I lose touch with myself as critic and interpreter and enter Miss Walker's created world of love and trouble.

Jerry H. Bryant, "The Outskirts of a New City," *Nation*, 12 November 1973, pp. 501–2.

GREIL MARCUS   At its best, ⟨. . .⟩ the tone of ⟨*Meridian* is⟩ flat, direct, measured, deliberate, with a distinct lack of drama. ⟨. . .⟩ And the tone is right; it's not the plot that carries the novel forward but *Meridian*'s attempt to resolve, or preserve the reality of, the questions of knowledge, history, and murder that Miss Walker introduces early on. The astonishing dramatic intensity that Walker brought to *The Third Life of Grange Copeland* would in *Meridian* blow those questions apart.

But such questions lead all too easily to high-flown language and to pretensions that fictional characters cannot support, which is why most "philosophical" novels are impossible to reread. Miss Walker does not always avoid this trap; though her tendency is to insist on the prosaic, to bring philosophy down to earth, *Meridian* at times seems to be floating straight to Heaven. The book tries to make itself a parable—more than a mere novel—or trades the prosaic for an inert symbolism that would seem to be intended to elevate the story but instead collapses it. In an early chapter, Meridian, age seven, finds a gold bar and rushes with it to her parents; they ignore her. She buries the gold (her unrecognized gifts) and finally forgets about it (and it will be years until she finds her gifts again). In college, as Meridian lies sick in bed, a halo forms around her head. Back in the South after the meeting in New York, she works alone persuading people, one at a time, to register to vote, organizing neighborhoods around local issues, and staging symbolic protests, which she calls, wonderfully, her "performances." This is beautifully presented and utterly convincing; each incident is memorable, shaped as a story in itself. But after every "performance" Meridian falls to the ground, paralyzed, and must be carried like a corpse back to wherever she is living. A hundred years ago, an author would simply have made Meridian an epileptic if we were meant to guess that she was sainted. ⟨. . .⟩

Meridian is interesting enough without all this—without symbolism and "higher meanings" that are one-dimensional and fixed. There is no mystery in these symbols—as there is in Meridian's ability to get through to Southern blacks, or in the questions of the rebel, murder, and limits—and a symbol without mystery, without suggestive power, is not really a symbol at all. But most of the book's scenes have the power its symbols lack, and its last chapters rescue Meridian's questions from a holy oblivion.

Greil Marcus, "Limits," *New Yorker*, 7 June 1976, p. 135

TRUDIER HARRIS   Walker's use of folk material is less prominent in her novel *The Third Life of Grange Copeland* (1970), but it is apparent. Folk material becomes significant in defining the relationship between

Grange and Ruth, his granddaughter. It is a way to seal the bond between them and to identify their unity against a hostile and un-understanding world. Even Josie, Grange's wife, is shut out of the bantering between Ruth and Grange, as she will later be physically excluded from their presence. Grange tells Ruth tales and generally entertains her on the nights when they sit around peeling oranges and shredding coconut in their Georgia farmhouse.

Although Grange knows "all the Uncle Remus stories by heart" and can produce even more exciting ones about John the trickster, he is not a mindless teller of tales solely for the sake of entertainment. Walker attributes to him the analytical ability that is often only implied in historical storytellers. Grange does not accept the benign Uncle Remus as historically accurate or even as having common sense. He criticizes Uncle Remus's stance and re-interprets it with political connotations and renewed emphasis on social awareness, especially black social awareness. ⟨. . .⟩ It is obvious from Grange's attitude that Walker does not view the folk culture as something separate from life, but as an integral part of one's existence. The change Grange would impose on Uncle Remus is synonymous with the changes that take place in the novel. From sharecropping with its shuffling, head-bowing, acquiescing days, Walker moves Grange and his family into the Sixties and the days of Martin Luther King. Marching, voting, and statesmanship do indeed replace the tendency to minstrelize.

Grange also tells Ruth stories about "two-heads and conjurers; strange men and women more sensitive than the average spook," but he laments that "folks what can look at things in more than one way is done got rare." Grange's feelings are again commensurate with the theme of change that Walker explores in the novel. ⟨. . .⟩

Alice Walker is assuredly in the literary and historical traditions of the recording and creative use of black folk materials. Like ⟨Charles W.⟩ Chesnutt, she uses such material for social commentary. But her environment allows more freedom of usage than did Chesnutt's; where he had to embed his statements about slavery in an elaborate framing device and filtered them through the eyes of a white Northerner, Walker can be obvious, blatant, and direct about social injustices. Like ⟨Zora Neale⟩ Hurston, Walker reflects a keen insight into the folk mind. As Hurston reflected the nuances of relationships between men and women in *Their Eyes Were Watching God* (1937) through the use of the folk culture, so too does Walker use this culture to reflect relationships between the characters in *The Third Life of Grange Copeland*.

Trudier Harris, "Folklore in the Fiction of Alice Walker: A Perpetuation of Historical and Literary Traditions," *Black American Literature Forum* 11, No. 1 (Spring 1977): 7–8

ROBERT TOWERS   In *The Color Purple* Alice Walker moves backward in time, setting her story roughly (the chronology is kept vague) between 1916 and 1942—a period during which the post-Reconstruction settlement of black status remained almost unaltered in the Deep South. Drawing upon what must be maternal and grandmaternal accounts as well as upon her own memory and observation, Miss Walker, who is herself under forty, exposes us to a way of life that for the most part existed beyond or below the reach of fiction, and that has hitherto been made available to us chiefly through tape-recorded reminiscences: the life of poor, rural Southern blacks as it was experienced by their womenfolk. Faulkner, to be sure, touches upon it in his rendering of the terrified Nancy in "That Evening Sun," but her situation, poignant though it is, comes to us largely through the eyes and ears of the white Compson children; similarly, the majestic figure of Dilsey in *The Sound and the Fury* is, for all its insight, sympathy, and closeness of observation, a white man's portrait of a house servant, idealized and, one imagines, subtly distorted by the omission of those moments of sickening rage (as distinct from exasperation) which must have been an ingredient in Dilsey's complex attitude toward the feckless and demanding family that employs her. The suffering, submissive women in Wright's *Native Son* are no doubt authentically portrayed—but again from a man's point of view; furthermore, they are city dwellers, poor but still different from the dirt-poor countryfolk. ⟨. . .⟩

I cannot gauge the general accuracy of Miss Walker's account or the degree to which it may be colored by current male-female antagonisms within the black community—controversial reports of which from time to time appear in print. I did note certain improbabilities: it seems unlikely that a woman of Celie's education would have applied the word "amazons" to a group of feisty sisters or that Celie, in the 1930s, would have found fulfillment in designing and making pants for women. In any case, *The Color Purple* has more serious faults than its possible feminist bias. Alice Walker

still has a lot to learn about plotting and structuring what is clearly intended
to be a realistic novel. The revelations involving the fate of Celie's lost
babies and the identity of her real father seem crudely contrived—the stuff
of melodrama or fairy tales. ⟨. . .⟩

Fortunately, inadequacies which might tell heavily against another novel
seem relatively insignificant in view of the one great challenge which Alice
Walker has triumphantly met: the conversion, in Celie's letters, of a subliter-
ate dialect into a medium of remarkable expressiveness, color, and poignancy.
I find it impossible to imagine Celie apart from her language; through it,
not only a memorable and infinitely touching character but a whole sub-
merged world is vividly called into being. Miss Walker knows how to avoid
the excesses of literal transcription while remaining faithful to the spirit
and rhythms of Black English. I can think of no other novelist who has so
successfully tapped the poetic resources of the idiom.

> Robert Towers, "Good Men Are Hard to Find," *New York Review of Books*, 12 August
> 1982, pp. 35–36

GERALD EARLY   ⟨. . .⟩ *The Color Purple* remains an inferior novel
not because it seems so self-consciously a "woman's novel" and not because
it may be playing down to its mass audience, guilty of being nothing more
than a blatant "feel-good" novel, just the sort of book that is promoted
among the nonliterary. *The Color Purple* is a poor novel because it ultimately
fails the ideology that it purports to serve. It fails to be subversive enough
in substance; it only *appears* to be subversive. Indeed, far from being a
radically feminist novel, it is not even, in the end, as good a bourgeois
feminist novel as *Uncle Tom's Cabin*, written 130 years earlier. Its largest
failure lies in the novel's inability to use (ironically, subversively, or even
interestingly) the elements that constitute it. Take, for instance, these
various Victorianisms that abound in the work: the ultimate aim of the
restoration of a gynocentric, not patriarchal family; the reunion of lost
sisters; the reunion of mother and children; the glorification of cottage
industry in the establishment of the pants business; bequests of money and
land to the heroine at novel's end; Celie's discovery that her father/rapist
is really a cruel stepfather; the change of heart or moral conversion of Mr.
Albert, who becomes a feminized man at the end; the friendship between
Shug Avery and Celie, which, despite its overlay of lesbianism (a tribute
to James Baldwin's untenable thesis that nonstandard sex is the indication

of a free, holy, thoroughly unsquare heterosexual heart), is nothing more than the typical relationship between a shy ugly duckling and her more aggressive, beautiful counterpart, a relationship not unlike that between Topsy and Little Eva. Shug convinces Celie that she is not black and ugly, that somebody loves her, which is precisely what Eva does for Topsy. For Walker, these clichés are not simply those of the Victorian novel but of the *woman's* Victorian novel. This indicates recognition of and paying homage to a tradition; but the use of these clichés in *The Color Purple* is a great deal more sterile and undemanding than their use in, say, *Uncle Tom's Cabin*. Together, for Walker, these clichés take on a greater attractiveness and power than for the female Victorian, since they are meant to represent a series of values that free the individual from the power of the environment, the whim of the state, and the orthodoxy of the institution. The individual still has the power to change, and that power supersedes all others, means more than any other. Human virtue is a reality that is not only distinct from all collective arrangements except family; in the end, it can be understood only as being opposed to all collective arrangements. But all of this is only the bourgeois fascination with individualism and with the ambiguity of Western family life, in which bliss is togetherness while having a room of one's own. ⟨. . .⟩

What Walker does in her novel is allow its social protest to become the foundation for its utopia. Not surprisingly, the book lacks any real intellectual or theological rigor or coherence, and the fusing of social protest and utopia is really nothing more than confounding and blundering, each seeming to subvert the reader's attention from the other. One is left thinking that Walker wishes to thwart her own ideological ends or that she simply does not know how to write novels. In essence, the book attempts to be revisionist salvation history and fails because of its inability to use or really understand history.

Gerald Early, "*The Color Purple* as Everybody's Protest Art," *Antioch Review* 44, No. 3 (Summer 1986): 271–73

LAUREN BERLANT   *The Color Purple*'s strategy of inversion, represented in its elevation of female experience over great patriarchal events, had indeed aimed to critique the unjust practices of racism and sexism that violate the subject's complexity, reducing her to a generic biological sign.

But the model of personal and national identity with which the novel leaves us uses fairy-tale explanations of social relations to represent itself: this fairy tale embraces America for providing the Afro-American nation with the right and the opportunity to own land, to participate in the free market, and to profit from it. In the novel's own terms, American capitalism thus has contradictory effects. On one hand, capitalism veils its operations by employing racism, using the pseudonatural discourse of race to reduce the economic competitor to a subhuman object. In Celie's parental history, *The Color Purple* portrays the system of representation characteristic of capital relations that *creates* the situation of nationlessness for Afro-Americans.

But the novel also represents the mythic spirit of American capitalism as the vehicle for the production of an Afro-American utopia. Folkpants, Unlimited is an industry dedicated to the reproduction and consumption of a certain system of representation central to the version of Afro-American "cultural nationalism" enacted by *The Color Purple*. But Folkpants, Unlimited also participates in the profit motive: the image of the commodity as the subject's most perfect self-expression is the classic fantasy bribe of capitalism. The illogic of a textual system in which the very force that disenfranchises Afro-Americans provides the material for their national reconstruction is neither "solved" by the novel nor raised as a paradox. The system simply stands suspended in the heat of the family reunion on Independence Day.

What saves Celie and Nettie from disenfranchisement is their lifelong determination to learn, to become literate: Nettie's sense that knowledge was the only route to freedom from the repressive family scene gave her the confidence to escape, to seek "employment" with Samuel's family, to record the alternative and positive truth of Pan-African identity, to face the truth about her own history, to write it down, and to send it to Celie, against all odds. Writing was not only the repository of personal and national hope; it became a record of lies and violences that ultimately produced truth.

Lauren Berlant, "Race, Gender, and Nation in *The Color Purple*," *Critical Inquiry* 14, No. 4 (Summer 1988): 857–58

J. M. COETZEE   Readers of *The Color Purple* will remember that part of the book—the less convincing part—consists of letters from Miss Celie's missionary sister about her life in Africa.

The Temple of My Familiar again bears a message from Africa, but this time in a far more determined manner. The message reaches us via Miss Lissie, an ancient goddess who has been incarnated hundreds of times, usually as a woman, sometimes as a man, once even as a lion. Less a character than a narrative device, Lissie enables Alice Walker to range back in time to the beginnings of (wo)man.

Here are just three of the ages in human evolution that Lissie lives through:

First, an age just after the invention of fire, when humanfolk live in separate male and female tribes, at peace with their animal "familiars." Here Lissie is incarnated as the first white-skinned creature, a man with insufficient melanin, who flees the heat of Africa for Europe. Hating the sun, he [invents] an alternative god in his own image, cold and filled with rage.

Next, an age of pygmies, when the man tribe and the woman tribe visit back and forth with each other and with the apes. This peaceful, happy age ends when men invent warfare, attack the apes and impose themselves on women as their sole familiars. Thus, says Ms. Walker (rewriting Rousseau and others), do patriarchy and the notion of private property come into being.

Third, the time of the war waged by Europe and monotheistic Islam against the Great Goddess of Africa. The instrument of the warfare is the slave trade (Lissie lives several slave lives). Its emblem is the Gorgon's head, the head of the Goddess, still crowned with the serpents of wisdom, cut off by the white hero-warrior Perseus.

These episodes from the past of (wo)mankind give some idea of the sweep of the myth Alice Walker recounts, a myth that inverts the places assigned to man and woman, Europe and Africa, in the male-invented myth called history. In Ms. Walker's counter-myth, Africa is the cradle of true religions and civilization, and man a funny, misbegotten creature with no breasts and an elongated clitoris. ⟨. . .⟩

History is certainly written by people in positions of power, and therefore principally by men. The history of the world—including Africa—is by and large a story made up by white males. Nevertheless, history is not just storytelling. There are certain brute realities that cannot be ignored. Africa has a past that neither the white male historian nor Ms. Walker can simply invent. No doubt the world would be a better place if, like Fanny and Suwelo, we could live in bird-shaped houses and devote ourselves to bread making and massage, and generally adopt Fanny's mother's gospel: "We are all of us in heaven already!" Furthermore, I readily concede that inventing a better world between the covers of a book is as much as even the most gifted of us can hope to do to bring about a better real world. But whatever new worlds and new histories we invent must carry conviction: they must be possible worlds, possible histories, not untethered fantasies; and they must be born of creative energy, not dreamy fads.

> J. M. Coetzee, "The Beginnings of (Wo)man in Africa," *New York Times Book Review*, 30 April 1989, p. 7

ALICE HALL PETRY   Walker's disinclination for exposition, and the concomitant impression that many of her stories are outlines or fragments of longer works, is particularly evident in a technique which mars even her strongest efforts: a marked preference for "telling" over "showing." This often takes the form of summaries littered with adjectives. In "Advancing Luna," for example, the narrator waxes nostalgic over her life with Luna in New York: "our relationship, always marked by mutual respect, evolved into a warm and comfortable friendship which provided a stability and comfort we both needed at that time." But since ⟨. . .⟩ the narrator comes across as vapid and self-absorbed, and since the only impressions she provides of Luna are rife with contempt for this greasy-haired, Clearasil-daubed, poor-little-rich-white-girl from Cleveland, the narrator's paean to their mutual warmth and friendship sounds ridiculous. No wonder critic Katha Pollitt stated outright that she "never believed for a minute" that the narrator and Luna were close friends. Even more unfortunate is Walker's habit of telling the reader what the story is about, of making sure that he doesn't overlook a single theme. For example, in "The Abortion," the heroine Imani, who is just getting over a traumatic abortion, attends the memorial service of a local girl, Holly Monroe, who had been shot to death while returning home from her high school graduation. Lest we miss the point, Walker spells it out for us: "every black girl of a certain vulnerable age *was* Holly Monroe. And an even deeper truth was that Holly Monroe was herself [i.e., Imani]. Herself shot down, aborted on the eve of becoming herself." Similarly transparent, here is one of the last remarks in the story "Source." It is spoken by Irene, the former teacher in a federally-funded adult education program, to her ex-hippie friend, Anastasia/Tranquility: " 'I was looking toward "government" for help; you were looking to Source [a California guru]. In both cases, it was the wrong direction—*any* direction that is away from ourselves is the wrong direction.' " The irony of their parallel situation is quite clear without having Irene articulate her epiphany in an Anchorage bar. Even at the level of charactonyms, Walker "tells" things to her reader. We've already noted the over-used "he"/"she" device for underscoring sex roles, but even personal names are pressed into service. For example, any reasonably perceptive reader of the vignette "The Flowers" will quickly understand the story's theme: that one first experiences reality in all its harshness while far from home, physically and/or experientially; one's immediate surroundings are comparatively "innocent." The reader would pick up on the innocence of nearsightedness even if the main character, ten-year-old Myop, hadn't been named after myopia. Likewise, "The Child Who Favored Daughter" is actually marred by having the father kill his daughter because he confuses her with his dead sister named "Daughter." The hints of incest, the unclear cross-generational identities, and the murky Freudian undercurrents are sufficiently obvious without the daughter/Daughter element: it begins to smack of Abbott and Costello's "Who's on First?" routine after just a few pages. Alice Walker's preference for telling over showing suggests a mistrust of her readers, or her texts, or both.

Alice Hall Petry, "Alice Walker: The Achievement of the Short Fiction," *Modern Language Studies* 19, No. 1 (Winter 1989): 21–22

CHARLES R. LARSON   Fiction and conviction make strange bedfellows. Nor am I convinced that novels that resurrect characters from a writer's earlier work are likely to be as imaginative and as artful as the result of the initial inspiration. But one does not have to read many pages of *Possessing the Secret of Joy* to realize that Alice Walker has not foisted her subject—female circumcision—upon us; instead, this writer of bold artistry challenges us to feel and to think. Here is a novel—and a subject—whose time has surely come. ⟨. . .⟩

The novel's ironic beginning is patently romantic. There is joy in Tashi and Adam's initial lovemaking, in spite of their conflicting backgrounds. Because of her conversion to Christianity, Tashi has not been traditionally circumcised. And Adam, the African-American missionary's son, appears not to harbor the Puritan layers of guilt typical of missionaries at the time—though Walker uses no dates, apparently the 1920s or '30s—the story begins.

What, in fact, can possibly diminish their happiness? The marriage appears destined to become a union of their complementary spirits and yearnings for togetherness.

But then Tashi wavers. As Adam's future wife, in America, shouldn't she attempt to retain as much of her African culture as possible? Should she be circumcised? The operation, she feels, will join her to her sisters, "whom she envisioned as strong, invincible. Completely woman. Completely African." ⟨. . .⟩

⟨. . .⟩ How is it possible, ⟨Tashi⟩ asks herself, that the person who administered her own excision ⟨. . .⟩ could be a woman? The question takes her back to Africa, to her Olinka people, and to the resolution of her fate. Though it would be unfair to reveal the end of her story—Tashi's final act of defiance—a part of her understanding of her ordeal can be noted: "The connection between mutilation and enslavement that is at the root of the domination of women in the world." It's a chilling realization, not simply related to Tashi's own culture, but central to images of female victimization worldwide. Tashi says: "It's in all the movies that terrorize women . . . The man who breaks in. The man with the knife . . . But those of us whose chastity belt was made of leather, or of silk and diamonds, or of fear and not of our own flesh . . . we worry. We are the perfect audience, mesmerized by our unconscious knowledge of what men, with the collaboration of our mothers, do to us."

Charles R. Larson, "Against the Tyranny of Tradition," Washington Post Book World, 5 July 1992, pp. 1, 14

DONNA HAISTY WINCHELL   The Alice Walker of the 1980s and early 1990s comes across as a woman at peace with herself. She has spent half a literary lifetime tracing women's search for self, including her own. Ironically, her harshest critics have focused on her portrayal not of women, but of men. One regret that she has is that such criticism merely succeeds once more in drawing attention away from injustices done to women. Another is that people tend to see only the negative behavior of her male characters.

Walker told Oprah Winfrey in 1989, "Why is it that they only see, they can only identify the negative behavior? . . . I think it's because it's the negative behavior, the macho behavior, that they see as male behavior and that when the men stop using that behavior, when the men become gentle, when the men become people you can talk to, when they are good grandparents, when they are gentle people, they are no longer considered men and there is an inability even to see them." Critics don't often "see," or at least don't remember, that near the end of *The Color Purple,* a reformed Albert asks Celie to marry him again, this time in spirit as well as flesh. They forget that Grange Copeland comes back from his "second life" in New York a new and responsible man—and a loving grandfather. Truman Held takes on the burden that Meridian finally puts down when she walks away, refusing to be a martyr. And Suwelo in *Temple of My Familiar* grows from using Carlotta's body without considering her pain to recognizing that she is far more than blind flesh, that indeed all women are. At the end of the novel, he has left university teaching and is learning carpentry, although he suffers pangs of guilt over the requisite slaughter of trees.

Walker already saw a "new man" beginning in some of her poetry from the 1970s. At first, she thought that new man would be one who, like Christ, put love in front and the necessary clenched fist behind, as she explains in "The Abduction of Saints." However, by the time she wrote the dedication to the 1984 volume that contains this poem, *Good Night, Willie Lee, I'll See You in the Morning,* she had set a slightly different standard for the new man. Her ideal man's rebellion now takes a more subtle form; he doesn't need fists. She calls him simply "the quiet man." Walker considers such a new, nurturing man essential for the survival of the planet.

Donna Haisty Winchell, *Alice Walker* (New York: Twayne, 1992), pp. 132–33

Bibliography

Once. 1968.

The Third Life of Grange Copeland. 1970.

Five Poems. 1972.

Revolutionary Petunias and Other Poems. 1973.

In Love and Trouble: Stories of Black Women. 1973.

Langston Hughes, American Poet. 1974.

Meridian. 1976.

The Women's Center Reid Lectureship, November 11, 1975: Papers (with June Jordan). 1976.

I Love Myself When I Am Laughing . . . and Then Again When I Am Looking
    Mean and Impressive: A Zora Neale Hurston Reader (editor). 1979.

Good Night, Willie Lee, I'll See You in the Morning. 1979.

Beyond What. 1980.

You Can't Keep a Good Woman Down. 1981.

The Color Purple. 1982.

In Search of Our Mothers' Gardens: Womanist Prose. 1983.

While Love Is Unfashionable. 1984.

Horses Make a Landscape Look More Beautiful. 1984.

The Alice Walker Calendar for 1986. 1985.

To Hell with Dying. 1987.

From Alice Walker. 1988.

Living by the Word: Selected Writings 1973–1987. 1988.

The Temple of My Familiar. 1989.

Finding the Green Stone. 1991.

Her Blue Body Everything We Know: Earthling Poems 1965–1990 Complete.
    1991.

Possessing the Secret of Joy. 1992.

Warrior Masks: Female Genital Mutilation and the Sexual Blinding of Women
    (with Pratibha Parmar). 1993.

Everyday Use. Ed. Barbara Christian. 1994.

Jay Wright

b. 1935

JAY WRIGHT was born on May 25, 1935, in Albuquerque, New Mexico, the son of Leona Dailey and Mercer Murphy Wright. Wright attended high school in San Pedro, California, and, after graduation, served in the U.S. Army. In 1961 he received a B.A. from the University of California at Berkeley, briefly attended the Union Theological Seminary in New York, and attended postgraduate courses at Rutgers University, earning an M.A. in 1966.

Wright has chiefly received critical attention for his poetry. He draws on his formal education and knowledge of European literary traditions as well as the history of black Americans and anthropological studies of African and New World civilizations. Ritual and mythology also find a place in his poems.

Wright's first published volume was a small chapbook of poems, *Death as History* (1967); it received little attention, but many of the poems included in it were reprinted in *The Homecoming Singer* (1971), Wright's first major collection. The poems are greatly influenced by events in Wright's life, especially his artistic and spiritual development. Unlike other black American writers who draw on cultural connections to the agrarian South or the industrialized North, Wright uses the geography of the Southwest to relate, symbolically, the social alienation experienced by blacks in America.

Many of the themes found in *The Homecoming Singer* reappear in *Soothsayers and Omens* (1976) and *Dimensions of History* (1976). These volumes reflect Wright's travels in Mexico and in Scotland, where he stayed from 1971 to 1973 as a Fellow in Creative Writing at Dundee University. The poems in these two collections unite a quest for personal identity with an exploration of a mythological world view.

It was not until the publication of *The Double Invention of Komo* (1980), however, that Wright's ambitious themes were more successfully synthesized into a historical ritualized mythology. This long and complex poem utilizes a cosmogony conceived by the Komo, an all-male society that exists within the Bambara tribe and other tribes in Africa. A young man's initiation into this society serves as a symbol for the emotional maturation of the individual.

Several other collections of poetry have appeared in the last decade: *Explications/Interpretations* (1984), *Elaine's Book* (1988), and *Boleros* (1991), all continuing the search for metaphysical truth by means of ritual and myth derived from a wide array of Eastern and Western cultures. A *Selected Poems* appearing in 1987 cemented Wright's reputation as a major American poet, in spite of frequent criticisms of the difficulty and obscurity of much of his work.

As a dramatist Wright has also been successful, although to date only one of his plays, *Balloons* (1968), has been published in book form. Other, briefer plays have appeared in periodicals: *Love's Equator* (*Callaloo*, Fall 1983), *The Death and Return of Paul Batuata* (*Hambone*, Fall 1984), and *The Adoration of Fire* (*Southern Review*, Summer 1985). These plays, and other unpublished ones, develop the same mythological and religious themes as his poetry. Wright also wrote some plays for California radio stations in the 1960s.

Wright has been poet in residence at Tougaloo College and has taught at Talladega College and Yale University. He was the recipient of a Hodder Fellow in Playwriting at Princeton University in 1970–71. He currently resides in Piermont, New Hampshire.

Critical Extracts

DAVID KALSTONE   Part of the point of Wright's title ⟨*The Homecoming Singer*⟩ is its tense. The homecoming singer is always approaching and never making the identifications he desires. His poems are about wishes to submerge himself, to recapture the affections of his old life or to be released into fiercer strength. His verse resembles prose; yet the lines pause at points where he branches out with participles and oddities of syntax to discover what energies are available in worlds he can't belong to. The rhythms—there are few full stops—deceive us into sharing others' dreams.

The book takes its most important turn when Wright comes to suspect his conjury and to see his freedom as thwarted vision:

You travel in cities
that travel in you,
lost in the ache
of knowing none.

Living in Mexico—the occasion for some of his best poems—chastens
and challenges him. Its foreignness heightens the pleasures and penalties
of living at a distance from his subjects. In the intense "Reflections Before
the Charity Hospital," he turns against his own vicarious impulses. After
some fierce attempts to imagine life inside the hospital walls, he sees his
own life as a kind of shrunken voyeurism:

It is not death
that I have felt within these walls.
It is the senseless, weightless,
time-denying feeling of not being here.

At this point *The Homecoming Singer* moves away from novelistic experience, the particulars of memory and description, to a technique more adven-
turous and visionary. The role of the youthful observer threatens to swallow
him; he turns to surrealistic landscapes of the mind.

David Kalstone, "Black Energies in a White Society," *New York Times Book Review*,
30 July 1972, pp. 4, 15

DUDLEY RANDALL   I was first struck by the length of the book
⟨*The Homecoming Singer*⟩. It has 95 pages of poetry. Then I was struck by
the length of the poems. There are no four-line or eight-line or even twelve-
or fourteen-line poems. One remembers how Catullus compressed a world
of excruciation into two lines, in *"odi et amo."* Most of these poems are a
page long. Some of them cover two or three pages, although I did read one
poem of 21 lines and another of 19.

But what has the length of a poem got to do with its quality? Doesn't a
poet have the right to make his poems as long as he wants to? Of course
he has. But it is also desirable to inspire the reader to turn the pages. There
must be some suspense in the action, some energy in the rhythm, some
power in the emotion, some surprise in the phrases, to motivate the reader
to turn the pages to see what is on the next one. I turned these pages very
slowly. That is why this review is so late.

But there were some poems that stimulated me to turn the pages rapidly.
"An Invitation to Madison County" has the same brooding sense of latent

terror that permeates Robert Hayden's "A Ballad of Remembrance" and
that a Black person feels in any Southern town.

> Fifteen minutes in the city,
> and nothing has happened.
> No one has asked me to move over
> for a small parade of pale women,
> or called me nigger, or asked me where I'm from.

Perhaps this was because of the shared Black experience. But "Jalapeña
Gypsies" was not about the Black experience, and I read it eagerly. And
the poems about Wright's father were moving.

Dudley Randall, [Review of The Homecoming Singer], Black World 22, No. 11 (September 1973): 90

HAROLD BLOOM   I have not read a contemporary black poet who
seems to me as important and permanent a writer as Jay Wright, whose
fourth book, *Soothsayers and Omens*, adds to a distinguished, difficult and
absurdly neglected body of work. Jay Wright is a learned, mythological poet,
whose difficulties rise not out of the initial strangeness of African mythology
but out of the intricate allegories of his interpretations.

Harold Bloom, "Harold Bloom on Poetry," New Republic, 26 November 1977, p. 26

DARRYL PINCKNEY   Much of what is widely admired in modern
poetry is difficult in one sense or another. But there is a kind of obscurity
that repels, one that has to do with deceit or delusion. Every poem has its
strategic laws, and unraveling them is part of the joy of reading. Then why
is it hard to care whether one can or cannot breathe the thin, piercing air
of Wright's lofty levels of meaning? The incredible monotony of this poem
⟨*The Double Invention of Komo*⟩ betrays the strain of the idea. It does not
have much convincing speculative force, and for all the intricacies of its
surface, the language of this poem does not speak to the ear with any
urgency, intimacy, or power.

   This is a poem about escape, rebirth, consciousness, discovery, framed
by stages of an initiation right. It begins "This is the language of desire /
bana yiri kqrq . . ." and ends "You present me to sacred things. / I am reborn

into a new life. / My eyes open to Komo" in the same key, in the same tone, part of the aggressive complacency of enlightenment or religious feeling. Throughout, there is a discourse with history, both general and private, and about modes of perception, dulled by an utter opacity, which may be a form of shrewdness. The lack of drama slows the movement of the poem, though voices call out from a wood, from a village, from Paris, from Los Angeles, Berlin, Rome, Florence, Venice, Bad Nauheim, Albuquerque, Mexico City. Perhaps this is a poem about naming things, identifying with things, becoming things, the thingness of things, oneness, or "coming into the word"—large abstractions broken into steps that are meant to correspond to the process of acquiring knowledge. The initiate is a pilgrim, a *peregrinus*, insistent on what might pass for the classical mood. But what is discovered seems predetermined. This initiate has no need for humility, awe, or passion. He can, after all, follow Dante into exile—"Let sister Florence / truss herself in virtue"—and not contract malaria.

⟨. . .⟩ Page after page of the merely declarative, very prose-like, passage after passage of symbols mercilessly recapitulated, of lines that do not form true images. "As your initiate's agent on creation's knife / I open the membrane of my celebrant's voice." Or: "There is a tree that is divine. / Its scalar leaves reveal / a scapulary mother at its base." It might not be to the point to ask to understand the lines but the inner landscape Wright, apparently, is trying to open isn't very evocative or intriguing. Surrealism, if anything, has made it difficult for the surreal to move us.

Darryl Pinckney, "You're in the Army Now," *Parnassus: Poetry in Review* 9, No. 1 (Spring–Summer 1981): 307–8

CHARLES H. ROWELL   ROWELL: Most of your poems published after 1971 force me to rethink and re-evaluate my own concept of *the poem* or of *poetry*. What is a poem—or, what do you, a working poet, conceive poetry to be? And what are its functions? My questions seem strange, I'm certain, in 1984, but your poetry evokes them from me. The main of your poetry after *The Homecoming Singer* (1971; the poems in section two of *Soothsayers and Omens*, 1976, are, however, similar to those in *The Homecoming Singer*) is quite different as constructs, for example, from the contemporary poetry I have read.

WRIGHT: Theory is the angel in twentieth century intellectual life, but I'll risk a hip. I sometimes enjoy setting forth my paradigmatic relationship to the words *poetry* and *poem*. I almost said derivational, but that leads us into the tricky area of fixed laws, and any conception of fixed law introduces the troubling necessity of finding the origin of such a law. I suppose I shouldn't worry about that. So much of Anglo-American, and, unfortunately, black Afro-American, talk about poetry simply ignores that problem, and sets out a comfortable notion of poetry that accepts unspecified (and, when specified, contradictory) compositional rules. In developing my theory, I've begun by asking whether it is not true that poetry is what a particular literary community at a particular time says it is. The literary histories available to us suggest that this is so, up to a point. I haven't gone far, but you can see that I've already begun by acknowledging that no poet can be without the civilizing impress of history and tradition. Clapping that mathematical word, derivational, on the table wasn't as ingenuous as it may have seemed to you. Poetry, if I may rearrange some bones for a moment, does deduce one function from another. In recent years, I've been energized by Samuel Akpabot's statement that "the African lives in music and number." My reading of history impels me to think that music, speech and calculation (the measuring of time and event) have been the complex relationships in which human spirit, action, social and political relationships have been most gloriously exemplified. I realize that asserting this makes literary phenomena seem primary. You would expect a poet to insist upon literature's central position in human affairs. We hardly apologize for this insistence any longer. But I should stop here to say that I include in the speech community all those practitioners of verbal art who are not normally included: the griot, the old Testament prophet, the ritual chanter, the fabulist, the legist, the chronicler, the preacher, even the mathematician, among others. Quite a list, you say. What's left out? Why, nothing. Not even poetry. Among various speech communities, poetry finds its voice, and its unique functions, which, nevertheless, are like those of other disciplines—the discovery, explication, interpretation, exploration and transformation of experience. I've now come to the point where I can set down the basic elements of my theory, the one by which I'm guided in writing poetry. Poetry is a concentrated, polysemous, literary act which undertakes the discovery, explication, interpretation, exploration and transformation of experience. It differs from some other forms of speech (such as that used by the legist, the chronicler, the mathematician) in that it handles its "facts" with more disdain, if I might put it that way, insisting upon spiritual resonance. It differs from some other forms of speech (such as that used by the preacher, the ritual chanter, the fabulist) in that it handles its spiritual domain with slightly more critical detachment than they do. The paradox of the extreme manipulative consciousness of the two domains—spiritual and material—indeed, their association to produce what is at least a third and unique domain—is what distinguishes poetry from the other forms of speech. I was almost going to say that I assume that we can recognize the formal differences between a poem and a statute, or a mathematical formula, or a sermon, but I would have left the field too soon. A poem distinguishes itself by rhythmic balance, accent and imaginative dissolution and reconstruction of its materials. It has a rhetoric we recognize as something peculiar to what we call a poem, irrespective of its line count, its imagery or lack of it, its rhyme or lack of it, its metaphor or absence of it, its adherence to any accepted paradigm. What the new poem tries to do is to establish itself as a member of that class of things to create the third domain. This ought to be an unremarkable statement. ⟨. . .⟩ What should be remarkable is that I consider poetry to have a functional value equivalent to all other forms of speech in a social and historical community. Putting things this way means that I consider poetry to have social and historical responsibilities. The poet cannot escape these. These responsibilities manifest themselves in the act of writing poetry and in the act of the poem.

Charles H. Rowell, " 'The Unraveling of the Egg': An Interview with Jay Wright," *Callaloo* 6, No. 3 (Fall 1983): 3–4

JOHN HOLLANDER   Jay Wright's poetry is some of the most original and powerful that is being written in America. He shares with Geoffrey Hill a secularized religious power that keeps him questing among the chapels of ruined tropes, but unlike Hill he contends not with English poetic history, but with a peculiarly American body of fate. It involves a totally unique vision of an imaginative heritage which is institutionally and politically designated as Afro-American: Jay Wright makes the phrase mean more than it ever has. His vision is more truly and deeply responsible to the conceptual realms on each side of the hyphen partly because it reinterprets the significance of each of them. Or, to put it another way, by being a true poet and not a writer of modern journalistic jingle or editorial, or stand-up seriocomic or diarist in verse, he gives to the hyphenation itself a unique relational profundity which makes us feel that he had invented its meaning and use for the first time. Learned, intellectual in the deepest sense, a musician, a studious recluse, Wright has explored a terrain disputed by the powers of anthropology and philosophy. His poems are often strong spiritual exercises and thought-experiments troped as tribal rites, whether West African or Mexican Indian. ⟨. . .⟩

Wright's narrative structures (I should rather say, formats) in his larger poems derive from Pound to some degree, but his language—and this is more important—grew out of a love of Rilke and Hart Crane, the American poet he is in some ways closest to. His new book, *Expectations/Interpretations* (Callaloo Poetry Series, University of Kentucky, 1984), moves beyond the framework of rituals and fables of the Dogon people of West Africa to generate some of its own ad hoc songs and epistemological dances. ⟨. . .⟩ His absorption in the relation of bodies and places stems from a philosophical initiation into the seriousness of certain kinds of questions which daily life might have to hold to be frivolous. But the initiates and public singers in so many of his poems are not chanting primal charms below what Stevens called "the tension of the lyre." Rather they are part of a remarkable poet's tracking down of what the idea of "one's world" might mean, and the stakes are so high, the poet's mind so complex, the realm of knowledge through which he moves so dense and varied in terrain, that it is understandable why he has not so far commanded the kind of popularity that other writers of his generation—anecdotal, narcissistic, polemical, ironically smarmy— elicit. What is a readership taught to absorb easily and piously the literal litanies and versified vignettes of most Afro- and non-Afro-American poetry to make, for example, of Wright's explorations of the tropes of bodily members in his "Twenty-Two Tremblings of the Postulant"?—or, even more, of the post-Poundian colloquy of voices and texts in which David Hume, Hugh McDiarmid (as sort of prototypical forger of a feigned Scottish language for a true poetry), and a Scots colonial administrator in West Africa all surround the poet in his struggle with scepticism ("There may be more light / in David's perpetual twilight / than in our hidden hope for light," he says at one point) in a fine poem called "MacIntyre, the Captain and the Saints"? Wright requires passionate and intelligent readers who can understand the ways in which the imagination can transform the materials of learning.

So much discourse in America today about ethnic origins and searches for meaning in genealogical lineage has degenerated into sleazy cant and travesties of treks toward inner freedom that when an important and enduring poet like Wright takes up the great romantic matter of the quest for true spiritual—as opposed to merely biological—ancestry it will go unnoticed at first. The beasts of detraction (Wright's phrase, "a derry of jackals," is applicable here) can only approach such an artistic quest with a deafened and deafening clamor.

John Hollander, "Poetry in Review," *Yale Review* 74, No. 1 (November 1984): xvi–xix

---

VERA M. KUTZINSKI   ⟨. . .⟩ there is one thing we can be certain about: Wright's poetry is obsessed with history and with the history of the New World in particular. To be more precise, it is motivated by the desire, and in fact the need, to comprehend the complex relations between history, myth, and literature as different forms of self-knowledge. Wright's poet's journeys are set in motion by the search for a language that accommodates both myth and history, that plays off one against the other without submitting to the constraints of either. This interplay of myth and history also offers a key to Wright's use of ritual. *The Double Invention of Komo*, for instance, is explicitly described as a poem that "risks ritual's arrogance." At the same time, it is important for us to understand that poetry, as Wright insists elsewhere, is not ritual. Yet ritual ⟨. . .⟩ can be used in poetry, Wright and ⟨Wilson⟩ Harris would agree, "not as something in which we situate ourselves absolutely, but an unravelling of self-deception within self-revelation as we see through the various dogmatic proprietors of the globe within a play of contrasting structures and anti-structures." It is this play of contrasting structures and antistructures (that is, of myth and history) that Wright's poetry seeks to articulate through linguistic and formal rigor. The results are spectacular: Wright is one of the poets is our recent literary history who, to use ⟨William Carlos⟩ Williams's words, is "making the mass in which some later Eliot will dig." In neglecting his poetry, the criticism of Afro-American (and American) literature(s) has deprived itself of one of the most fascinating and fertile resources for a true critical revisionism. ⟨. . .⟩

Wright's work offers one of the most remarkable examples of an Afro-American poet maintaining a very active dialogue with a variety of traditions while at the same time confronting the problems posed by the idea of writing within the specific context of Afro-American culture. Wright is a most skillful weaver of poetic textures that well deserve to be called mythological in that they embrace both the timelessness of mythical discourse and the radical and inevitable historicity induced by the act of writing itself. There is no doubt that Wright is creating a mythology of Afro-American writing, but he is also constantly reminding himself and his readers of the precariousness of such an endeavor. His best poetry emerges from a confrontation—or what Ralph Ellison would call an "antagonistic cooperation"—between history and myth, in which myth is rendered historical and history mythical.

> Vera M. Kutzinski, "The Black Limbo: Jay Wright's Mythology of Writing," *Against the American Grain: Myth and History in William Carlos Williams, Jay Wright, and Nicolás Guillén* (Baltimore: Johns Hopkins University Press, 1987), pp. 50–51, 55

ROBERT B. STEPTO   For Wright as for Ellison—and others, too, including William Carlos Williams—the weave of community, history, and space is "already woven," and it is the poet's task to "uncover the weave." But what distinguishes Wright from these authors, and from many of his contemporaries as well, is that the weave he seeks to unveil or possibly reenact is from a loom of much larger scale. Whereas Ellison pursues the weave of a pluralized vernacular America ("America" meaning the United States), and speaks continually of the "fate" of that national geography, Wright unveils the strands and textures of the various transatlantic traditions of culture and consciousness.

Over the years, Wright has become more explicitly attentive to the tangle of black traditions binding the Americas to West Africa. One is therefore tempted to argue that from the view of literary history the poem behind Wright's art is Robert Hayden's "Middle Passage." It is worth suggesting that Wright's poetic act unlocks a Hayden line such as "Shuttles in the rocking loom of history." But claims of this sort for Wright's art are too culturally provincial and based upon too narrow a notion of what may constitute a precursory text. Wright has been "energized," as he likes to say, by texts and discourses as various as Dante's *Commedia*, Willard Van Orman Quine's work in logic, Benjamin Banneker's letters to Thomas Jefferson, J. B. Danquah's *Akan Doctrine of God*, and the jazz discourses of Albert Ayler and John Coltrane. In his art Wright is perhaps most obviously for New World readers an heir or sibling of Banneker, Hayden, Wilson Harris,

Alejo Carpentier, Eliot, Hart Crane, and Nicolás Guillén. But Augustine, Goethe, Rilke, and unnumbered, anonymous griots, singers, musicians, and the like also figure in his ancestral community. To argue, as Wright has argued, that poetic discourse is that which handles its facts with more disdain than that of, say, the mathematician or chronicler is to argue as well a rather specific definition of who the poets are or have been. This suggests the sweep and shape, as well as the discipline and drive, of Wright's aesthetic eclecticism. It suggests as well why he is now gaining the audience he has long deserved: Wright invites us to roam the cultures of the transatlantic world, to speak and know many tongues, to partake of the rituals through which we may be initiated into modes of individual and communal enhancement. In yet another age of great uncertainty, Wright enables us to imagine that breaking the vessels of the past is more an act of uncovering than sheer destruction, and that we need not necessarily choose between an intellectual and a spiritual life, for both can still be had.

Robert B. Stepto, "Introduction," *Selected Poems of Jay Wright* (Princeton: Princeton University Press, 1987), x–xi

---

HAROLD BLOOM   In Wright's powerful book, *Soothsayers and Omens*, the final chant, "The Dead," gives the central statement of his poetics, at least as I comprehend his vision. After admonishing his readers that our learning alone cannot suffice, since "it is not enough / to sip the knowledge / of our failings," the poet chants an intricate rhapsody of the self's return from its own achieved emptiness:

> The masks dance
> on this small point, and lead
> this soul, these souls,
> into the rhythm
> of the eye stripped of sight,
> the hand stripped of touch,
> the heart stripped of love,
> the body stripped of its own beginning,
> into the rhythm
> of emptiness and return,
> into the self
> moving against itself,
> into the self
> moving into itself,
> the word, and the first design.

The *askesis* here is Wright's characteristic apotropaic gesture toward tradition, toward all his traditions. As an immensely learned poet, Wright tries to defend himself against incessant allusiveness by stripping his diction, sometimes to an astonishing sparseness. The same movement in W. S. Merwin has damaged the art of one of our strongest contemporary poets, but Wright's minimalism is fortunately not nearly so prevalent. His most characteristic art returns always to that commodious lyricism I associate with American poetry at its most celebratory, in Whitman, in Stevens, in Crane, in Ashbery. ⟨. . .⟩

It is not to be believed, by me, that a verbal art this absolute will continue to suffer neglect. A Pindaric sublimity that allies Hölderlin, Rilke, and Hart Crane with Jay Wright is not now much in fashion, but that mode of high song always returns to us again. As an authentic poet of the Sublime, Wright labors to make us forsake easier pleasures for more difficult pleasures. Wright's reader is taught by him what Hölderlin and Rilke wished us to learn, which is that poetry compels us to answer the fearful triple question: more? equal to? or less than? Self is set against self, or an earlier version of the self against a later one, or culture against culture, or poem against poem. Jay Wright is a permanent American poet because he induces us to enter that agon—with past strength, our own or others'; with the desolations of culture; with the sorrows of history—and because he persuades us also that "it is not enough / to sip the knowledge / of our failings."

Harold Bloom, "Afterword," *Selected Poems of Jay Wright* (Princeton: Princeton University Press, 1987), pp. 195–97

ROBERT B. SHAW   Jay Wright is a difficult poet who makes few concessions to readers uneducated in the sources upon which his work has increasingly relied. These sources are anthropological. Wright's extensive knowledge of West African and Latin American cultures informs the structures and imbues the substance of many of his more elaborate pieces. As a black American born in New Mexico, Wright is well situated to explore cultural diversity, and as a poet he is equipped as well with a wide array of rhetorical skills. He seems in many ways a belated High Modernist; certainly his appropriation of myth and some of his particular kinds of stylistic density put one in mind of Eliot or, even more, Hart Crane, as the critics in this volume ⟨*Selected Poems of Jay Wright*⟩ both note.

I have found in this book some poems I was moved by, a great many more I was intrigued by, but not many that I am certain I understand. It is typically Wright's earlier poems which I accept (and enjoy) with fewer questions. These include some mordant descriptions of Mexican scenes, and some subtle, incisive attempts at self-definition. In these latter pieces Wright adds something of his own to the strong tradition of American poets seeking, questioning, and embracing their vocation. ⟨. . .⟩

In the later work, roughly the second half of the book, the content is frequently more esoteric and the rigor of the style does not relax to provide a helpful context in which references might be understood. ⟨. . .⟩ My distrust of the oracular increases year by year, and yet I do not wish to dismiss these poems. I would like to suggest that judgments of their value will be hard to form without the benefit of more commentary.

Robert B. Shaw, [Review of *Selected Poems of Jay Wright*], *Poetry* 152, No. 1 (April 1988): 45–46

RON WELBURN   In the two later collections, *Elaine's Book* and *Boleros*, one realizes that Wright's quest for metaphysically derived properties of truth have indeed been assimilated, so that their subtle incorporation into individual poems and shorter poem-sequences betrays nothing of pretense. *Elaine's Book* contains the thematically engaging "Zapata and the Egungun Mask," its longest poem, in which the famed Mexican revolutionary who was a campesino addresses the Yoruba ritual mask that represents the intermediation between forces living and non-living. We are apt to find language in these two collections that is richer in metaphor than Wright's earlier poems, if that seems possible! He freely personifies inanimate objects and physical sensations: "No ruffled lace guitars clutch at the darkened windows" ("Madrid"); or the women who, knowing the autumnal flight of geese, "tell us that, if you listen, you can hear / their dove's voices ridge the air." Indeed, two of the book's short sequences, "Desire's Persistence"—whose "Winter" section contains the last example—and "The Anatomy of Resonance," are concerned with aural and visual perceptions. Several of the thirty-nine poems in *Boleros* lack titles outright, Wright preferring numbers to identify them instead. Spanish phrases, some idiomatically obscure, characterize many. Again, history, reality and myth blend without clear demarcations. Saints' days, the Muses, New England, and a Moorish-Iberian point of reference that stimulates thoughts about the cultures of the Americas are its themes. Wright's use of color is not as vivid as Wallace Stevens's, for example, but he responds to a symbolist's influence on the intellect and the senses without any lack of discipline in how he selects his images. The cover design of *Boleros* makes obvious Jay Wright's ideals of fusion and the kind of intellectual and metaphysical terrain he is willing to risk: a *bolero* is a Spanish dance at slow tempo; the figures depicted on the cover are a man and a woman in an African carving and they are playing a *balafon*, a precursor to the xylophone. Together constituting an image and impression on the senses, they demand that artist and public depend on an interactive freedom in order to attain a spiritual unity.

> Ron Welburn, "Jay Wright's Poetics: An Appreciation," *MELUS* 18, No. 3 (Fall 1993): 68

Bibliography

Death as History. 1967.
Balloons. 1968.
The Homecoming Singer. 1971.
Soothsayers and Omens. 1976.
The Albuquerque Graveyard. 1976.
Dimensions of History. 1976.
The Double Invention of Komo. 1980.
Explications/Interpretations. 1984.
Selected Poems. 1987.
Elaine's Book. 1988.
Boleros. 1991.